Close-up

COMPANION B2

Jennifer Heath

SECOND EDITION

Australia • Brazil • Mexico • Singapore • United Kingdom • United States

Close-up B2 Companion, Second Edition
Jennifer Heath

Publisher: Sharon Jervis

Development Editor: Kayleigh Buller

Editorial Assistant: Georgina McComb

Cover Designer: Ken Vail Graphic Design Ltd

Compositor: MPS Limited

Content Project Manager: Jon Ricketts

Acknowledgements

Recording and production at Matinee Sound and Vision Ltd

Editorial Development by Liz Gardiner

© 2015 National Geographic Learning, a Cengage Learning Company

ALL RIGHTS RESERVED. No part of this work covered by the copyright herein may be reproduced or distributed in any form or by any means, except as permitted by U.S. copyright law, without the prior written permission of the copyright owner.

"National Geographic", "National Geographic Society" and the Yellow Border Design are registered trademarks of the National Geographic Society ® Marcas Registradas

---

For product information and technology assistance, contact us at
Cengage Learning Customer & Sales Support, cengage.com/contact

For permission to use material from this text or product,
submit all requests online at **cengage.com/permissions**
Further permissions questions can be emailed to
permissionrequest@cengage.com

ISBN: 978-1-4080-9578-2

National Geographic Learning
Cheriton House, North Way, Andover, Hampshire, SP10 5BE
United Kingdom

National Geographic Learning, a Cengage Learning Company, has a mission to bring the world to the classroom and the classroom to life. With our English language programs, students learn about their world by experiencing it. Through our partnerships with National Geographic and TED Talks, they develop the language and skills they need to be successful global citizens and leaders.

Locate your local office at **international.cengage.com/region**

Visit National Geographic Learning online at **NGL.Cengage.com/ELT**
Visit our corporate website at **www.cengage.com**

Photo credits

Cover image: © WLADIMIR BULGAR/Science Photo Library/Corbis

To access the Close-up B2 Companion audio go to **ngl.cengage.com**

Search for **Close-up B2** with **ESL/ELT** selected from the dropdown menu. Then click on the **Student Companion Site** link

To access the Grammar and Vocabulary section Answer Keys go to **ngl.cengage.com**

Search for **Close-up B2** with **ESL/ELT** selected from the dropdown menu. Then click on the **Teacher Companion Site** link (Teacher access only)

Printed in Greece by Bakis SA
Print Number: 05   Print Year: 2017

Contents

Unit	Page
Note to Teachers	4
Terms & Abbreviations	4
Key to pronunciation and phonetic symbols	4
1 Personally Speaking	5
Vocabulary	5
Grammar	13
2 One World?	19
Vocabulary	19
Grammar	27
3 Star Quality	31
Vocabulary	31
Grammar	40
4 City Living	43
Vocabulary	43
Grammar	50
5 Tied to Technology	56
Vocabulary	56
Grammar	63
6 Fun, Fun, Fun!	68
Vocabulary	68
Grammar	75
7 Right or Wrong?	80
Vocabulary	80
Grammar	88
8 Environmental Affairs	91
Vocabulary	91
Grammar	98
9 And What Do You Do?	102
Vocabulary	102
Grammar	110
10 Learn to Learn!	113
Vocabulary	113
Grammar	119
11 Wish You Were Here!	124
Vocabulary	124
Grammar	131
12 Fit for Life	135
Vocabulary	135
Grammar	142
Alphabetical Word List	146

Note to Teachers

Close-up B2 Companion provides students with everything they need to understand the vocabulary and grammar in the *Close-up B2 Student's Book*.

In the vocabulary section, words and phrases are listed in order of appearance together with their parts of speech and IPA. Each entry includes a clear explanation of the headword, an example sentence, derivatives (appropriate for the level) and the Greek translation of the word or phrase as it is used in the context of the Student's Book. For some entries there are special notes. These include antonyms, synonyms and expressions. At the end of the word lists for most sections, there are word sets that help students learn related words or phrases more easily. The vocabulary section ends with a variety of tasks that practise many of the new words and phrases of that unit.

In the grammar section, there are comprehensive grammar explanations in Greek with plenty of topic-related example sentences. The grammar section ends with tasks that practise the grammar of that unit. Each unit of the companion ends with a Use Your English exam task which is based on the grammar and vocabulary of the unit. Answer keys to these tasks are available here: ngl.cengage.com

At the back of the book, there is a complete list of all the words and phrases in the companion in alphabetical order with their entry number. This helps teachers and students to locate words easily, for example, if they want to refer to a word they learnt in another unit, or if they come across any difficulties.

Finally, *Close-up B2 Companion* is accompanied by audio, which contains the accurate pronunciation of each headword. You can find the audio here: ngl.cengage.com

Terms & Abbreviations

Terms / Abbreviations		Όροι / Συντομεύσεις
n	noun	ουσιαστικό
v	verb	ρήμα
phr v	phrasal verb	περιφραστικό ρήμα
adj	adjective	επίθετο
adv	adverb	επίρρημα
det	determiner	προσδιοριστικό
pron	pronoun	αντωνυμία
prep	preposition	πρόθεση
conj	conjunction	σύνδεσμος
expr	expression	έκφραση
excl	exclamation	επιφώνημα
Opp	opposite	αντίθετο
Syn	synonym	συνώνυμο
abbr	abbreviation	συντόμευση

Key to pronunciation and phonetic symbols

Consonants					
p	pen	/pen/	tʃ	chain	/tʃeɪn/
b	bad	/bæd/	dʒ	jam	/dʒæm/
t	tea	/tiː/	f	fall	/fɔːl/
d	did	/dɪd/	v	van	/væn/
k	cat	/kæt/	θ	thin	/θɪn/
g	get	/get/	ð	this	/ðɪs/

Vowels and diphthongs					
iː	see	/siː/	ɜː	fur	/fɜː/
i	happy	/ˈhæpi/	ə	about	/əˈbaʊt/
ɪ	sit	/sɪt/	eɪ	say	/seɪ/
e	ten	/ten/	əʊ	go	/ɡəʊ/
æ	cat	/kæt/	aɪ	my	/maɪ/
ɑː	father	/ˈfɑːðə/	ɔɪ	boy	/bɔɪ/
ɒ	got	/ɡɒt/	aʊ	now	/naʊ/
ɔː	saw	/sɔː/	ɪə	near	/nɪə/
ʊ	put	/pʊt/	eə	hair	/heə/
u	actual	/ˈæktʃuəl/	ʊə	pure	/pjʊə/
uː	too	/tuː/	ʌ	cup	/kʌp/

1 Personally Speaking

Reading — page 6

1.1 emotion (n) /ɪˈməʊʃən/
a feeling, e.g. happiness, fear, sadness ● *I can't describe my emotions when my dog died.*
➢ emotional (adj) ❖ συναίσθημα

1.2 facial expression (n) /ˈfeɪʃl ɪksˈpreʃn/
what you are feeling or thinking shown on your face ● *You could tell he had heard good news from his happy facial expression.*
❖ έκφραση προσώπου

1.3 body language (n) /ˈbɒdi ˈlæŋgwɪdʒ/
what you are feeling or thinking shown by the position of your body ● *Her body language showed she was confident: she stood up straight and held her head high.* ❖ γλώσσα του σώματος

1.4 communicate (v) /kəmˈjuːnɪkeɪt/
share information with sb ● *I communicate with my sister by email.* ➢ communication (n), communicative (adj) ❖ επικοινωνώ

1.5 disgust (n) /dɪsˈgʌst/
a feeling that sth is unpleasant ● *She felt disgust when she saw the dirty food.* ➢ disgust (v), disgusting, disgusted (adj) ❖ αηδία

1.6 anxiety (n) /æŋˈzaɪəti/
a feeling of worry ● *Try to control any anxiety you feel before exams.* ➢ anxious (adj)
❖ άγχος, ανησυχία

1.7 guess (v) /ges/
form an opinion without having full knowledge of a situation ● *I guessed she was angry as she didn't talk to me all afternoon.* ➢ guess (n)
❖ μαντεύω

1.8 find out (phr v) /faɪnd aʊt/
discover ● *The neuroscientist wants to find out what happens in our brains when we experience fear.*
❖ διαπιστώνω, ανακαλύπτω

1.9 spread (v) /spred/
reach a large number of people ● *Fear quickly spread in the bank when a man with a gun walked in.* ➢ spread (n) ❖ εξαπλώνομαι
✎ Also: rumours spread like wildfire

Word Focus — page 6

1.10 neuroscientist (n) /njʊərəʊˈsaɪəntɪst/
a scientist who studies the brain and nervous system ● *The neuroscientist gave a talk about how the brain works.* ➢ neuroscience (n)
❖ νευροεπιστήμονας

1.11 nervous system (n) /ˈnɜːvəs ˈsɪstəm/
all the nerves in your body ● *The nervous system allows the brain to send messages to the body so it can move.* ❖ νευρικό σύστημα

1.12 study (n) /ˈstʌdi/
a particular piece of research ● *The neuroscience student read many studies on the nervous system.*
➢ study (v) ❖ μελέτη

1.13 particular (adj) /pəˈtɪkjʊlə/
used to emphasise that you are talking about one thing; specific ● *I remember what happened one particular day; it was 2nd July.* ➢ particularly (adv)
❖ συγκεκριμένος

1.14 automatic (adj) /ɔːtəˈmætɪk/
done without thinking ● *Breathing is an automatic function of the body.*
➢ automatically (adv) ❖ αυτόματος

1.15 instinctively (adv) /ɪnˈstɪŋktɪvli/
(acting) without thinking ● *The cat ran instinctively when it saw the angry dog.*
➢ instinct (n), instinctive (adj) ❖ ενστικτωδώς

1.16 neutral (adj) /ˈnjuːtrəl/
neither positive nor negative ● *He didn't take my side in the argument or hers. He remained neutral.* ➢ neutrality (n), neutrally (adv)
❖ ουδέτερος

1.17 motor (adj) /ˈməʊtə/
relating to muscles, nerves and parts of the brain that control movement ● *Our motor skills develop slowly, so children take time to learn how to hold a pencil.* ❖ κινητικός

1.18 muscle (n) /ˈmʌsl/
a part of body that holds bones together and makes them move ● *The leg muscles of a track athlete are very strong.* ➢ muscular (adj) ❖ μυς

1.19 nerve (n) /nɜːv/
a long fibre along which messages are sent from your brain to a part of your body or from a part of your body to your brain ● *If you damage a nerve, you might be paralysed.* ❖ νεύρο

1.20 mechanism (n) /ˈmekənɪzəm/
an aspect of your behaviour which helps you deal with a situation ● *Crying is an automatic mechanism which happens when you feel sad.*
❖ μηχανισμός

1.21 deal with (phr v) /diːl wɪð/
recognise sth like an unpleasant emotion or a difficult situation and remain in control of yourself in spite of it ● *He couldn't deal with the death of his mother and was depressed for a long time.*
❖ αντιμετωπίζω

Reading — pages 6–7

1.22 fearful (adj) /ˈfɪəfʊl/
showing or feeling fear ● *Her body language showed how fearful she was of dogs.* ➢ fear (v, n)
❖ έντρομος

1.23 posture (n) /ˈpɒstʃə/
the way you stand • *Dancers tend to have good posture and stand up straight.* ❖ στάση του σώματος

1.24 process (v) /ˈprəʊses/
deal with sth in a systematic way • *The brain processes information it receives so a person knows how to react.* ➢ process (n) ❖ επεξεργάζομαι

1.25 lead (to) (v) /liːd (tuː)/
cause • *Too much fear can lead to a panic attack.* ❖ οδηγώ (σε)

1.26 response (n) /rɪˈspɒns/
a reaction • *A common response to danger is to run away fast.* ➢ respond (v), responsive (adj) ❖ αντίδραση

1.27 visual (adj) /ˈvɪʒʊəl/
relating to sight or things you can see • *Artists have a very good visual imagination.* ➢ vision (n) ❖ οπτικός

1.28 conscious (adj) /ˈkɒnʃəs/
aware • *Your conscious mind is the part of your brain that you use to think.* ➢ consciousness (n), consciously (adv) ❖ συνειδητός 🗐 Opp: unconscious

1.29 mind (n) /maɪnd/
thoughts • *Her mind told her not to be afraid of the dark, but her instincts said otherwise.* ❖ μυαλό, νους

1.30 aware (of) (adj) /əˈweə (ɒv)/
knowing about sth • *I'm aware it's late but I don't want to go to bed yet.* ➢ awareness (n) ❖ γνώστης, (αυτός) που γνωρίζει

1.31 concentrate (on) (v) /ˈkɒnsəntreɪt (ɒn)/
focus on sth • *The neuroscientist's study concentrates on how we deal with fear.* ➢ concentration (n) ❖ εστιάζω, επικεντρώνω

1.32 react (v) /rɪˈækt/
behave in a certain way towards sth or sb • *Police officers are trained to react calmly in dangerous situations.* ➢ reaction (n), reactionary (adj) ❖ αντιδρώ

1.33 still (adj) /stɪl/
not moving • *Don't move! Stay still!* ❖ ακίνητος, ακούνητος

1.34 image (n) /ˈɪmɪdʒ/
a picture; a photo • *Some journalists take images of world events on their mobile phones.* ❖ φωτογραφία, εικόνα

1.35 carry out (phr v) /ˈkæri aʊt/
do or complete sth • *Research is being carried out on how we react to frightening situations.* ❖ διεξάγω, εκτελώ

1.36 prove (v) /pruːv/
show to be true • *The scientists hope to prove that there is life on other planets.* ➢ proof (n) ❖ επιβεβαιώνω, αποδεικνύω

1.37 observer (n) /əbˈzɜːvə/
sb who watches or notices sth • *A few observers saw the boy stealing the shoes from the shop.* ➢ observe (v) ❖ παρατηρητής

1.38 still (n) /stɪl/
a photograph taken from a film for publicity purposes • *Look at these stills and tell me if you recognise any of the actors.* ➢ still (adj) ❖ φωτογραφία, καρέ, εικόνα

1.39 participant (n) /pɑːˈtɪsɪpənt/
sb who takes part • *The participants in the study had to look at stills of scared people.* ➢ participate (v), participation (n) ❖ συμμετέχων

1.40 armed robber (n) /ɑːmd ˈrɒbə/
sb who robs a person or place using a gun or other weapon • *The armed robber shot the bank manager and ran off with the money.* ❖ ένοπλος ληστής

1.41 pour (v) /pɔː/
put (liquid) in a cup or glass • *He poured me a cup of tea, but I was too shaken to hold the cup.* ❖ σερβίρω, βάζω (τσάι, καφέ, νερο, κλπ σε φλυτζάνι, ποτήρι)

1.42 region (n) /ˈriːdʒən/
area • *She felt a sudden pain in the region of her stomach.* ➢ regional (adj) ❖ περιοχή

1.43 connected (to) (adj) /kəˈnektɪd (tuː)/
related to • *The way we react to films is often connected to the type of music we can hear.* ➢ connect (v), connection (n) ❖ σχετίζομαι (με), συνδέομαι (με)

1.44 responsible (for) (adj) /rɪˈspɒnsəbl (fɔː)/
causing • *The nervous system is responsible for transmitting messages from the brain to the body.* ➢ responsibility (n) ❖ υπεύθυνος (για)

1.45 activate (v) /ˈæktɪveɪt/
make sth start to work • *Scary images activate the visual part of the brain and we then feel fear.* ➢ activation (n), activated (adj) ❖ ενεργοποιώ 🗐 Opp: deactivate

1.46 flock (n) /flɒk/
a group of birds, sheep or goats • *A flock of birds flew inland to escape the dangerous storm at sea.* ➢ flock (v) ❖ σμήνος, κοπάδι

1.47 take off (phr v) /teɪk ɒf/
leave the ground • *Hundreds of birds took off and flew away when they heard the gunshot.* ➢ take-off (n) ❖ απογειώνομαι

1.48 extremely (adv) /ɪkˈstriːmli/
very much • *'It is extremely important to catch this dangerous armed robber,' said the police officer.* ➢ extreme (n, adj) ❖ εξαιρετικά

1.49 evolutionary (adj) /iːvəˈluːʃənri/
relating to gradual change • *At some point in their evolutionary history, dolphins returned to the sea.* ➢ evolve (v), evolution (n) ❖ εξελικτικός

1.50 prey (n) /preɪ/
an animal hunted by another • *Mice are the prey of many large birds.* ➢ prey (v) ❖ λεία, θήραμα

1.51 fraction (n) /ˈfrækʃn/
a very small amount ● *In a fraction of a second, panic spread through the room.*
❖ κλάσμα

1.52 evaluate (v) /ɪˈvæljueɪt/
judge ● *The bank manager evaluated the situation and called the police when she realised that someone had stolen the money.* ➢ evaluation (n)
❖ αξιολογώ

1.53 break out (phr v) /breɪk aʊt/
start suddenly ● *The building was totally destroyed by the fire that broke out.* ❖ ξεσπώ

1.54 adopt (v) /əˈdɒpt/
copy; start to use ● *The child soon adopted the bad behaviour of his new classmates.*
➢ adoption (n) ❖ υιοθετώ

1.55 rationalise (v) /ˈræʃənəlaɪz/
think of reasons to justify or explain sth
● *He tried to rationalise his fears, but he failed.*
➢ rational (adj), rationally (adv)
❖ λογικοποιώ

1.56 focus (on) (v) /ˈfəʊkəs (ɒn)/
concentrate on ● *In this study, we focus on the nervous system.* ➢ focus (n) ❖ εστιάζω (σε)

1.57 enable (v) /ɪnˈeɪbl/
allow to happen ● *These experiments enable scientists to learn more about the brain.*
❖ επιτρέπω, δίνω δυνατότητα

1.58 robotic (adj) /rəʊˈbɒtɪk/
mechanical, functioning automatically
● *In Japan, robotic companions are being created to help care for the elderly.* ➢ robot (n)
❖ ρομποτικός

1.59 perceive (v) /pəˈsiːv/
see and understand ● *People and insects perceive their surroundings in different ways.*
➢ perception (n), perceptive (adj)
❖ αντιλαμβάνομαι

1.60 respond (to) (v) /rɪˈspɒnd (tuː)/
react; take action ● *He responded well to the bad news and remained calm.* ➢ response (n)
❖ αντιδρώ

1.61 express (v) /ɪksˈpres/
show what you think or feel ● *She is rather shy and doesn't express her feelings well.*
➢ expression (n), expressive (adj)
❖ εκφράζω

1.62 speech (n) /spiːtʃ/
words; talking ● *Sign language is a form of speech without sound.* ❖ ομιλία

Brain and body
body language	nerve
facial expression	nervous system
mind	posture
muscle	speech

Vocabulary page 8

1.63 be in agony (expr) biː/ɪn ˈægəni/
be in a lot of pain ● *He was in agony after breaking his arm.* ❖ έχω φριχτούς πόνους

1.64 out of curiosity (expr) /aʊt əv kjʊəriˈɒsəti/
from a desire to know ● *Out of curiosity, can I see a photo of your brother?* ➢ curious (adj)
❖ από περιέργεια

1.65 on the edge of (my) seat (expr)
/ɒn ðiː edʒ əv (maɪ) siːt/
thrilled, very excited ● *I was on the edge of my seat at the end of the match when the score was still 1-1.*
❖ κάθομαι στα καρφιά, ενθουσιασμένος

1.66 at a loss for words (expr) /æt ə lɒs fə wɜːdz/
not knowing what to say ● *I was at a loss for words when I heard the bad news and couldn't speak.*
❖ μένω άναυδος, δεν ξέρω τι να πω

1.67 with regret (expr) /wɪð rɪˈgret/
with sadness ● *It is with regret that I must announce I am no longer getting married.*
❖ με λύπη

1.68 announce (v) /əˈnaʊns/
tell people sth publicly or officially ● *The judges are going to announce the winner of the competition.* ➢ announcer, announcement (n)
❖ ανακοινώνω

1.69 get under (my) skin (expr)
/get ˈʌndə (maɪ) skɪn/
annoy ● *That annoying kid at school really gets under my skin.* ❖ με εκνευρίζει

1.70 amazement (n) /əˈmeɪzmənt/
great surprise ● *We watched John in amazement when he picked up the spider he was terrified of.*
➢ amaze (v), amazing, amazed (adj), amazingly (adv) ❖ κατάπληξη

1.71 confidence (n) /ˈkɒnfɪdəns/
belief in (your) abilities ● *John has a lot of confidence and never feels unsure about himself.*
➢ confident (adj), confidently (adv)
❖ αυτοπεποίθηση

1.72 fury (n) /ˈfjʊəri/
great anger ● *He was red with fury when he found out that his money had been stolen.*
➢ furious (adj), furiously (adv) ❖ οργή

1.73 joy (n) /dʒɔɪ/
happiness ● *She was filled with joy when she became a grandmother.* ➢ joyful (adj)
❖ χαρά

1.74 misery (n) /ˈmɪzəri/
great sadness ● *Losing his dog caused him terrible misery.* ➢ miserable (adj)
❖ θλίψη, δυστυχία

1.75 shame (n) /ʃeɪm/
an uncomfortable feeling of embarrassment
● *Sam felt full of shame when her friends found out she was a shoplifter.* ➢ shameful, ashamed (adj)
❖ ντροπή

1.76 **obvious** (adj) /ˈɒbvɪəs/
easy to see or understand • *It's obvious that he's lying! Look at his face!* ➢ obviously (adv)
❖ εμφανής, προφανής

1.77 **poverty** (n) /ˈpɒvəti/
the state of being very poor • *There is so much poverty here that people cannot even buy food to eat.* ➢ poor (adj) ❖ φτώχεια

1.78 **experience** (v) /ɪkˈspɪəriəns/
feel or be affected by sth • *He experienced a terrible feeling of panic when he got stuck in the lift.* ➢ experience (n) ❖ βιώνω, ζω κάτι

1.79 **beloved** (adj) /bɪˈlʌvɪd/
A beloved person or thing is sb or sth that you love a lot • *Her beloved cat means everything to Nancy.* ❖ αγαπημένος

1.80 **go missing** (expr) /ɡəʊ ˈmɪsɪŋ/
disappear • *The police are looking for an elderly woman who went missing yesterday evening.* ❖ αγνοούμαι

1.81 **overcome** (adj) /əʊvəˈkʌm/
be unable to think clearly • *They were overcome with joy when they won the lottery.* ❖ συγκλονισμένος, συνεπαρμένος, κυριευμένος

1.82 **cheat** (v) /tʃiːt/
behave dishonestly to gain an advantage in an exam, competition, etc • *He passed the exam because he cheated.* ➢ cheat (n) ❖ κλέβω

1.83 **affect** (v) /əˈfekt/
make a change to sb/sth • *If somebody starts crying, affects Sharon and she starts to cry too.* ❖ επηρεάζω

1.84 **effect** (n) /ɪˈfekt/
the change that one thing has on sth else • *Phobias can have a bad effect on your social life.* ➢ effective (adj), effectively (adv)
❖ αποτέλεσμα, επίδραση

1.85 **alone** (adv) /əˈləʊn/
on your own • *She went to the cinema alone because all her friends were busy.* ❖ μόνος

1.86 **lonely** (adj) /ˈləʊnli/
unhappy because you are alone • *He felt lonely after his wife left him.* ➢ loneliness (n)
❖ μοναχικός

1.87 **convey** (v) /kənˈveɪ/
communicate feelings or information • *He conveyed his best wishes to the happy couple by email.* ❖ μεταφέρω

1.88 **fright** (n) /ˈfraɪt/
a strong feeling of fear • *I got a fright when Ted jumped out from behind the door.* ➢ frighten (v), frightening, frightened (adj) ❖ τρομάρα

1.89 **experience** (n) /ɪkˈspɪəriəns/
a particular event, feeling, etc that sb has had • *My last holiday was the best experience of my life.* ➢ experience (v) ❖ εμπειρία

1.90 **award** (n) /əˈwɔːrd/
sth you given to sb to reward them for sth they have done • *He won an award for best actor in a play.* ➢ award (v) βραβείο

1.91 **proud** (adj) /praʊd/
pleased with yourself or sb else • *We were proud when our son passed all his exams.*
➢ pride (n), proudly (adv) ❖ υπερήφανος

1.92 **optimism** (n) /ˈɒptɪmɪzm/
hopefulness; the tendency to expect the best to happen • *Your optimism makes everyone feel positive too.* ➢ optimistic (adj) ❖ αισιοδοξία
✎ Opp: pessimism

1.93 **enthusiasm** (n) /ɪnˈθjuːziæzm/
great interest • *The boy's enthusiasm for football meant that he trained every day.* ➢ enthusiastic (adj), enthusiastically (adv) ❖ ενθουσιασμός

1.94 **slam** (v) /slæm/
close loudly • *Don't slam the door. Close it quietly!* ➢ slam (n) ❖ βροντάω (πόρτα), κτυπώ δυνατά

1.95 **annoy** (v) /əˈnɔɪ/
make angry • *Her younger brother always tried to annoy her by putting spiders in her bed.* ➢ annoyance (n), annoying, annoyed (adj), annoyingly (adv) ❖ ενοχλώ

1.96 **eager** (adj) /ˈiːɡə/
keen; willing • *She was eager to do well, so she worked very hard.* ➢ eagerness (n), eagerly (adv) ❖ πρόθυμος

Adjective endings

-ed	-ous
armed	anxious
beloved	disastrous
disappointed	
terrified	**-ble**
	terrible
-al	uncontrollable
cultural	
facial	**-ic**
irrational	automatic
neutral	robotic
visual	specific

Grammar page 9

1.97 **left-handed** (adj) /left-ˈhændɪd/
using your left hand to write • *I'm left-handed and can't write at all with my right hand.*
➢ left-handedness (n) ❖ αριστερόχειρας
✎ Opp: right-handed

1.98 **trait** (n) /treɪt/
a quality, good or bad, in sb's character • *Personality traits such as optimism tend to run in families.* ❖ γνώρισμα, χαρακτηριστικό

1.99 **pass on** (phr v) /pɑːs ɒn/
to go from one generation to another ● *She passed on her blue eyes to two of her children.*
❖ μεταβιβάζω, περνώ (στην επόμενη γενιά)
✎ Syn: pass down

1.100 **gene** (n) /dʒiːn/
a part of a chromosome which contains genetic information ● *The colour of your eyes and hair is determined by your genes.* ❖ γονίδιο

1.101 **tend (to)** (v) /tend tuː/
often do a particular thing ● *People who are creative tend to become artists, writers, actors or musicians.* ➢ tendency (n)
❖ τείνω (να), έχω την τάση (να)

1.102 **occur** (v) /əˈkɜː/
happen ● *What time did the accident occur?*
➢ occurrence (n) ❖ συμβαίνω

1.103 **stressed** (adj) /strest/
so worried that you cannot relax ● *I got stressed in the heavy traffic as I knew I would be late for work.* ➢ stress (v, n), stressful (adj) ❖ αγχωμένος, πιεσμένος

1.104 **cliff** (n) /klɪf/
a high area of land next to the sea ● *There are high cliffs on the island of Santorini.*
❖ γκρεμός

Listening — page 10

1.105 **freak out** (phr v) /friːk aʊt/
suddenly feel shocked; become angry ● *Dad freaked out when I crashed his car.* ❖ φρικάρω

1.106 **weird** (adj) /wɪəd/
very strange ● *It's weird that Ken knew about the party because I didn't tell him.* ➢ weirdly (adv)
❖ παράξενος, αλλόκοτος

1.107 **turn up** (phr v) /tɜːn ʌp/
come; appear ● *To my surprise, my friends turned up at the airport to say goodbye.*
❖ εμφανίζομαι

1.108 **cheer up** (phr v) /tʃɪər ʌp/
feel better ● *She cheered up when she heard that she hadn't done badly in the test.* ❖ κάνω κουράγιο, νιώθω καλύτερα

1.109 **terrified** (adj) /ˈterɪfaɪd/
very frightened ● *He won't swim in the sea because he's terrified of sharks.* ➢ terrify (v), terrifying (adj)
❖ τρομοκρατημένος

1.110 **disappointed** (adj) /dɪsəˈpɔɪntɪd/
sad because sth you expected did not happen ● *I felt disappointed because I wasn't invited to the party.* ➢ disappoint (v), disappointment (n)
❖ απογοητευμένος

1.111 **absence** (n) /ˈæbsəns/
being away from a place ● *She's got loads of absences from school, so she might have to repeat the class.* ➢ absent (adj) ❖ απουσία

1.112 **inability** (n) /ɪnəˈbɪləti/
being unable to do sth ● *He regretted his inability to speak German when he went to Frankfurt.*
❖ ανικανότητα ✎ Opp: ability

1.113 **poor** (adj) /pɔː/
bad ● *Since you stopped studying, your grades have become poor.* ➢ poorly (adj) ❖ κακός

1.114 **severe** (adj) /sɪˈvɪə/
very bad; serious ● *She has a severe phobia of open spaces and never leaves the house.*
➢ severity (n) ❖ ακραίος, πολύ σοβαρός

1.115 **extreme** (adj) /ɪkˈstriːm/
very great in degree or intensity; more severe or unusual than you would expect ● *We have had extreme weather recently, with freezing temperatures.* ➢ extremely (adv)
❖ ακραίος, υπερβολικός

1.116 **irrational** (adj) /ɪˈræʃənl/
not based on reason ● *Jumping out the window was an irrational reaction to the small fire.*
➢ irrationality (n), irrationally (adv)
❖ παράλογος ✎ Opp: rational

1.117 **anxious** (adj) /ˈæŋkʃəs/
nervous or worried ● *She felt anxious before her driving lesson, but in the end there was nothing to worry about.* ➢ anxiety (n), anxiously (adv)
❖ ανήσυχος, αγχωμένος

1.118 **over-rated** (adj) /əʊvəˈreɪtɪd/
reported to be better than it actually is
● *Everyone said that the book is good, but I thought it was over-rated and didn't like it at all.*
➢ over-rate (v) ❖ υπερτιμημένος

1.119 **lack (of)** (n) /læk (ɒv)/
not having any or enough ● *She refused to lend Jack her car as she had a lack of confidence in his driving abilities.* ➢ lack (v) ❖ έλλειψη

1.120 **overhear** (v) /əʊvəˈhɪə/
hear without sb knowing you are listening
● *He overheard his teacher and the headmaster talking about his grades.* ❖ ακούω τυχαία

Grammar — page 12

1.121 **sore** (adj) /sɔː/
painful ● *I've got a sore throat and a headache.*
❖ πονεμένος, ερεθισμένος

1.122 **pale** (adj) /peɪl/
lacking colour ● *She was tired and looked pale.*
❖ χλωμός

1.123 **explode** (v) /ɪkˈspləʊd/
burst with great violence ● *When the bomb exploded, it destroyed the house.* ➢ explosion (n), explosive (adj) ❖ εκρήγνυμαι

1.124 **downtown** (adj) /ˈdaʊntaʊn/
situated in the central part of a city ● *They took a taxi to downtown Chicago.* ➢ downtown (n, adv)
❖ (που βρίσκεται στο) κέντρο της πόλης, κεντρικός

1.125 **down** (adj) /daʊn/
depressed; very sad • *The constant rain made me feel down.* ❖ απογοητευμένος

1.126 **starving** (adj) /ˈstɑːvɪŋ/
very hungry • *I'm starving. What's for supper?* ➢ starve (v), starvation (n)
❖ πολύ πεινασμένος

Phrasal verbs

bottle up	cheer up	pass on
break out	chicken out	take off
burst into	find out	turn up
calm down	freak out	
carry out	get away	

Use your English — page 13

1.127 **bottle up** (phr v) /ˈbɒtl ʌp/
not express your feelings • *Harry bottled up his feelings so nobody knew how sad he was.*
❖ καταπνίγω, συγκρατώ

1.128 **burst into** (phr v) /bɜːst ˈɪntuː/
show sudden emotion • *Little Mary burst into tears when she fell over.* ❖ ξεσπώ σε

1.129 **calm down** (phr v) /kɑːm daʊn/
stop being angry or excited • *Stop shouting and try to calm down.* ❖ ηρεμώ

1.130 **chicken out** (phr v) /ˈtʃɪkɪn aʊt/
be too scared to do sth • *He wanted to ask her on a date, but chickened out when he saw her talking to another boy.* ❖ δειλιάζω

1.131 **loneliness** (n) /ˈləʊnlinəs/
a feeling of sadness because you are alone • *The old lady had no family and suffered from loneliness.*
➢ lonely (adj) ❖ μοναξιά

1.132 **depression** (n) /dɪˈpreʃn/
a serious feeling of sadness • *People who suffer from depression feel very low and they need medical treatment.* ➢ depress (v), depressed, depressing (adj) ❖ κατάθλιψη

1.133 **specific** (adj) /spəˈsɪfɪk/
particular • *The scientist gave his assistant specific instructions.* ➢ specify (v), specifically (adv)
❖ συγκεκριμένος

1.134 **acrophobia** (n) /ˌækrəˈfəʊbiə/
fear of heights • *He suffers from acrophobia, so he cannot go near the edge of the balcony.*
➢ acrophobic (adj) ❖ υψοφοβία, ακροφοβία

1.135 **claustrophobia** (n) /ˌklɒstrəˈfəʊbiə/
fear of closed-in places • *I won't take the lift as I have claustrophobia and I panic in small spaces.*
➢ claustrophobic (adj) ❖ κλειστοφοβία

1.136 **excessive** (adj) /ɪkˈsesɪv/
more than is reasonable • *An excessive fear of crowds means he cannot go to the town centre.*
➢ excess (n), excessively (adv) ❖ υπερβολικός

1.137 **disastrous** (adj) /dɪˈzɑːstrəs/
having very bad consequences • *The storm was disastrous and destroyed all the farmers' crops.* ➢ disaster (n), disastrously (adv)
❖ καταστροφικός

1.138 **involve** (v) /ɪnˈvɒlv/
be a necessary part or consequence of sth
• *Getting over a phobia often involves facing the thing you fear.* ➢ involvement (n)
❖ περιλαμβάνω, συνεπάγομαι, εμπεριέχω

1.139 **rapid** (adj) /ˈræpɪd/
quick • *The athlete has very rapid reactions.*
➢ rapidity (n), rapidly (adv) ❖ γρήγορος

1.140 **breathe** (v) /briːð/
take in and let out air from your lungs
• *We couldn't breathe as there was so much dust in the air.* ➢ breath (n) ❖ αναπνέω

1.141 **uncontrollable** (adj) /ˌʌnkənˈtrəʊləbl/
If sth is uncontrollable, you cannot control it.
• *Panic is an uncontrollable feeling of great fear.*
➢ uncontrollably (adv) ❖ ανεξέλεγκτος
✎ Opp: controllable

1.142 **desire** (n) /dɪˈzaɪə/
a wish; a need • *She looked so funny that I had a strong desire to laugh.* ➢ desirable (adj), desire (v)
❖ επιθυμία

1.143 **get away** (phr v) /get əˈweɪ/
escape • *The armed robber got away from the police in a fast car.* ❖ ξεφεύγω

1.144 **treat** (v) /triːt/
give medical care; try to cure or heal sth or sb
• *Doctors can treat depression with drugs.*
➢ treatment (n) ❖ κουράρω, περιποιούμαι

1.145 **cope (with)** (v) /kəʊp (wɪð)/
deal with something difficult successfully
• *It's difficult to cope with twins when they are babies.* ❖ αντεπεξέρχομαι, διαχειρίζομαι

Writing: an informal letter / email — pages 14–15

1.146 **inappropriate** (adj) /ˌɪnəˈprəʊpriət/
not suitable • *T-shirts and jeans are inappropriate clothes for a job interview.* ➢ inappropriately (adv)
❖ ακατάλληλος ✎ Opp: appropriate

1.147 **hilarious** (adj) /hɪˈleəriəs/
very funny • *She tells hilarious jokes.*
❖ ξεκαρδιστικός

1.148 **chatty** (adj) /ˈtʃati/
having a friendly, informal style • *I wrote my grandparents a long, chatty email with all our news.*
➢ chat (n, v) ❖ φλύαρος, φιλικός, πολύλογος

1.149 **attend** (v) /əˈtend/
be present at an event • *How many people attended your cousin's wedding?* ➢ attendance (n)
❖ παρευρίσκομαι, παρίσταμαι, έρχομαι

1.150 recommend (v) /rekəˈmend/
suggest • *I recommend that you take up a sport in order to keep fit.* ➤ recommendation (n)
❖ προτείνω

1.151 grateful (adj) /ˈgreɪtfʊl/
feeling thankful because sb has done sth for you • *I'm grateful for all your help.* ➤ gratitude (n)
❖ ευγνώμων ✎ Opp: ungrateful

1.152 plus (prep) /plʌs/
as well as; and also • *I really like Alan. He's very good-looking. Plus, he's clever and kind.*
❖ επίσης, συν (ότι)

1.153 distinct (adj) /dɪˈstɪŋkt/
clearly different • *He spoke with a distinct American accent.* ➤ distinctly (adv)
❖ ξεχωριστός, ευδιάκριτος ✎ Opp: indistinct

1.154 achieve (v) /əˈtʃiːv/
succeed in doing sth • *She achieved her success because of her hard work and talent.*
➤ achievement (n), achievable (adv) ❖ καταφέρνω

Video: A Chinese Artist in Harlem page 16

1.155 custom (n) /ˈkʌstəm/
tradition • *Cooking lamb on a spit at Easter is a Greek custom that goes back many centuries.*
➤ customary (adj) ❖ έθιμο

1.156 portrait (n) /ˈpɔːtrɪt/
a painting or photograph of a person • *The artist painted a beautiful portrait of my mother.*
❖ πορτρέτο, προσωπογραφία

1.157 cultural ambassador (n) /ˈkʌltʃərəl æmˈbæsədə/
sb who promotes the culture of a particular place • *Georgios Dalaras is a respected cultural ambassador of Greek music.* ❖ πολιτιστικός πρέσβης

1.158 immigrant (n) /ˈɪmɪgrənt/
sb who comes to live in a country from a different one • *Many immigrants from Europe went to Australia to start new lives in the 1950s.*
➤ immigrate (v), immigration (n)
❖ μετανάστης

1.159 multicultural (adj) /mʌltiˈkʌltʃərəl/
with many people of different cultures • *New York is a multicultural city with people from all over the world.* ❖ πολυπολιτισμικός

1.160 landscape (n) /ˈlændskeɪp/
a picture of the countryside • *Can you please paint a landscape of my garden?* ❖ τοπίο

1.161 run (v) /rʌn/
be in charge of a business, etc • *They run a bakery in the centre of town.* ❖ διευθύνω

1.162 background (n) /ˈbakgraʊnd/
a person's family, culture, education, etc • *She came from a poor working-class background.*
❖ παρελθόν, ιστορικό

1.163 benefit (v) /ˈbenɪfɪt/
be helped by sth; help sb • *The English course benefits immigrants to the UK who don't speak the language.* ➤ benefit (n), beneficial (adj) ❖ ωφελώ

1.164 cosmopolitan (adj) /kɒzməˈpɒlɪtən/
with many people from different places and of different cultures • *Many large European cities are cosmopolitan places with people from all over the world.* ❖ κοσμοπολίτικος

1.165 ethnicity (n) /eθˈnɪsɪti/
membership of a particular group of people who have common characteristics • *She was born in Africa and she says her ethnicity was important to her.* ➤ ethnic (adj) ❖ εθνότητα

1.166 introduce (v) /ɪntrəˈdjuːs/
cause sb to experience sth for the first time • *Television introduced many people to images of other parts of the world.*
➤ introduction (n) ❖ εισάγω

1.167 practise (v) /ˈpræktɪs/
do an activity • *She's a doctor and has been practising medicine for 20 years.* ❖ ασκώ, εξασκώ (επάγγελμα)

1.168 community (n) /kəˈmjuːnəti/
the people living in an area • *We live in a friendly community where people help each other out.*
❖ κοινωνία, κοινότητα

1.169 make a living (expr) /meɪk ə ˈlɪvɪŋ/
work and earn money • *He makes a living as a doctor.* ❖ κερδίζω τα προς το ζην

1.170 field (n) /fiːld/
an area in which you work or study • *My field is neuroscience and I study how people experience fear.* ❖ πεδίο, τομέας

1.171 train (v) /treɪn/
teach • *I have trained my dog to bring me the newspaper!* ➤ training, trainer (n) ❖ εκπαιδεύω

1.173 regard (v) /rɪˈgɑːd/
consider • *He regards Einstein as the greatest physicist of the last century.* ❖ θεωρώ

1.174 beyond (prep) /bɪˈjɒnd/
on the further side of sth • *The explorer wanted to explore the area beyond the mountains.*
❖ πέρα από

1.175 culture (n) /ˈkʌltʃə/
the beliefs and arts of a civilisation • *You should buy a book about the culture of the country you are going to visit.* ➤ cultural (adj)
❖ κουλτούρα

Vocabulary Exercises

A Match.

1. Don't bottle
2. She burst
3. You must calm
4. Cheer
5. Did he chicken
6. Mum freaked
7. I should carry
8. Birds can take
9. If a fire breaks
10. We pass
11. The robber got
12. Did anyone turn

a. down.
b. up, everyone!
c. up your feelings.
d. off from the water.
e. out, leave the building.
f. up at the meeting?
g. out some tests.
h. on traits in our genes.
i. out when the vase broke.
j. away in a blue car.
k. out in the end?
l. into tears.

B Complete the table.

Adjective	Noun
responsible	1
fearful	2
anxious	3
amazed	4
excessive	5
proud	6
starving	7
stressed	8

C Read the definition and complete the words.

1. what you are feeling or thinking shown on your face: f _ _ _ _ _ _   e _ _ _ _ _ _ _ _ _ _
2. the way you stand: p _ _ _ _ _ _ _
3. what you are feeling or thinking shown by the position of your body: b _ _ _   l _ _ _ _ _ _ _ _
4. all the nerves in your body: n _ _ _ _ _ _ _   s _ _ _ _ _ _
5. thoughts: m _ _ _
6. words, talking: s _ _ _ _ _ _
7. part of the body that holds bones together and makes them move: m _ _ _ _ _ _
8. your ethnic group: e _ _ _ _ _ _ _ _ _
9. part of a chromosome: g _ _ _
10. writing with your left hand: l _ _ _-h _ _ _ _ _ _

D Circle the odd one out.

1. respond   react   process
2. joy   depression   misery
3. over-rated   multicultural   cosmopolitan
4. poor   proud   severe
5. fear   phobia   trait
6. fearful   irrational   terrified
7. achieve   cheat   benefit
8. convey   experience   express

1 Grammar

1.1 Present Simple

Κατάφαση
I/we/you/they talk
he/she/it talk**s**

Άρνηση
I/we/you/they **don't** talk
he/she/it **doesn't** talk

Ερώτηση
Do I/we/you/they talk?
Does he/she/it talk?

Σύντομες απαντήσεις	
Yes, I/we/you/they **do**.	No, I/we/you/they **don't**.
Yes, he/she/it **does**.	No, he/she/it **doesn't**.

Χρησιμοποιούμε **Present Simple** για:
γεγονότα ή γενικές αλήθειες.
→ The sun **rises** in the east and it **sets** in the west.
ρουτίνες ή συνήθειες (συχνά με adverbs of frequency).
→ My grandmother **always combs** her hair in the morning.
μόνιμες καταστάσεις.
→ She **works** for a research lab.
προγράμματα, ώρες έναρξης/λήξης/άφιξης/αναχώρησης στο μέλλον.
→ The lesson **starts** at 9 am on Monday.
αφηγήσεις (μια ιστορία, ένα ανέκδοτο, μια πλοκή, μια αθλητική αναμετάδοση, κλπ)
→ He steals the ball and **races** down the field.

Σημείωση: Χρονικές εκφράσεις που χρησιμοποιούνται συχνά με Present Simple είναι *every day/week/month/summer, every other day, once a week, twice a month, in the morning/afternoon/evening, at night, at the weekend, in April, on Mondays, on Sunday mornings,* κλπ.
→ Jacob writes his blog **every other day**.

Θυμήσου: Χρησιμοποιούμε συχνά adverbs of frequency με Present Simple. Μπαίνουν πριν από το κύριο ρήμα, αλλά μετά από το ρήμα *be*.
→ I **usually study** in the evening.
→ Actors **often give** interviews.
→ Brian **is never** afraid of anything.

Συνηθισμένα adverbs of frequency είναι:

				rarely	
				hardly ever	
always	usually	often	sometimes	seldom	never
100% -- 0%

1.2 Present Continuous

Κατάφαση
I **am** (**'m**) talking
he/she/it **is** (**'s**) talk**ing**
we/you/they **are** (**'re**) talk**ing**

Άρνηση
I **am** (**'m**) not talk**ing**
he/she/it **is not** (**isn't**) talking
we/you/they **are not** (**aren't**) talk**ing**

Ερώτηση
Am I talk**ing**?
Is he/she/it talk**ing**?
Are we/you/they talk**ing**?

Σύντομες απαντήσεις	
Yes, I **am**.	No, I'm **not**.
Yes, he/she/it **is**.	No, he/she/it **isn't**.
Yes, we/you/they **are**.	No, we/you/they **aren't**.

Ορθογραφία:
giv**e** → giv**ing**   trave**l** → trave**lling**   tid**y** → tid**ying**

Χρησιμοποιούμε **Present Continuous** για:
πράξεις που συμβαίνουν την ώρα που μιλάμε.
→ My mother **is practising** her calligraphy right now.

1 Grammar

πράξεις που εξελίσσονται γύρω από την ώρα που μιλάμε, αλλά όχι αυτή τη στιγμή.
→ I **am studying** the effects of phobias this year.
καταστάσεις που είναι προσωρινές.
→ She'**s using** her sister's laptop this week.
ενοχλητικές συνήθειες (συχνά με τα *always, continually, constantly* και *forever*).
→ Gwen **is always borrowing** my mobile phone.
να περιγράψουμε μια εικόνα.
→ In this picture, a woman **is giving** a talk on India.
σχέδια και ότι έχουμε κανονίσει για το μέλλον.
→ We **are starting** a new experiment next week.
καταστάσεις που μεταβάλλονται ή εξελίσσονται στο παρόν.
→ More and more people **are suffering** from stress.

Σημείωση: Κάποιες συνηθισμένες χρονικές εκφράσεις που χρησιμοποιούνται συχνά με Present Continuous είναι *now, at the moment, for the time being, this morning/afternoon/evening/week/month/year, today,* κλπ.
→ A flock of birds is flying over our house **at the moment**.

1.3 Stative Verbs

Κάποια ρήματα συνήθως δεν χρησιμοποιούνται στους χρόνους διαρκείας (continuous). Ονομάζονται **stative verbs** διότι περιγράφουν καταστάσεις (states) και όχι πράξεις. Τα πιο συνηθισμένα από αυτά είναι:
ρήματα συναισθημάτων: *hate, like, love, need, want, prefer*.
→ I **like** portraits.
ρήματα αισθήσεων: *feel, hear, see, seem, smell, sound, taste*.
→ I **feel** sad today.
ρήματα που έχουν σχέση με τη νόηση: *believe, doubt, forget, imagine, know, remember, suppose, think, understand*.
→ I **know** a phobia is an irrational fear.
ρήματα κτήσης/ιδιοκτησίας: *belong to, have, own, possess*.
→ **Does** this laptop **belong to** you?
άλλα ρήματα: *be, consist, contain, cost, include, mean*.
→ This website **contains** information unsuitable for children.

Κάποια ρήματα μπορούν να περιγράφουν καταστάσεις (stative verbs) και πράξεις (action verbs), αλλά έχουν διαφορετική σημασία. Τα πιο συνηθισμένα από αυτά είναι:
be
→ Miss Reeves **is** calm. (είναι (περιγράφει χαρακτηριστικό)
→ You **are being** rude. (συμπεριφέρομαι)
expect
→ I **expect** you are interested in science. (νομίζω ή πιστεύω)
→ I'**m expecting** two friends for lunch. (περιμένω)
have
→ She **has** three digital cameras. (have = έχω, κατέχω)
→ She'**s having** problems with two new students. (have = βιώνω μια εμπειρία)
look
→ You **look** furious. (look = δείχνω, φαίνομαι)
→ They **are looking** at the portraits in the exhibition. (look = κοιτάζω)
taste
→ This bread **tastes** delicious. (taste = έχω (κάποια ιδιαίτερη) γεύση)
→ I'**m tasting** the salad; maybe it needs more lemon. (taste = δοκιμάζω τη γεύση)
think
→ I **think** Mary is upset about something. (think = νομίζω)
→ Dad **is thinking** of buying a faster PC. (think = σκέπτομαι, προσπαθώ να αποφασίσω)
see
→ I **don't see** what all the fuss is about. (see = καταλαβαίνω)
→ We **are seeing** our cousins tomorrow. (see = συναντώ)

smell
→ Your perfume **smells** wonderful. (smell = έχω (συγκεκριμένη) μυρωδιά)
→ I'**m smelling** the cheese. I think it has gone off. (smell = μυρίζω: η πράξη της όσφρησης)
weigh
→ This mobile phone **weighs** 120 grams. (weigh = έχω (συγκεκριμένο) βάρος)
→ The nurse **is weighing** the baby. (weigh = ζυγίζω: μετρώ το βάρος του)

1.4 Present Perfect Simple

Κατάφαση
I/we/you/they **have ('ve) driven**   he/she/it **has ('s) driven**
Άρνηση
I/we/you/they **have not (haven't) driven**   he/she/it **has not (hasn't) driven**
Ερώτηση
Have I/we/you/they **driven**?   **Has** he/she/it **driven**?
Σύντομες απαντήσεις

Yes, I/we/you/they **have**. **Yes**, he/she/it **has**.	**No**, I/we/you/they **haven't**. **No**, he/she/it **hasn't**.

Ορθογραφία:
look → look**ed**   travel → trave**lled**   st**ay** → stay**ed**   wast**e** → wast**ed**   tr**y** → tr**ied**

Σημείωση: Κάποια ρήματα είναι ανώμαλα και δεν ακολουθούν αυτούς τους ορθογραφικούς κανόνες. Δες τη λίστα των ανωμάλων ρημάτων και τις παθητικές μετοχές (past participles) στις σελ. 176-177 του Student's Book.

Χρησιμοποιούμε **Present Perfect Simple**:
για κάτι που ξεκίνησε στο παρελθόν και συνεχίζεται ως τώρα.
→ I'**ve had** this phobia for a year.
για κάτι που έγινε στο παρελθόν αλλά δε γνωρίζουμε ή δεν αναφέρουμε ακριβώς πότε 'έγινε.
→ Derek **has studied** how the brain reacts to fear.
για κάτι που έγινε στο παρελθόν και το αποτέλεσμα επηρεάζει το παρόν.
→ She **has eaten** three ice creams. That's why she feels sick!
για πράξεις που έχουν μόλις τελειώσει.
→ He **has just finished** doing the dishes and will now watch a film.
για εμπειρίες και επιτεύγματα.
→ Mario **has visited** most European countries.
για κάτι που έγινε αρκετές φορές στο παρελθόν.
→ Larry **has tried** again and again to overcome his fear of cats.
με τον υπερθετικό των επιθέτων (superlatives), και με τις φράσεις *the first time/the second time*, κλπ.
→ It's the best study on brain activity I **have ever read**.

Σημείωση: Κάποιες συνηθισμένες χρονικές εκφράσεις που χρησιμοποιούνται με Present Perfect Simple είναι *already, ever, for, for a long time/ages, just, never, once, recently, since 2003/October, so far, twice, four times, until now, yet*, κλπ.
→ Humans have communicated using language **for ages**.

Θυμήσου: Χρησιμοποιούμε *have been* όταν κάποιος έχει πάει κάπου και τώρα έχει επιστρέψει, αλλά χρησιμοποιούμε *have gone* όταν κάποιος έχει πάει κάπου και βρίσκεται ακόμα εκεί.
→ We'**ve been** to the cultural festival, but now we're on our way home.
→ Angela **has gone** to the shops, but she'll be back in an hour.

1 Grammar

1.5 Present Perfect Continuous

Κατάφαση
I/we/you/they **have ('ve) been** driv**ing** he/she/it **has ('s) been** driv**ing**
Άρνηση
I/we/you/they **have not (haven't) been** driv**ing** he/she/it **has not (hasn't) been** driv**ing**
Ερώτηση
Have I/we/you/they **been** driv**ing**? **Has** he/she/it **been** driv**ing**?
Σύντομες απαντήσεις
Yes, I/we/you/they **have**. **No**, I/we/you/they **haven't**. **Yes**, he/she/it **has**. **No**, he/she/it **hasn't**.

Ορθογραφία:
make → mak**ing**   let → le**tting**   cry → cry**ing**

Χρησιμοποιούμε **Present Perfect Continuous** για:
πράξεις που ξεκίνησαν στο παρελθόν και είναι ακόμα σε εξέλιξη ή που είναι επαναλαμβανόμενες μέχρι τώρα.
→ I **have been studying** fears and phobias for a long time.
πράξεις που έγιναν πολλές φορές στο παρελθόν και έχουν ολοκληρωθεί πρόσφατα, αλλά έχουν αποτελέσματα που επηρεάζουν το παρόν.
→ She is worried because she **has been getting** bad headaches recently.
να τονίσουμε για πόσο καιρό είναι σε εξέλιξη μια πράξη.
→ I **have been living** alone since I was twenty.
μια πράξη που είναι πρόσφατη ή που δεν έχει ολοκληρωθεί.
→ Our teacher **has been discussing** modern Chinese culture with us.

Σημείωση: Κάποιες συνηθισμένες χρονικές εκφράσεις που χρησιμοποιούνται συχνά με Present Perfect Continuous είναι *all day/night/week, for years/a long time/ages, lately, recently, since*. Μπορούμε να χρησιμοποιήσουμε *How long...?* με Present Perfect Continuous σε ερωτήσεις.
→ Ingrid has been bottling up her feelings **lately**. It's not good for her.
→ Mr. Romano has been teaching photography **for years**.
→ **How long** have they been studying calligraphy?

1.6 Present Perfect Simple & Present Perfect Continuous

Χρησιμοποιούμε **Present Perfect Simple** για να μιλήσουμε για κάτι που έχουμε κάνει ή έχουμε πετύχει, ή για μια πράξη που έχει ολοκληρωθεί. Τον χρησιμοποιούμε επίσης για να πούμε πόσες φορές έχει συμβεί κάτι.
→ She **has spoken** to all the students about their progress.
→ The shop **has sold** twenty copies of the new CD already.

Χρησιμοποιούμε **Present Perfect Continuous** για να δείξουμε για πόσο καιρό συμβαίνει κάτι. Δεν έχει σημασία αν η πράξη έχει ολοκληρωθεί ή όχι.
→ I**'ve been having** problems with my best friend for a week now.
→ She**'s been trying** to call James all day.

Grammar Exercises

A Choose the correct answers.

1 Some people ___ how lucky they are!
   a don't know   b aren't knowing

2 The university ___ a neuroscience department.
   a has   b is having

3 Charlie ___ a blood test tomorrow.
   a has   b is having

4 In this still, we can see a child who ___.
   a cries   b is crying

5 I ___ house at the moment, so I can't make it to your party.
   a move   b am moving

6 Our science lesson ___ every Tuesday morning.
   a takes place   b is taking place

7 They ___ to the library every Friday.
   a go   b are going

8 He ___ more and more down.
   a feels   b is feeling

9 In this film, an armed robber ___ a bank.
   a holds up   b is holding up

10 At present, she ___ medicine.
   a studies   b is studying

B Match.

1 More and more immigrants   ☐   a is taking off.
2 This photo depicts a flock of birds which   ☐   b introduces us to a world of information.
3 An average new-born baby   ☐   c are you doing?
4 The Internet   ☐   d are arriving in our country every day.
5 His annoying sister   ☐   e is always getting under his skin.
6 Our train   ☐   f are studying the brain.
7 In our next biology lesson, we   ☐   g weighs about three kilos.
8 What   ☐   h leaves tomorrow at midday.

C Complete the sentences using the Present Perfect Simple or Present Perfect Continuous of the verbs in brackets.

1 He _____ (paint) this landscape all morning and now it's ready.
2 The rules _____ (not affect) all of us, only the new pupils.
3 This is the first time I _____ (see) such terrible poverty.
4 _____ (you/write) that report all day?
5 Janet _____ (work) as a doctor for only a few months.
6 We _____ (just/hear) some more specific information about the robbery.
7 _____ (you/ever/be) to New York?
8 She _____ (paint) her bedroom all day, so she's tired.

1 Grammar

D Put the words in the correct order.

1 lecture / gone / to / the / physics / John / has
_____

2 learning / they / have / calligraphy / about / been
_____

3 has / Stan / ambassador / been / years / a / cultural / for / country / for / his
_____

4 felt / you / claustrophobic / ever / have / ?
_____

5 out / early / why / gone / so / Kelly / has / ?
_____

6 they / been / neuroscience / studying / for / long / very / haven't
_____

7 had / my / I / never / the / to / write / hand / have / with / left / ability
_____

8 computer / has / playing / been / games / morning / she / all / ?
_____

Use your English

Exam Task

For questions **1–12**, read the text below and decide which answer (**A**, **B**, **C** or **D**) best fits each gap.

Mouth and Foot Painting Artists

There are many disabled artists who have **(1)** ___ support from mouth and foot painting organisations over the last fifty years. Some of these artists have **(2)** ___ disabled since birth, while others have suffered accidents which have **(3)** ___ their ability to use their hands. The organisations **(4)** ___ the word about what they do for people with disabilities and introduce them to their **(5)** ___ side. They build up people's confidence and **(6)** ___ them to paint with their feet or mouth. The aim is to **(7)** ___ the artists to earn money so they can make a **(8)** ___ and remain as independent as possible.

Once a year, from one of these organisations, I receive greeting cards and a calendar which I am free to buy or return by post. Personally, I buy them and I always **(9)** ___ that other people do the same. Why? Well, mainly because I like the art, especially some of the beautiful **(10)** ___. Also, I know that my small contribution **(11)** ___ a community that deserves support. The art isn't restricted to cards, though. Go online and you can **(12)** ___ out more about these artists.

1	A found	B perceived	C gone	D responded
2	A done	B gone	C had	D been
3	A processed	B affected	C led	D proven
4	A spread	B process	C carry out	D communicate
5	A irrational	B specific	C creative	D rapid
6	A regard	B practise	C experience	D train
7	A enable	B focus	C activate	D achieve
8	A life	B living	C live	D work
9	A express	B recommend	C adopt	D regard
10	A studies	B participants	C immigrants	D landscapes
11	A benefits	B guesses	C slams	D moves
12	A break	B carry	C find	D freak

2 One World?

Reading — page 18

2.1 availability (n) /əˈveɪləˈbɪlɪti/
how easy it is obtain or get sth ● *The availability of fresh fruit in winter was limited in the past.* ➤ available (adj) ❖ διαθεσιμότητα

2.2 goods (pl n) /gʊdz/
things made to be sold ● *This shop sells leather goods such as bags, shoes and boots.*
❖ εμπορεύματα

2.3 service (n) /ˈsɜːvɪs/
an organisation or system that provides sth to the public ● *The bus service is good in our area.*
❖ υπηρεσία

2.4 globalisation (n) /ˈgləʊbəlaɪˈzeɪʃn/
making something such as business operate in a lot of different countries all over the world
● *Globalisation has led to people all over the world working together, often using English to communicate.* ➤ global (adj)
❖ παγκοσμιοποίηση

Word Focus — page 19

2.5 source (n) /sɔːs/
the place or thing from which sth originates
● *Lack of money is a source of unhappiness for most people.* ❖ πηγή

2.6 profit (n) /ˈprɒfɪ/
the amount of money you gain when you are paid more for sth than it cost ● *The company made a huge profit selling clothes for teenagers.*
➤ profitable (adj), profitably (adv), profit (v)
❖ κέρδος ✎ Opp: loss

2.7 boundary (n) /ˈbaʊndəri/
an imaginary line that separates one area of land from another ● *We planted a hedge at the boundary between our houses.* ❖ όριο, σύνορο

2.8 edge (n) /ɛdʒ/
the place or line where sth stops ● *Don't walk near the edge of the cliff! You might fall!*
❖ άκρη, χείλος

2.9 tolerance (n) /ˈtɒlərəns/
willingness to accept the things people do or say even if you do not agree with them ● *Tolerance is important if we want to live together peacefully.*
➤ tolerant (adj), tolerate (v) ❖ ανεκτικότητα
✎ Opp: intolerance

2.10 willingness (n) /ˈwɪlɪŋnəs/
not minding doing sth; not objecting to doing sth
● *I appreciate your willingness to help, but I can do the work by myself.* ➤ willing (adj), willingly (adv)
❖ θέληση

2.11 lyrics (pl n) /ˈlɪrɪks/
the words of a song ● *The lyrics of this song are in German, so I can't understand them.*
❖ στίχοι τραγουδιού

Reading — page 18–19

2.12 destroy (v) /dɪsˈtrɔɪ/
ruin ● *Online bullying destroyed her confidence and she no longer wanted to go out.* ➤ destruction (n), destructive (adj) ❖ καταστρέφω

2.13 employment (n) /ɪmˈplɔɪmənt/
having a paid job ● *There are few employment opportunities for young people these days.*
➤ employ (v), employer, employee (n)
❖ απασχόληση, εργασία
✎ Opp: unemployment

2.14 manufacture (v) /mænjʊˈfæktʃə/
make things in a factory ● *Delta is a company that manufactures dairy products.* ➤ manufacturer (n)
❖ κατασκευάζω

2.15 ship (v) /ʃɪp/
send things by sea ● *It took two weeks to ship our things from Greece to the UK.* ➤ ship, shipping (n)
❖ στέλνω (μέσω θαλάσσης)

2.16 unemployed (adj) /ʌnɪmˈplɔɪd/
not having a job even though you want one
● *Unemployed workers can become depressed if they don't find another job quickly.*
➤ unemployment (n) ❖ άνεργος

2.17 give up (phr v) /gɪv ʌp/
stop doing or having sth ● *The work was difficult, but they didn't give up and succeeded in the end.*
❖ σταματώ, τα παρατώ

2.18 barely (adv) /ˈbɛəlɪ/
used to say that sth is only just true or possible
● *He spoke so softly that I could barely hear him.*
❖ μετά βίας, με δυσκολία

2.19 survive (v) /səˈvaɪv/
stay alive ● *All the passengers survived the coach crash.* ➤ survival, survivor (n) ❖ επιβιώνω

2.20 support (v) /səˈpɔːt/
provide sb with money or the things they need
● *She works hard to support her family.*
➤ support, supporter (n) ❖ υποστηρίζω συντηρώ

2.21 foreign (adj) /ˈfɒrən/
from another country ● *Foreign tourists always want to visit the Acropolis before they return to their own countries.* ➤ foreigner (n) ❖ ξένος

2.22 company (n) /ˈkʌmpəni/
business ● *Microsoft is one of the most profitable companies in the world.* ❖ εταιρεία

2.23	**connect** (v) /kəˈnɛkt/ join • *You can connect to the Internet at any Internet café.* ➣ connection (n) ❖ συνδέω	2.36	**impact** (n) /ˈɪmpækt/ having a strong effect on sb or sth • *The economic crisis has had an impact on most people's lives.* ❖ αντίκτυπο
2.24	**identity** (n) /aɪˈdɛntəti/ who sb is • *The cultural identity of many people is reflected in their music.* ➣ identify (v), identification (n) ❖ ταυτότητα	2.37	**wealthy** (adj) /ˈwɛlθi/ rich • *Jack is a wealthy man who gives a lot of his money to charity.* ➣ wealth (n) ❖ πλούσιος
2.25	**respect** (n) /rɪˈspɛkt/ not doing things that other people dislike or regard as wrong • *You must show respect to other people and be polite to them.* ➣ respect (v), respectful, respectable (adj) ❖ σεβασμός ✎ disrespect	2.38	**co-operation** (n) /kəʊˌɒpəˈreɪʃən/ working with sb and helping them • *There's a lot of work to do and I'd appreciate your co-operation.* ➣ co-operate (v), co-operative (adj) ❖ συνεργασία
2.26	**climate change** (n) /ˈklaɪmət tʃeɪndʒ/ changing global weather patterns • *Scientists predict that climate change will cause difficult weather conditions for the world in the future.* ❖ κλιματική αλλαγή	2.39	**dietary** (n) /ˈdaɪətəri/ relating to the kind of food you eat • *She doesn't have any special dietary requirements; she eats most things.* ➣ diet (n, v) ❖ διατροφικός
2.27	**local** (adj) /ˈləʊkl/ from the place you are in • *We tried local dishes like moussaka when we visited Greece.* ➣ locally (adv) ❖ τοπικός	2.40	**international** (adj) /ɪntəˈnæʃənl/ involving different countries • *International travel became possible for people when the cost of air travel fell.* ❖ διεθνής
2.28	**chain** (n) /tʃeɪn/ many shops, hotels etc of the same kind • *Zara is a chain, so you can find Zara shops in many places.* ❖ αλυσίδα	2.41	**trade** (v) /treɪd/ buy and sell • *Kotsovolos is a chain of shops that trade in electrical goods.* ➣ trade (n), trader (n) ❖ εμπορεύομαι
2.29	**catch on** (phr v) /kætʃ ɒn/ become popular • *The new fashion quickly caught on and soon everyone was wearing the same style.* ❖ 'πιάνω', γίνομαι δημοφιλής	2.42	**mayor** (n) /mɛə/ a person who has been elected to represent a town or city • *The mayor of our town opened the new library.* ❖ δήμαρχος
2.30	**dairy product** (exp) /ˈdɛːri ˈprɒdʌkt/ a food such as butter, cheese or yoghurt • *I love eating dairy products like cheese and yoghurt.* ❖ γαλακτοκομικό προϊόν	2.43	**event** (n) /ɪˈvɛnt/ a planned, organised occasion such as a party or sports competition • *I love going to events like weddings or formal parties.* ❖ εκδήλωση, γεγονός
2.31	**uniqueness** (n) /juːˈniːknəs/ being the only one of its kind • *The uniqueness of this object makes it valuable. It is the only one in existence.* ➣ unique (adj), uniquely (adv) ❖ μοναδικότητα	2.44	**conditions** (pl n) /kənˈdɪʃənz/ the things in people's lives that affect their comfort, safety or success • *The people lived in terrible conditions: their houses were dirty and they didn't have clean drinking water.* ❖ περιστάσεις
2.32	**lifestyle** (n) /ˈlaɪfstaɪl/ how sb lives • *Many people envy the lifestyle of the rich and famous.* ❖ τρόπος ζωής		
2.33	**similar** (adj) /ˈsɪmələ/ almost the same • *We have similar interests, which is why we get on so well.* ➣ similarity (n) ❖ παρόμοιος ✎ Opp: dissimilar		
2.34	**potential** (n) /pə(ʊ)ˈtɛnʃəl/ the ability to be useful or successful in the future • *You have the potential to be a good musician, but you have to practise harder.* ➣ potential (adj), potentially (adv) ❖ προδιαγραφή, προοπτική		
2.35	**concern** (v) /kənˈsɜːn/ If sth concerns you, it worries you. • *Climate change concerns me; it's a very serious problem.* ➣ concern (n), concerned (adj) ❖ απασχολώ, ανησυχώ		

Business

availability	import
chain	manufacture
company	outsourcing
do business	professional
employment	profit
export	service
globalisation	trade
goods	unemployed

Vocabulary   page 20

2.45	**universal** (adj) /juːnɪˈvɜːsəl/ relating to everyone and everything • *Climate change is a universal problem that affects us all.* ➣ universe (n), universally (adv) ❖ παγκόσμιος

2.46 knowledge (n) /ˈnɒlɪdʒ/
information you have about sth ● *Before the Internet, people has less knowledge of the world and other cultures.* ➢ know (v), knowledgeable (adj)
❖ γνώση

2.47 society (n) /səˈsaɪəti/
a group of people living in same place with a similar way of life ● *Western society focuses too much on money and success.*
➢ social (adj), socially (adv) ❖ κοινωνία

2.48 belief (n) /bɪˈliːf/
a feeling that sth is true ● *It is my belief that the climate will change our lives this century.*
➢ believe (v) ❖ πεποίθηση, πίστη ✎ Opp: disbelief

2.49 concept (n) /ˈkɒnsept/
idea ● *Dad says youngsters have no concept of what life was like before the Internet.*
❖ ιδέα, έννοια

2.50 aspect (n) /ˈæspekt/
part ● *The best aspect of our visit was the delicious food.* ❖ πλευρά

2.51 occurrence (n) /əˈkʌrəns/
sth that happens ● *Floods didn't use to be such a frequent occurrence.* ➢ occur (v)
❖ περιστατικό, συμβάν

2.52 phenomenon (n) /fɪˈnɒmɪnən/
a fact or event in nature or society, usually one not fully understood ● *Weather is a natural phenomenon which humans cannot control.*
➢ phenomenal (adj) ❖ φαινόμενο
✎ NB: Plural = phenomena

2.53 expand (v) /ɪksˈpænd/
become bigger ● *The company has expanded and now has two new offices in the UK.*
➢ expansion (n) ❖ επεκτείνω, διευρύνω

2.54 extend (v) /ɪkˈstend/
stretch ● *The Roman Empire extended across much of Europe and parts of northern Africa.*
➢ extent, extension (n), extensive (adj)
❖ εκτείνομαι

2.55 exchange (v) /ɪksˈtʃeɪndʒ/
change for sth else ● *I exchanged email addresses with my new colleagues in our Paris office.*
➢ exchange (n) ❖ ανταλλάσσω

2.56 provide (v) /prəˈvaɪd/
give ● *Does this hotel provide free Wi-Fi or do I have to go to an Internet café?* ➢ provision (n) ❖ παρέχω

2.57 swap (v) /swɒp/
change one thing for another ● *We swapped email addresses so we could keep in touch.* ❖ ανταλάσσω

2.58 reindeer (n) /ˈreɪndɪə/
a deer with horns that lives in northern countries ● *Rudolph is a famous reindeer with a red nose!*
❖ τάρανδος

2.59 canal (n) /kəˈnæl/
a long, man-made stretch of water for boats to travel on ● *We travelled in a gondola along the canals of Venice.* ❖ κανάλι

2.60 spice (n) /spaɪs/
powder or seeds from a plant with a strong taste or smell used in cooking ● *Cumin is a strong spice which you can put in meatballs to make them tasty.*
➢ spicy (adj) ❖ μπαχαρικό

2.61 highway (n) /ˈhaɪˌweɪ/
a main road, one that usually connects towns or cities ● *It takes only fifteen minutes to get to my house if you drive on the highway.*
❖ λεωφόρος, αυτοκινητόδρομος

2.62 drive-through (n) /ˈdraɪv-θruː/
a restaurant where you buy your food from your car and then drive away with it ● *We got burgers at the drive-through and didn't even have to get out of the car.* ❖ εστιατόριο όπου ο πελάτης εξυπηρετείται μένοντας μέσα στο αυτοκίνητό του

2.63 windmill (n) /ˈwɪndmɪl/
a tall building with sails that turn as the wind blows ● *There are windmills on the island of Mykonos.* ❖ ανεμόμυλος

2.64 mummy (n) /ˈmʌmi/
a dead body that was preserved long ago by being rubbed with oils and wrapped in a cloth
● *The archaeologist found a number of mummies in the pyramid.* ➢ mummify (v) ❖ μούμια

2.65 cuisine (n) /kwɪˈziːn/
a region's characteristic style of cooking ● *I love Italian cuisine, especially the dishes of Sicily.* ❖ κουζίνα, φαγητό

2.66 dog sledding (n) /dɒg ˈslədɪŋ/
a sport where dogs pull a sled along the snow
● *There are dog-sledding competitions in Canada every winter.* ❖ έλκηθρο με σκύλους

2.67 civilisation (n) /sɪvəlaɪˈzeɪʃn/
organised human society ● *The civilisation of Ancient Greece had a great influence on the world.*
➢ civilise (v), civilised (adj) ❖ πολιτισμός

2.68 export (n) /ˈekspɔːt/
selling goods to another country ● *China's exports include clothes an electrical goods.* ➢ export (v)
❖ εξαγωγή

2.69 homeland (n) /ˈhəʊmlænd/
native country ● *I live abroad, but one day I will return to my homeland.* ❖ πατρίδα

2.70 influence (n) /ˈɪnfluəns/
affecting the way people think or act
● *Powerful countries often want to have an influence on other countries and control them.*
➢ influence (v), influential (adj) ❖ επιρροή

2.71 network (n) /ˈnetwɜːk/
a large number of roads that cross and meet at many points ● *Germany has an excellent transport network.* ❖ δίκτυο

2.72 port (n) /pɔːt/
a town by the sea with a harbour ● *The ferry docked at the port of Piraeus.* ❖ λιμάνι

2.73 roadway (n) /ˈrəʊdweɪ/
the part of a road used by vehicles ● *You'll need a jeep in the countryside because there isn't a good roadway.* ❖ δρόμος, κατάστρωμα (δρόμου)

2.74 **proper** (adj) /ˈprɒpə/
appropriate; correct • *There wasn't any proper heating in the hotel and we were very cold.* ➢ properly (adv) ❖ κατάλληλος

2.75 **efficient** (adj) /ɪˈfɪʃnt/
having or producing the best result • *The most efficient way get across Athens is to use the Metro.* ➢ efficiency (n), efficiently (adv) ❖ αποτελεσματικός ✎ Opp: inefficient

2.76 **extensive** (adj) /ɪksˈtensɪv/
very great • *The fire caused extensive damage and it cost a lot of money to repair the house.* ➢ extend (v), extent (n) ❖ εκτενής

2.77 **import** (n) /ˈɪmpɔːt/
bringing goods from another country • *The import of goods such as clothes from Bangladesh is common in the UK.* ➢ import (v) ❖ εισαγωγή

2.78 **trade route** (n) /treɪd ruːt/
the way goods travel from one place to another • *One famous trade route was the Silk Road, which enabled trade between Asia and Europe.* ❖ διαδρομή του εμπορίου

2.79 **land** (n) /lænd/
area of ground • *The Silk Road was an important trade route over land that connected Europe to Asia.* ❖ γη

2.80 **conduct** (v) /kənˈdʌkt/
organise or do sth • *The scientist conducted a number of experiments.* ❖ διεξάγω

2.81 **caravan** (n) /ˈkærəvæn/
a group of people, animals and vehicles travelling together • *Caravans have been travelling across deserts for centuries.* ❖ καραβάνι

2.82 **domesticate** (v) /dəˈmestɪkeɪt/
tame an animal and keep it as a pet or on a farm • *Humans domesticated the dog thousands of years ago.* ➢ domesticated (adj), domestic (adj) ❖ εξημερώνω

2.83 **transfer** (v) /trænsˈfɜː/
move sth from one place to another • *We transferred our bags to a taxi when we got off the ferry.* ➢ transfer (n) ❖ μεταφέρω

2.84 **found** (v) /faʊnd/
start sth like a a city, business etc • *The Romans founded the city of Londinium, known today as London.* ➢ founder (n) ❖ θεμελιώνω, ιδρύω

2.85 **textile** (n) /ˈtekstaɪl/
cloth; material • *Polyester is a modern synthetic textile.* ❖ ύφασμα

2.86 **pottery** (n) /ˈpɒtəri/
plates, dishes etc made from clay and then baked • *We saw lots of ancient pottery in the museum, but my favourite was a beautiful dish.* ❖ είδη αγγειοπλαστικής, πήλινα, κεραμικά

Traded products
dairy product   pottery
spice   textile

Grammar page 21

2.87 **tribe** (n) /traɪb/
a group of people of the same race, language and customs • *The cultures of the different Amazonian tribes are very interesting.* ➢ tribal (adj) ❖ φυλή

2.88 **elect** (n) /ɪˈlekt/
If people elect sb, they choose a person to represent them by voting. • *The people of the village elected Mrs Browne as mayor.* ➢ election (n) ❖ εκλέγω

2.89 **conquer** (n) /ˈkɒŋkə/
If one country or group of people conquers another, they take complete control of their land. • *The Romans conquered Britain in the first century AD.* ➢ conqueror, conquest (n) ❖ κατακτώ

2.90 **spill** (n) /spɪl/
If you spill a liquid, it accidentally flows over the edge of its container. • *I spilt coffee all over the cream-coloured carpet.* ❖ χύνω

2.91 **contribute** (v) /kənˈtrɪbjuːt/
help to make sth happen • *The army contributed to the expansion of the Roman Empire.* ➢ contribution (n) ❖ συμβάλλω

2.92 **form** (n) /fɔːm/
type • *Early forms of writing look like pictures rather than letters.* ➢ form (v) ❖ μορφή

2.93 **record** (n) /ˈrekɔːd/
an account of sth in writing, photographs etc so that you can refer to it later • *Records of births and deaths are kept at the local council.* ❖ αρχεία

2.94 **establish** (v) /ɪsˈtæblɪʃ/
create sth like a city, system or organisation • *Many cities established themselves along rivers where traders passed.* ❖ θεσπίζω, ιδρύω, εδραιώνομαι

2.95 **spring up** (phr v) /sprɪŋ ʌp/
suddenly start to exist • *A new block of flats has sprung up in our neighbourhood.* ❖ ξεφυτρώνω

2.96 **position** (n) /pəˈzɪʃn/
place • *Can you find your position on the map?* ➢ position (v) ❖ θέση

2.97 **waterway** (n) /ˈwɔːtəweɪ/
a river, canal, or other route for travel by water • *The Corinth Canal is a narrow waterway.* ❖ υδάτινη οδός, δίαυλος

2.98 **come up with** (phr v) /kʌm ʌp wɪð/
think of • *The Arabs first came up with the concept of zero.* ❖ επινοώ (ιδέα, λύση κλπ)

2.99 **farming** (n) /ˈfɑːmɪŋ/
growing crops and raising animals • *Farming is difficult as working on the land is backbreaking work.* ➢ farm, farmer (n) ❖ γεωργία

2.100 **handle** (v) /ˈhændl/
cope with • *People from the north tend to handle the cold winter weather better than southerners.* ❖ αντιμετωπίζω, χειρίζομαι

2.101 **regular** (adj) /ˈrɛgjʊlə/
happening at equal intervals • *She has regular, twice-yearly appointments at the dentist because she wants to have healthy teeth.* ➢ regularly (adv) ❖ τακτός, τακτικός

2.102 **flood** (n) /flʌd/
a large amount of water that covers an area that is usually dry • *Every year there are floods after the first rains because so many trees are lost in forest fires.* ➢ flood (v) ❖ πλημμύρα

2.103 **agriculture** (n) /ˈægrɪkʌltʃə/
farming • *He is a farmer and has always worked in agriculture.* ➢ agricultural (adj) ❖ γεωργία

2.104 **incredible** (adj) /ɪnˈkrɛdɪbl/
unbelievable • *It is incredible that the Ancient Egyptians built the pyramids with simple tools* ➢ incredibly (adv) ❖ απίστευτος

2.105 **advancement** (n) /ədˈvɑːnsmənt/
progress • *He owes his rapid career advancement to hard work.* ➢ advance (n, v) ❖ πρόοδος

2.106 **archaeologist** (n) /ˌɑːkɪˈɒlədʒɪst/
sb who studies the past by examining ruins and objects found in the ground • *British archaeologists found the ancient city of Pavlopetri in 1967.* ➢ archaeology (n), archaeological (adj) ❖ αρχαιολόγος

2.107 **dig** (v) /dɪg/
make a hole in the ground • *The archaeologist dug carefully and found a skeleton.* ❖ σκάβω

2.108 **ruin** (n) /ˈruːɪn/
a building that has been partly destroyed • *The ruins of the temple of Poseidon at Sounion are very beautiful.* ➢ ruin (v) ❖ ερείπιο, χαλάσματα

2.109 **temple** (n) /ˈtɛmpl/
religious building where people worship • *The temple of Poseidon is at Sounion.* ❖ ναός

2.110 **depiction** (n) /dɪˈpɪkʃən/
representing sb or sth in painting, drawing or writing • *I thought the novelist's depiction of the hero was excellent.* ➢ depict (v) ❖ απεικόνιση

2.111 **Assyrian** (n) /əˈsɪrɪən/
a person from the ancient kingdom of Mesopotamia, which stretched from Egypt to the Persian Gulf • *The culture of the Assyrian Empire produced great art.* ➢ Assyria (n) ❖ ασσυριακός

2.112 **warrior** (n) /ˈwɒrɪə/
a fighter; a soldier • *The warriors fought with swords.* ➢ war (n) ❖ πολεμιστής

> **Synonyms**
> call for = require   call off = cancel
> extend = stretch   farming = agriculture

Listening page 22

2.113 **house** (v) /haʊz/
If a building, place or container houses sth, it is kept there. • *Hundreds of famous paintings are housed in the Louvre.* ❖ στεγάζω

2.114 **date back (to)** (phr v) /deɪt bæk (tuː)/
exist from a time in the past • *The Parthenon dates back to the 5th century BC.* ❖ χρονολογούμαι από

2.115 **major** (adj) /ˈmeɪdʒə/
important • *Brussels is a major European city where many important decisions are made.* ❖ σημαντικός, μεγάλος

2.116 **illuminate** (v) /ɪˈluːmɪˌneɪt/
light up; decorate with lights • *The Parthenon is illuminated at night.* ➢ illumination (n) ❖ φωτίζω

Grammar page 24

2.117 **air force** (n) /ɛə fɔːs/
the part of a country's military organisation that is concerned with fighting in the air • *He joined the air force and flew planes during the war.* ❖ (πολεμική) αεροπορία

2.118 **oversleep** (n) /ˌəʊvəˈsliːp/
sleep for longer than you intended to • *She overslept and missed the bus.* ❖ παρακοιμάμαι

Use your English page 25

2.119 **call round** (phr v) /kɔːl raʊnd/
visit • *Let's call round at Tina's house and see if she wants to come out with us.* ❖ επισκέπτομαι

2.120 **call back** (phr v) /kɔːl bæk/
phone later • *I have to go now, but I'll call you back.* ❖ ξανατηλεφωνώ

2.121 **call off** (phr v) /kɔːl ɒf/
cancel • *The visit to the museum was called off because there was a strike.* ❖ ακυρώνω

2.122 **call up** (phr v) /kɔːl ʌp/
phone • *I called up Wendy, but she didn't answer her phone.* ❖ τηλεφωνώ

2.123 **call out** (phr v) /kɔːl aʊt/
say aloud • *Mr Jones called out all the pupils' names.* ❖ διαβάζω δυνατά

2.124 **call on** (phr v) /kɔːl ɒn/
ask sb to do sth • *The boss called on me to prepare the agenda for the monthly meeting.* ❖ ζητώ από κάποιον να κάνει κάτι

2.125 **call for** (phr v) /kɔːl fɔː/
require • *Dealing with climate change calls for action from governments worldwide* ❖ απαιτώ

2.126 **call in** (phr v) /kɔːl ɪn/
ask sb to come to a particular place to do sth for you • *She called in a plumber to fix the kitchen tap.* ❖ καλώ, ζητώ τις υπηρεσίες κάποιου

2.127 **electrician** (n) /ɪlekˈtrɪʃn/
sb who installs and mends electrical equipment • *An electrician fitted new lights for us.* ➢ electricity (n), electric (adj) ❖ ηλεκτρολόγος

2.128 **require** (v) /rɪˈkwaɪə/
need • *This job requires good computing skills.* ➢ requirement (n) ❖ απαιτώ

2.129 **honesty** (n) /ˈɒnəsti/
being honest; telling the truth • *People trust him because of his honesty; he always tells the truth.* ➢ honest (adj), honestly (adv) ❖ ειλικρίνεια ✎ Opp: dishonesty

2.130 **responsibility** (n) /rɪˌspɒnsəˈbɪləti/
duty • *It is the responsibility of the crew to make sure that passengers wear their seat belts.* ➢ responsible (adj) ❖ ευθύνη
✎ Opp: irresponsibility

2.131 **cancel** (v) /ˈkænsl/
call off; decide that sth will not take place • *The concert was cancelled because the lead singer was sick.* ➢ cancellation (n) ❖ ακυρώνω

2.132 **reputation** (n) /repjʊˈteɪʃn/
the opinion people have of sb • *He has built a reputation as a hard-working employee.* ➢ reputable (adj) ❖ φήμη

2.133 **empire** (n) /ˈempaɪə/
all the countries under the control of one ruler • *The Romans created an enormous empire that stretched across much of Europe.* ➢ emperor (n), imperial (adj)
❖ αυτοκρατορία

2.134 **impression** (n) /ɪmˈpreʃn/
Your impression of sb or sth is what you think they are like. • *His untidy clothes made a bad impression on the interviewer.* ➢ impress (v), impressive (adj) ❖ εντύπωση

2.135 **space** (n) /speɪs/
place; area • *We saved space by buying a small sofa.* ➢ spacious (adj) ❖ χώρος

2.136 **stretch** (v) /stretʃ/
extend • *White cliffs stretch along the south coast of England.* ➢ stretch (n) ❖ εκτείνομαι

2.137 **medical condition** (n) /ˈmedɪkəl kənˈdɪʃən/
a problem with your health • *Stephen Hawking suffers from a severe medical condition.*
❖ πρόβλημα υγείας

2.138 **relief** (n) /rɪˈliːf/
If you feel relief from pain, you no longer feel pain. • *Take some aspirin; it will give you relief from your headache.* ➢ relieve (v)
❖ ανακούφιση

2.139 **professional** (adj) /prəˈfeʃənl/
doing a job to earn money • *Some professional football players make a lot of money.*
➢ profession (n), professional (n)
❖ επαγγελματίας

Writing: an opinion essay
pages 26–27

2.140 **sum up** (phr v) /sʌm ʌp/
briefly describe the main features of sth • *He summed up the main ideas at the end of the lesson.* ❖ συνοψίζω

2.141 **grasp** (v) /ɡrɑːsp/
understand • *He just couldn't grasp the rules of the game.* ❖ καταλαβαίνω, αντιλαμβάνομαι

2.142 **view** (n) /vjuː/
opinion • *My view is that wealthy people should help the poor.* ❖ γνώμη

2.143 **to my mind** (exp) /tə maɪ maɪnd/
in my opinion • *To my mind, she is a great artist, but perhaps you disagree.* ❖ κατά τη γνώμη μου

2.144 **do business** (exp) /duː ˈbɪznɪs/
work or trade with • *Many Greek companies do business in the UK and you can buy Greek foods in British supermarkets.* ❖ συνεργάζομαι

2.145 **pleasure** (n) /ˈpleʒə(r)/
happiness, enjoyment or satisfaction • *He gets a lot of pleasure from his work.*
➢ please (v), pleased (adj), pleasant (adj)
❖ ευχαρίστηση, αναψυχή

2.146 **be worth the effort** (expr) /biː wɜːθ ðiː ˈefət/
be a good idea to try sth • *It was worth the effort to climb to the top of the mountain because the view was amazing.* ❖ αξίζει τον κόπο

2.147 **effectively** (adv) /ɪˈfektɪvli/
in a way that gets the result you wanted • *They dealt with the problem effectively.*
➢ effect (n), effective (adj) ❖ αποτελεσματικά

2.148 **recent** (adj) /ˈriːsənt/
happening a short time ago • *How was your recent visit to London?* ➢ recently (adv) ❖ πρόσφατος

2.149 **cultural awareness** (n) /ˈkʌltʃərəl əˈweənɪs/
knowing about and understanding a different culture • *Reading books by foreign writers has increased my cultural awareness.*
❖ πολιτισμική συνείδηση

2.150 **key** (n) /kiː/
the way to achieve sth • *The key to enjoying your trip is to find out a bit about the place you are going to visit.* ❖ κλειδί

2.151 **enrich** (v) /ɪnˈrɪtʃ/
improve the quality of sth • *Doing a course in pottery-making has enriched her life by giving her a new interest.* ➢ enrichment (n)
❖ εμπλουτίζω

2.152 conclude (v) /kənˈkluːd/
finish • *To conclude, I want to thank you all for coming.* ➢ conclusion (n), conclusive (adj) ❖ καταλήγω

2.153 abroad (adv) /əˈbrɔːd/
in another country • *She moved abroad and had to learn the language of the country.*
❖ στο εξωτερικό

Phrasal verbs

all back	call on	come up with
call for	call out	date back (to)
call in	call round	spring up
call off	call up	sum up

Video: A Special Type of Neighbourhood page 28

2.154 neighbourhood (n) /ˈneɪbəhʊd/
part of a town • *We live in a friendly neighbourhood and we know everyone there.* ➢ neighbour (n)
❖ γειτονιά

2.155 immigrate (v) /ˈɪmɪgreɪt/
come to live or work in a foreign country
• *We immigrated from India to the USA ten years ago, so our six-year-old was born here.*
➢ immigration, immigrant (n) ❖ μεταναστεύω

2.156 community member (n) /kəˈmjuːnəti ˈmembə/
sb who is part of a social group in a particular area • *Community members met at the town hall to discuss rising crime in the area.*
❖ μέλος της κοινότητας

2.157 relative (n) /ˈrelətɪv/
a family member • *Her oldest relative is her great-grandfather.* ❖ συγγενής

2.158 organisation (n) /ˌɔːgənaɪˈzeɪʃn/
an official group • *WWF is an organisation that tries to save animals.* ➢ organise (v) ❖ οργάνωση

2.159 district (n) /ˈdɪstrɪkt/
area • *There are many homeless people in the poorer districts of the city.* ❖ συνοικία

2.160 mural (n) /ˈmjʊərəl/
a painting or other work of art on a wall
• *Many murals are really good graffiti.*
❖ τοιχογραφία

2.161 raise (v) /reɪz/
collect (money) • *Our school raised money for poor families.* ❖ συγκεντρώνω

2.162 reflect (v) /rɪˈflekt/
show what sth is like • *His books reflect life in the poorer districts of Chicago.* ➢ reflection (n)
❖ απεικονίζω, αντικατοπτρίζω

2.163 choir (n) /kwaɪə/
a group of people who sing together. • *Our choir sang at the school concert.* ❖ χορωδία

2.164 natural disaster (n) /ˈnætrl dɪˈzɑːstə/
an event like an earthquake, flood, storm or fire that causes destruction and injuries or death
• *The earthquake in Japan was a terrible natural disaster.* ❖ φυσική καταστροφή

2.165 nation (n) /ˈneɪʃn/
an individual country • *Greece is a small European nation.* ➢ national (n) ❖ έθνος

2.166 lively (adj) /ˈlaɪvli/
interesting and exciting • *The tarantella is a lively Italian dance.* ❖ ζωηρός, έντονος

2.167 fairness (n) /ˈfeənɪs/
being fair or just • *The teacher treated us with fairness and listened to all of our views.*
➢ fair (adj) ❖ αμεροληψία, δικαιοσύνη

Vocabulary Exercises

A Complete the sentences with these words.

back call catch date for give in spring sum up

1 You should _____ up your ideas in the conclusion.
2 He really ought to _____ up eating so many sweets.
3 They might _____ off the match because of snow.
4 Being an archaeologist calls _____ patience and attention to detail.
5 Have you come _____ with any good ideas for the school magazine?
6 Did all those houses just _____ up overnight?
7 I don't think bright green will _____ on this year.
8 I can't speak now so I will call you _____ tomorrow.
9 They had to call _____ an electrician to fix the wiring.
10 These vases _____ back to classical Greece.

B Match.

1 natural   a through
2 community   b change
3 dog   c disaster
4 drive-   d sledding
5 cultural   e route
6 climate   f member
7 trade   g product
8 dairy   h awareness

C Circle the correct words.

1 The world has become a smaller place as a result of globalisation / organisation.
2 Countries that produce little rely on exports / imports from other countries.
3 She is talented and has the tolerance / potential to be a great actress.
4 A new facility / chain of menswear shops has opened across the country.
5 Europeans only discovered the source / influence of the Blue Nile in the nineteenth century.
6 The Panama Canal is a major waterway / roadway.
7 That fence marks the edge / boundary between our farm and theirs.
8 We had to transfer / exchange our luggage to another coach when the first one broke down.
9 This city was stretched / founded many centuries ago as a place of trade.
10 What concept / aspect of the situation most concerns you?

D Complete the sentences with the correct form of the words in capitals.

1 Modern _____ owes a lot to ancient teachings.   CIVILISE
2 It is essential that you show complete _____ in court.   HONEST
3 These companies are _____; they both sell electrical goods.   SIMILARITY
4 The boss showed _____ in the way he dealt with employees.   FAIR
5 What sort of _____ did you make at the interview?   IMPRESS
6 Is it your _____ that globalisation is a positive thing?   BELIEVE
7 Unemployment is a _____ problem these days.   UNIVERSE
8 Running a department is a great _____.   RESPONSIBLE
9 He seems to try hard, but I'm afraid he isn't very _____.   EFFICIENCY
10 The fire caused _____ damage.   EXTEND

2 Grammar

2.1 Past Simple

Κατάφαση
I/he/she/it/we/you/they work**ed**
Άρνηση
I/he/she/it/we/you/they **didn't** work
Ερώτηση
Did I/he/she/it/we/you/they work?
Σύντομες απαντήσεις
Yes, I/he/she/it/we/you/they **did**.   **No**, I/he/she/it/we/you/they **didn't**.

Ορθογραφία:

sol**ve** → sol**ved**   trave**l** → trave**lled**   stud**y** → stud**ied**   st**ay** → stay**ed**

Σημείωση: Κάποια ρήματα είναι ανώμαλα και δεν ακολουθούν αυτούς τους ορθογραφικούς κανόνες. Δες τη λίστα των ανωμάλων ρημάτων στις σελ. 176-177 του Student's Book.

Χρησιμοποιούμε **Past Simple** για:
κάτι που ξεκίνησε και τελείωσε στο παρελθόν.
→ *Michael Jackson **died** in 2009.*
ρουτίνες και συνήθειες που είχαμε στο παρελθόν (συχνά με επιρρήματα συχνότητας).
→ *People often **migrated** to find work.*
καταστάσεις στο παρελθόν.
→ *We **were** so happy to see them after such a long time.*
πράξεις που έγιναν η μία μετά την άλλη στο παρελθόν, για παράδειγμα όταν λέμε μια ιστορία.
→ *She **got** home, **sat** on the sofa and **switched on** the TV.*

Σημείωση: Κάποιες συνηθισμένες χρονικές εκφράσεις που χρησιμοποιούνται συχνά με Past Simple είναι *yesterday, last night/week/month/summer, a week/month/year ago,* κλπ.
→ *We watched a documentary on globalisation **last night**.*

2.2 Past Continuous

Κατάφαση
I/he/she/it **was** work**ing**   we/you/they **were** work**ing**
Άρνηση
I/he/she/it **was not (wasn't)** work**ing**   we/you/they **were not (weren't)** work**ing**
Ερώτηση
Was I/he/she/it work**ing**?   **Were** we/you/they work**ing**?
Σύντομες απαντήσεις
Yes, I/he/she/it **was**.   **No**, I/he/she/it **wasn't**.   **Yes**, we/you/they **were**.   **No**, we/you/they **weren't**.

Ορθογραφία:

gi**ve** → giv**ing**   trave**l** → trave**lling**   p**ay** → pay**ing**

Χρησιμοποιούμε **Past Continuous** για:
πράξεις που ήταν σε εξέλιξη σε συγκεκριμένη χρονική στιγμή στο παρελθόν.
→ *I **was reading** an article on immigration at 5 pm yesterday.*
δύο ή περισσότερες πράξεις που ήταν σε εξέλιξη την ίδια χρονική στιγμή στο παρελθόν.
→ *Tom **was talking** on his mobile phone while I **was reading** a Japanese comic book.*

2 Grammar

να περιγράψουμε το σκηνικό μιας ιστορίας.
→ *The sun **was rising** and the caravans **were starting** their journey across the desert.*
μια πράξη που ενώ ήταν σε εξέλιξη στο παρελθόν, διακόπηκε από μια άλλη.
→ *Ricardo **was reading** about Alexander the Great when his son **came** to talk to him.*

Σημείωση: Κάποιες συνηθισμένες χρονικές εκφράσεις που χρησιμοποιούνται συχνά με Past Continuous είναι *while, as, all day/week/month/year, at ten o'clock last night, last Sunday/week/month/year, this afternoon,* κλπ.
→ *They were walking around the abandoned city **this afternoon**.*

2.3 Used to & Would

Χρησιμοποιούμε *used to* + bare infinitive (απαρέμφατο χωρίς *to*) για:
πράξεις που κάναμε συχνά στο παρελθόν, αλλά δεν κάνουμε τώρα πια.
→ *Victoria **used to work** for a bank.*
καταστάσεις που υπήρχαν στο παρελθόν αλλά δεν υπάρχουν τώρα.
→ *My sister **used to be** very funny, but now she's serious.*

Χρησιμοποιούμε *would* + bare infinitive (απαρέμφατο χωρίς *to*) για πράξεις που κάναμε συχνά στο παρελθόν, αλλά δεν κάνουμε τώρα πια. Δεν το χρησιμοποιούμε για καταστάσεις που υπήρχαν στο παρελθόν.
→ *When I was a teenager, I **would spend** hours watching TV every day.*

2.4 Past Simple ή Present Perfect Simple

Χρησιμοποιούμε **Past Simple** για πράξεις που έγιναν σε συγκεκριμένη στιγμή στο παρελθόν, και για πράξεις ή καταστάσεις που ολοκληρώθηκαν στο παρελθόν.
→ *A lot of businesses **moved** to developing countries last year.*
→ *The archaeologist **worked** in the desert for three years.* (Δεν εργάζεται εκεί τώρα πια.)

Χρησιμοποιούμε **Present Perfect Simple** για πράξεις που έγιναν σε απροσδιόριστο χρόνο στο παρελθόν, και για πράξεις ή καταστάσεις που ξεκίνησαν στο παρελθόν και είναι ακόμα σε εξέλιξη.
→ *Mum **has bought** a book on Chinese spices.* (Δεν γνωρίζουμε ή δεν λέμε πότε.)
→ *The professor **has been** in his office all morning.* (Ακόμα είναι εκεί.)

Grammar Exercises

A Complete the dialogue using the Past Simple or Past Continuous of the verbs in brackets.

Larry: Am I late? What time **(1)** _____ (your lecture/finish), Martha?

Martha: We **(2)** _____ (not have) a lecture after all as Professor Barnes is sick.

Larry: But you **(3)** _____ (not wait) here a while ago, were you? I **(4)** _____ (sit) at the table just over there at nine.

Martha: No, I **(5)** _____ (study) in the library and trying to finish my paper on globalisation.

Larry: Right. So how's your paper getting on?

Martha: Not that well, really. It **(6)** _____ (require) a lot of research at the start and there **(7)** _____ (not be) many books in the library. I **(8)** _____ (find) some studies on the Internet and then I **(9)** _____ (order) some books from another library, but that **(10)** _____ (take) a week. So now I have all the information I need, but the paper has to be handed in on Friday.

Larry: I bet you **(11)** _____ (work) on it all night.

Martha: Absolutely. I'm exhausted, and it's still not finished.

B Circle the correct words.

1 He used to / would be a student, but now he works at a bank.
2 She used / would often watch the canal boats when she was a child.
3 Did you use / used to live in Egypt?
4 She would call / called round at her aunt's once a week.
5 Martin didn't use to / wouldn't be interested in archaeology when he was younger.
6 I use to / would first get an idea and then draw the mural.
7 Used / Would they meet at the Internet café regularly in those days?
8 We didn't use to liked / like the neighbourhood, but it's grown on us.

C Complete the sentences using the Past Simple or Present Perfect Simple of the verbs in brackets.

1 The Nile _____ (be) a major trade route for years and remains so today.
2 The canal _____ (close) last year because of complaints from the community.
3 _____ (you/ever/look up) your ancestors in the local records?
4 _____ (he/cancel) the meeting yesterday?
5 Actually, Lars _____ (never/visit) Norway, even though he is half Norwegian.
6 We _____ (go) to the exhibition on climate change last week.
7 I _____ (read) two chapters of this book already.
8 No, she _____ (not start) her archaeology course yet.

D Choose the correct answers.

1 Many companies ___ and now operate from less developed countries.
   a have outsourced
   b outsourced
   c were outsourcing

2 This port ___ itself centuries ago.
   a used to establish
   b established
   c has established

3 The historian ___ the tour of the site yesterday.
   a would conduct
   b has conducted
   c conducted

4 China ___ in silk for centuries and it is still big business nowadays.
   a has traded
   b was trading
   c would trade

5 In the past, trade routes ___ for hundreds of miles over land.
   a stretched
   b have stretched
   c were stretching

6 We ___ bags because mine is so heavy.
   a used to exchange
   b have exchanged
   c were exchanging

7 At the time, he ___ for a local news network.
   a has worked
   b was working
   c would work

8 This company ___ very successful, but now it isn't doing well.
   a would be
   b has been
   c used to be

Use your English

Exam Task

For questions **1–12**, read the text below and think of the word which best fits each gap. Use only **one** word in each gap.

The Silk Road

The Silk Road **(1)** _____ a major trade route and dates **(2)** _____ to the ancient Chinese Han dynasty. **(3)** _____ stretched from China to the Mediterranean passing through India and Persia. Traders **(4)** _____ travel in caravans along the route, which called **(5)** _____ courage because it was often dangerous: tribes used **(6)** _____ attack them to steal their valuable silk and other goods.

The Indians were proficient traders and successfully **(7)** _____ business with the Chinese, exchanging precious stones and metals for silk. But India was not the only place of trade. Cities established **(8)** _____ along the route and trading posts sprung **(9)** _____ in the new cities. China was also opening up because the Silk Road **(10)** _____ bringing visitors into China itself, leading to an exchange of knowledge between East and West.

However, the Silk Road declined as shipping trade increased and travelling by road was no longer worth **(11)** _____ effort. Imagine traders refusing to travel **(12)** _____ land and declaring, 'Not for all the tea China!'.

3 Star Quality

Word Focus — page 32

3.1 **heir** (n) /eə/
the person who takes sb's place or title when that person dies • *Prince Charles is the heir to the British throne and will become king when his mother dies.* ❖ κληρονόμος

3.2 **title** (n) /ˈtaɪtl/
a word like Mr or Mrs that is used before sb's name • *In the box on this form where it says "title", you should write Mrs, Miss or Ms.* ❖ τίτλος

3.3 **barricade** (v) /ˈbærɪkeɪd/
prevent people from coming into a place by blocking the entrance • *The armed robbers barricaded the door of the bank to keep the police out.* ➣ barricade (n)
❖ φράζω, κλείνω με οδόφραγμα

3.4 **venom** (n) /ˈvenəm/
poison from a snake, insect or spider • *The venom of many snakes is fatal unless you have an antidote.* ➣ venomous (adj) ❖ δηλητήριο

3.5 **quest** (n) /kwest/
a search • *Archaeologists are on a quest for knowledge about the past.* ❖ αναζήτηση

3.6 **sacred** (adj) /ˈseɪkrɪd/
holy; connected to God • *Some animals are considered to be sacred.* ❖ ιερός

3.7 **holy** (adj) /ˈhəʊli/
connected to God • *The old lady kissed the holy icon.* ➣ holiness (n) ❖ ιερός, άγιος

Reading — pages 32–33

3.8 **burial place** (n) /ˈberɪəl pleɪs/
where sb who has died is buried; a grave • *The Pyramids of Giza in Egypt are the burial places of pharaohs.* ❖ τόπος ταφής

3.9 **celebrity** (n) /səˈlebrəti/
a famous person • *My favourite celebrity is George Clooney.* ➣ celebrate (v), celebration (n), celebratory (adj) ❖ διασημότητα

3.10 **household name** (n) /ˈhaʊshəʊld neɪm/
well-known person • *Julius Caesar is a household name, being one of the most famous ancient Romans.* ❖ πασίγνωστο όνομα

3.11 **stage** (n) /steɪdʒ/
the place where actors perform in a theatre • *Our theatre seats were at the front, so we had a good view of the stage.* ❖ σκηνή

3.12 **royal** (adj) /ˈrɔɪəl/
connected to a king or queen • *King Juan Carlos was the head of the Spanish royal family.* ➣ royal, royalty (n) ❖ βασιλικός

3.13 **inspiration** (n) /ɪnspəˈreɪʃn/
sth that gives you a new idea • *Ancient Egypt has been the inspiration for many Hollywood movies.* ➣ inspire (v), inspirational (adj)
❖ έμπνευση

3.14 **monitor** (v) /ˈmɒnɪtə/
check the progress of sb or sth • *This machine monitors the changes in temperature during the day.* ❖ παρακολουθώ

3.15 **orbit** (v) /ˈɔːbɪt/
move around a planet, moon or sun • *A new satellite has been launched and will orbit Earth for the next ten years.* ➣ orbit (n)
❖ κινούμαι σε τροχιά

3.16 **asteroid** (n) /ˈæstərɔɪd/
a rock in space • *Some scientists believe an asteroid fell to Earth and ended the age of the dinosaurs.*
❖ αστεροειδής

3.17 **silhouette** (n) /sɪluˈet/
a dark shape seen against a light background • *Behind the curtain, I could see a silhouette moving.*
❖ σιλουέτα, φιγούρα

3.18 **coin** (n) /kɔɪn/
a piece of metal which is money • *I paid for my coffee with a two-euro coin.*
❖ κέρμα

3.19 **persuasiveness** (n) /pəˈsweɪsɪvnəs/
the ability to influence sb's ideas, opinions or actions • *With great persuasiveness she got her dad to let her go on holiday with her friends.* ➣ persuade (v), persuasion (n), persuasive (adj), persuasively (adv) ❖ πειστικότητα

3.20 **pleasant** (adj) /ˈpleznt/
friendly and polite • *Her son seemed a pleasant young man.* ➣ please (v), pleased (adj), pleasure (n) ❖ ευγενικός, ευχάριστος

3.21 **stringed instrument** (n) /strɪŋd ˈɪnstrəmənt/
a musical instrument with strings, e.g. a violin • *He plays two stringed instruments, the guitar and the cello.* ❖ έγχορδο όργανο

3.22 **charm** (n) /tʃɑːm/
a quality which makes you like or feel attracted to sb or sth • *He has a lot of charm and everyone enjoys his company.* ➣ charm (v), charming (adj)
❖ γοητεία

3.23 **looks** (pl n) /lʊks/
appearance • *Some people try to improve their looks with expensive plastic surgery.*
❖ εμφάνιση

3.24 **murder** (n) /ˈmɜːdə/
the crime of killing a person • *The murder of John Lennon shocked the world.* ➣ murder (v), murderer (n) ❖ δολοφονία

3.25	**decade** (n) /ˈdekeɪd/ a period of ten years • *The country's economy has improved in the past decade.* ❖ δεκαετία		3.39	**man-made** (adj) /ˈmæn-meɪd/ caused by people • *Pollution is a man-made problem caused partly by the burning fossil fuels.* ❖ ανθρωπογενής
3.26	**forces** (pl n) /ˈfɔːsɪz/ army (a group of soldiers) • *Alexander the Great led his forces into battle against the Persians.* ❖ στρατιωτικές δυνάμεις		3.40	**excavation** (n) /ekskəˈveɪʃn/ digging for antiquities • *In 1922, an excavation in Egypt revealed the tomb of the Pharoah Tutankhamun.* ➣ excavate (v) ❖ ανασκαφή
3.27	**defeat** (v) /dɪˈfiːt/ beat • *The Allies defeated the Germans in both world wars of the twentieth century.* ➣ defeat (n) ❖ νικώ		3.41	**fail (to)** (v) /feɪl (tə)/ be unsuccessful when you try to do sth • *They failed to come up with a better plan.* ➣ failure (n) ❖ δεν καταφέρνω, αποτυγχάνω ✎ Opp: succeed (in)
3.28	**mausoleum** (n) /mɔːzəˈliːəm/ a building where the members of a rich family are buried • *The dead king was placed in the mausoleum with his ancestors.* ❖ μαυσωλείο		3.42	**tomb** (n) /tuːm/ a large grave • *The tomb of Philip II was excavated by Manolis Andronikos.* ❖ τάφος
3.29	**commit suicide** (expr) /kəˈmɪt ˈsuːɪsaɪd/ kill yourself • *It is said that Marilyn Monroe committed suicide. However, some people think she didn't actually kill herself, but was murdered.* ❖ αυτοκτονώ		3.43	**put forward** (phr v) /pʊt ˈfɔːwʊd/ suggest for discussion • *The student put forward the idea that a field trip to the site would be interesting.* ❖ προτείνω (μια ιδέα)
3.30	**bury** (v) /ˈberi/ put sb who has died in a grave • *When she died, her family buried her next to her husband.* ➣ burial (n) ❖ θάβω, ενταφιάζω		3.44	**lecturer** (n) /ˈlektʃərə/ a teacher at a university • *Professor Stems is a university lecturer in biology.* ➣ lecture (v, n) ❖ λέκτορας
3.31	**location** (n) /ləʊˈkeɪʃn/ the place where sth is situated • *I would love to discover the location of the tomb of Alexander the Great.* ➣ locate (v) ❖ τοποθεσία		3.45	**antiquities** (n) /ænˈtɪkwətiːz/ objects from ancient times • *The museum has an amazing collection of Greek antiquities.* ➣ antique (n, adj) ❖ αρχαιότητες, αρχαιολογικά ευρήματα
3.32	**grave** (n) /greɪv/ the place where a dead person is buried • *We placed flowers on the grave and said our goodbyes to Grandma.* ❖ τάφος		3.46	**access** (n) /ˈækses/ the right or ability to enter a place • *The only Access to the tomb is down this ladder and through that tunnel.* ➣ access (v), accessible (adj) ❖ πρόσβαση
3.33	**remain** (v) /rɪˈmeɪn/ continue to be sth • *The situation remains unchanged.* ❖ παραμένω		3.47	**mention** (v) /ˈmenʃn/ talk about • *The lecturer mentioned that we should go to the library for more information.* ❖ αναφέρω
3.34	**ancestor** (n) /ˈænsestə/ a member of your family who lived a long time ago • *Queen Victoria was the ancestor of Queen Elizabeth II.* ❖ πρόγονος		3.48	**in advance** (expr) /ɪn ədˈvɑːns/ before something happens • *We booked tickets for the concert a month in advance.* ❖ προκαταβολικά, εκ των προτέρων
3.35	**site** (n) /saɪt/ a place where something important happened • *The Pyramids are This is one of the most well-known archaeological sites in the world.* ❖ τοποθεσία		3.49	**convinced** (adj) /kənˈvɪnst/ feeling certain that sth is true • *The archaeologist was convinced that there were more tombs in the area.* ➣ convince (v), convincing (adj) ❖ πείθομαι
3.36	**earthquake** (n) /ˈɜːθkweɪk/ shaking of the ground • *The earthquake shook our flat and all my books fell off the shelf.* ❖ σεισμός		3.50	**lie** (v) /laɪ/ be located in a particular place • *Epidavros lies to the south of Corinth.* ❖ βρίσκομαι
3.37	**tidal wave** (n) /ˈtaɪdl weɪv/ a very large wave often caused by an earthquake at sea; a tsunami • *An earthquake and tidal wave hit Japan in 2011.* ❖ παλιρροιακό κύμα		3.51	**alongside** (prep) /əˌlɒŋˈsaɪd/ next to • *You can park your car alongside ours.* ❖ δίπλα σε
3.38	**rising seas** (pl n) /ˈraɪsɪŋ siːz/ ocean levels which are going up • *Rising seas could lead to flooding in many coastal cities.* ❖ ανερχόμενη στάθμη των θαλασσών		3.52	**victorious** (adj) /vɪkˈtɔːriəs/ having won • *The victorious forces marched through the streets of the city they had taken.* ➣ victory, victor (n) ❖ νικηφόρος

3.53 enemy (n) /ˈenəmi/
sb who is against you • *France and Germany were enemies during World War II.* ❖ εχθρός

3.54 (the) press (n) /(ðə) pres/
newspapers and magazines • *She said she'd go to the press with her story unless they gave her money.* ❖ τύπος

People
celebrity household name
heir ancestor

Archaeology
burial place   site   tomb
coin   excavation

Vocabulary   page 34

3.55 accomplishment (n) /əˈkʌmplɪʃmənt/
sth that is successful; sth that is achieved after a lot of work • *Winning an Oscar is an accomplishment for filmmakers.* ➢ accomplish (v), accomplished (adj) ❖ επίτευγμα, κατόρθωμα

3.56 effort (n) /ˈefət/
trying hard • *John made an effort to be nice even though he didn't want to be at the social event.* ➢ effortless (adj) ❖ προσπάθεια, κόπος

3.57 victory (n) /ˈvɪktəri/
winning; success in a war • *The winning forces celebrated their victory with a parade.* ➢ victor (n), victorious (adj) ❖ νίκη

3.58 chatter (n) /ˈtʃætə/
talk • *The teacher asked us to stop our chatter and pay attention.* ➢ chatter (v) ❖ φλυαρία

3.59 gossip (n) /ˈɡɒsɪp/
talk about other people's lives • *There is lots of gossip about famous people on morning TV shows.* ➢ gossip (v) ❖ κουτσομπολιό

3.60 rumour (n) /ˈruːmə(r)/
sth a lot of people are talking about that may not be true • *I heard a rumour that he is leaving the team.* ❖ φήμη

3.61 massive (adj) /ˈmæsɪv/
enormous; huge • *Elvis Presley was a massive star.* ➢ mass (n), massively (adj) ❖ εντυπωσιακός, σπουδαίος, τεράστιος

3.62 hit (n) /hɪt/
success • *My favourite band is Depeche Mode; they've had loads of hits over the years.* ❖ επιτυχία

3.63 figure (n) /ˈfɪɡə(r)/
sb who is important or famous in some way • *J.F. Kennedy was one of the most important political figures of his time.* ❖ φιγούρα, μορφή

3.64 influential (adj) /ɪnfluˈenʃl/
having an influence on people • *The Dalai Lama is an influential figure who many people respect.* ➢ influence (v, n) ❖ που ασκεί επιρροή

3.65 marked (adj) /mɑːkt/
noticeable • *You have shown a marked improvement in your school work.* ❖ αξιοσημείωτος

3.66 notorious (adj) /nəʊˈtɔːriəs/
famous for a bad reason • *George Karagounis is notorious for falling over in every match.* ➢ notoriety (n) ❖ διαβόητος

3.67 gifted (adj) /ˈɡɪftɪd/
naturally talented • *Manos Hatzidakis was a gifted composer who wrote many beautiful pieces of music.* ➢ gift (n) ❖ προικισμένος

3.68 qualified (adj) /ˈkwɒlɪfaɪd/
having passed the necessary exams; having the necessary experience • *He is a qualified history teacher with a degree from Athens University.* ➢ qualify (v), qualifications (pl n) ❖ πτυχιούχος, έχων τα προσόντα ✎ Opp: unqualified

3.69 accomplished (adj) /əˈkʌmplɪʃt/
talented • *Thanassis Vegos was an accomplished actor and comedian.* ➢ accomplish (v), accomplishment (n) ❖ σπουδαίος

3.70 guarantee (v) /ɡærənˈtiː/
promise sth • *With Jose Mourinho as coach, I guarantee that the team will win the championship.* ➢ guarantee (n) ❖ εγγυώμαι

3.71 sponsor (v) /ˈspɒnsə/
support financially in order to get publicity • *Vodafone sponsors the football team Olympiakos.* ➢ sponsor, sponsorship (n) ❖ είμαι χορηγός, είμαι σπόνσορας

3.72 match-fixing (n) /mætʃ ˈfɪksɪŋ/
arranging the result of a match before it takes place, usually to make money from betting • *People were shocked to learn about match-fixing in football.* ❖ στήσιμο αγώνων

3.73 disgrace (n) /dɪsˈɡreɪs/
a disrespectful or shameful action that brings strong disapproval • *The terrible behaviour of the football fans was a disgrace.* ➢ disgrace (v), disgraceful (adj) ❖ ντροπή, αίσχος
✎ Also: to be in disgrace

3.74 scandal (n) /ˈskændl/
a shocking event • *Why do so many politicians become involved in scandals and yet few of them go to prison?* ➢ scandalise (v), scandalous (adj) ❖ σκάνδαλο

3.75 have stars in one's eyes (expr) /hæv stɑːz ɪn wʌnz aɪz/
dream of being famous • *She's got stars in her eyes and dreams of winning Greek Idol.* ❖ ονειρεύομαι την δημοσιότητα

3.76 publicity (n) /pʌbˈlɪsəti/
attention from the public • *Many stars appear on talk shows to get publicity for their new films.*
❖ δημοσιότητα

3.77 PR (abbreviation) /piː aː/
public relations; explaining to the public what an organisation does so that they will approve of it • *Ronald deals with the celebrity's PR and talks to the press for him.*
❖ δημόσιες σχέσεις

3.78 social networking (n) /ˈsəʊʃl ˈnetwɜːkɪŋ/
socialising with people online • *Social networking is a way of keeping in touch with all your friends.*
❖ κοινωνική δικτύωση

3.79 release (v) /rɪˈliːs/
make sth available for people to buy or see • *The band have just released their new CD.* ➢ release (n) ❖ κυκλοφορώ

3.80 supporter (n) /səˈpɔːtə(r)/
sb who likes a particular sports team or political party • *Thousands of Liverpool supporters watched the final.* ➢ support (v, n)
❖ οπαδός, υποστηρικτής

3.81 fan (n) /fæn/
a supporter; an admirer • *She's a fan of Madam Lala and has all her CDs.*
❖ θαυμαστής

3.82 account (n) /əˈkaʊnt/
a regular online service • *I don't have a Facebook account because I don't want to be like everyone else.* ❖ λογαριασμός

3.83 comment (n) /ˈkɒment/
sth you say; a remark • *The prime minister made a comment about the debt crisis on his blog.*
➢ comment (v) ❖ σχόλιο

3.84 privacy (n) /ˈprɪvəsi/
when you are alone and other people cannot see or hear you • *The problem with being famous is that you rarely get any privacy.* ➢ private (adj)
❖ ιδιωτική ζωή

3.85 in the public eye (expr) /ɪn ðə ˈpʌblɪk aɪ/
receiving a lot of attention in newspapers, on TV, etc. • *As the President's wife, she is constantly in the public eye.*
❖ στο φως της δημοσιότητας

3.86 reveal (v) /rɪˈviːl/
make people aware of sth • *The newspaper revealed the star's secret.* ➢ revelation (n)
❖ αποκαλύπτω

3.87 highly (adv) /ˈhaɪli/
very • *Dolphins are highly intelligent animals.*
❖ πολύ, ιδιαίτερα

3.88 guard (v) /ɡɑːd/
keep sb or sth safe from other people or danger • *The house was guarded by a large dog.*
➢ guard (n) ❖ προφυλάσσω, φρουρώ

Adjectives to describe people
accomplished   notorious
gifted   qualified
influential

Grammar page 35

3.89 review (n) /rɪˈvjuː/
a report in the media giving an opinion of a book, film, etc • *The reviews for Joanne Harris' new book are mixed, but the Guardian recommends it.* ➢ review (v), reviewer (n)
❖ κριτική

3.90 contestant (n) /kənˈtestənt/
sb who takes part in a competition • *The contestant who won received 5,000 euros.*
➢ contest (n) ❖ διαγωνιζόμενος

3.91 go around (phr v) /ɡəʊ əˈraʊnd/
circulate • *There's a rumour going around that the famous couple is splitting up.*
❖ κυκλοφορώ

3.92 stadium (n) /ˈsteɪdiəm/
a building for sports with a playing field surrounded by many seats • *We watched the athletics at the Olympic stadium.* ❖ στάδιο

3.93 start out (phr v) /stɑːt aʊt/
begin • *He started out as a mechanic, but ended up as a Formula 1 driver.* ❖ ξεκινώ

3.94 land (n) /lænd/
a country or region • *People say that America is the land of freedom.* ❖ χώρα, πατρίδα

3.95 aviator (n) /ˈeɪvieɪtə/
a pilot • *Amelia Earhart was the first woman aviator to fly solo across the Atlantic.* ➢ aviation (n)
❖ πιλότος

3.96 explorer (n) /ɪkˈsplɔːrə/
sb who travels to new places to find out about them • *Dutch explorers were the first Europeans to discover Australia and they named it New Holland.*
➢ explore (v), exploration (n) ❖ εξερευνητής

3.97 amateur (adj) /ˈæmətə/
doing an activity for pleasure, not as a job • *He is an amateur photographer but hopes to become professional one day.* ➢ amateur (n)
❖ ερασιτέχνης

3.98 parachute (n) /ˈpærəʃuːt/
a large piece of cloth which allows you to float to the ground from a plane • *He made his first parachute jump from a plane when he was twenty.*
➢ parachute (v), parachutist (n) ❖ αλεξίπτωτο

3.99 cosmonaut (n) /ˈkɒsmənɔːt/
an astronaut from the former Soviet Union • *Yuri Gagarin was the first cosmonaut to go into space.* ❖ κοσμοναύτης

3.100 spacecraft (n) /ˈspeɪskrɑːft/
a vehicle designed to travel in space
• *The Americans sent the first spacecraft to the moon in 1969.* ❖ διαστημόπλοιο

3.101 launch (v) /lɔːntʃ/
send a spacecraft into the sky or into space
• *Spacecraft need tons of fuel to be launched into space.* ➢ launch (n) ❖ εκτοξεύω

3.102 mission (n) /ˈmɪʃn/
an important job that involves travelling somewhere • *The astronaut's mission was to repair part of the space station.* ❖ αποστολή

More people

agent	explorer
aviator	fan
contestant	lecturer
cosmonaut	warlord
enemy	

Listening page 36

3.103 royalty (n) /ˈrɔɪəlti/
kings, queens and their families • *The event was attended by royalty and politicians.* ➢ royal (adj) ❖ μέλος βασιλικής οικογένειας

3.104 fixed (adj) /fɪkst/
not changing • *She has fixed ideas about how children should be brought up.* ❖ αμετάκλητος

3.105 entertainment (n) /entəˈteɪnmənt/
performances that give people pleasure
• *That film was great entertainment.* ➢ entertain (v), entertainer (n), entertaining (adj)
❖ ψυχαγωγία

3.106 industry (n) /ˈɪndəstri/
the companies and people involved in producing a particular type of thing or providing a particular service • *The tourist industry is important to the country's economy.* ➢ industrial (adj)
❖ βιομηχανία

3.107 live up to (expr) /lɪv ʌp tuː/
be as good as sb hopes • *I expected a great film, but the last Harry Potter movie didn't live up to my expectations.* ❖ ανταποκρίνομαι

3.108 resemble (n) /rɪˈzembl/
look like sb or sth • *Mandy resembles her mother.*
➢ resemblance (n) ❖ μοιάζω (με)

Speaking page 37

3.109 have in common (expr) /həv ɪn ˈkɒmən/
have the same interests as sb; be like sb in a certain way • *I like spending time with her – we have a lot in common.*
❖ έχω κοινά σημεία

Grammar page 38

3.110 vanish without a trace (expr) /ˈvænɪʃ wɪˈðaʊt ə treɪs/
disappear suddenly without leaving any sign • *Many ships have vanished without a trace in the Bermuda Triangle.* ❖ χάνομαι από προσώπου γης, εξαφανίζομαι χωρίς να αφήσω ίχνη

3.111 break in (phr v) / breɪk ɪn/
enter a place by force, usually in order to steal sth • *Somebody broke into my office and stole my laptop.* ➢ break-in (n)
❖ διαρρηγνύω, παραβιάζω

3.112 regret (v) /rɪˈɡret/
feel sorry about sth you did or did not do
• *I don't regret what I said to him, so I'm not going to apologise.* ➢ regret (n), regretful (adj)
❖ μετανιώνω

3.113 remove (v) /rɪˈmuːv/
take off (e.g. clothes, glasses) • *Please remove your shoes before you enter.* ➢ removal (n)
❖ βγάζω, αφαιρώ

3.114 audition (v) /ɔːˈdɪʃn/
give a short performance so that sb can judge if you are good enough to act in a play, sing in a concert etc • *You will have to audition for the role.* ➢ audition (n)
❖ κάνω δοκιμαστικό

3.115 lamp post (n) /læmp pəʊst/
a tall pole that supports a light over a public area • *The street lights on the lamp posts light up after dark.* ❖ φανοστάτης, στύλος ηλεκτρικού

Use your English page 39

3.116 come in for (phr v) /kʌm ɪn fɔː/
receive • *People didn't like his latest film and it came in for a lot of criticism.*
❖ γίνομαι αποδέκτης

3.117 look down on (phr v) /lʊk daʊn ɒn/
have a low opinion of • *Dad looks down on pop musicians, but I really admire them.*
❖ έχω άσχημη γνώμη για, περιφρονώ

3.118 circulate (v) /ˈsɜːkjʊleɪt/
go around • *News of the scandal circulated fast as soon as the press got hold of it.*
❖ κυκλοφορώ

3.119 trend (n) /trend/
the way sth is changing or developing
• *There's a trend towards more violent computer games.* ➢ trendy (adj)
❖ τάση, μόδα

3.120 meet expectations (expr) /miːt ˌekspekˈteɪʃnz/
be as good as sb hopes • *The film met my expectations and I enjoyed it as much as I thought I would.* ❖ ανταποκρίνομαι στις προσδοκίες

3.121 criticism (n) /ˈkrɪtɪsɪzm/
disapproval; judgement • *The documentary about the Greek Revolution of 1821 received a lot of criticism.* ➣ criticise (v), critic (n), critical (adj) ❖ κριτική, επίκριση

3.122 split up (phr v) /splɪt ʌp/
separate • *Many Hollywood couples split up; it seems the pressure of fame makes it hard to stay in a relationship.* ❖ χωρίζω

3.123 in public (expr) /ɪn ˈpʌblɪk/
If you do something in public, you do it where people can see you. • *Michael Jackson sometimes wore masks when he went out in public.* ❖ δημόσια

3.124 in private (expr) /ɪn ˈpraɪvɪt/
If you do something in private, you do it where people cannot see you. • *The star is much friendlier in private in the comfort of his own home.* ❖ ιδιωτικά

3.125 under pressure (expr) /ˈʌndə ˈpreʃə/
feeling stressed • *On the opening night of the play, the actors felt under pressure to perform well.* ❖ υπό πίεση

3.126 at a price (expr) /æt ə praɪs/
not for free • *You lose your privacy when you become famous, which is why they say fame comes at a price.* ❖ με κόστος

3.127 agent (n) /ˈeɪdʒənt/
sb who represents sb else and helps them find work • *The first thing you must do is get an agent who will find acting work for you.* ➣ agency (n) ❖ αντιπρόσωπος, ατζέντης

3.128 on sb's behalf (expr) /ɒn ˈsʌmbədɪz bɪˈhɑːf/
instead of sb • *Martin can't be here tonight, so on his behalf I want to thank you for this award.* ❖ εκ μέρους του/της

3.129 press conference (n) /pres ˈkɒnfərəns/
a meeting when an important person answers reporters' questions • *The mayor held a press conference to announce the new plan.* ❖ συνέντευξη τύπου

3.130 to one's astonishment (expr) /tʊ wʌnz əˈstɒnɪʃmənt/
to sb's great surprise • *To our astonishment, Rihanna walked into the shop.* ❖ προς μεγάλη μου έκπληξη

3.131 by all accounts (expr) /baɪ ɑːl əˈkaʊnts/
according to a lot of people • *By all accounts, he is an unpleasant man, but I will decide when I meet him.* ❖ σύμφωνα με όλους

3.132 behind the scenes (expr) /bɪˈhaɪnd ðə siːnz/
when nobody is looking • *The actors seemed to get on well together, but behind the scenes they fought all the time.* ❖ στα παρασκήνια

3.133 without a doubt (expr) /wɪðˈaʊt ə daʊt/
for certain • *Without a doubt, Martin Scorsese is a gifted director.* ❖ χωρίς αμφιβολία ✎ Also: doubtless

Phrasal verbs
come in for	split up
live up to	start out
look down on	turn out
look forward to	turn to
put forward	

Writing: a story pages 40–41

3.134 shock (n) /ʃɒk/
emotional upset • *It was a shock to hear that the young actor had committed suicide.* ➣ shock (v), shocking, shocked (adj) ❖ σοκ

3.135 rip (v) /rɪp/
tear • *She ripped the paper into tiny pieces.* ➣ rip (n) ❖ σκίζω

3.136 envelope (n) /ˈenvələʊp/
a flat paper cover you put a letter in before you post it • *Don't forget to write your address on the envelope.* ❖ φάκελος

3.137 shake like a leaf (expr) /ʃeɪk laɪk ə liːf/
tremble from excitement or fear • *She was shaking like a leaf before she went on her first date.* ❖ τρέμω σαν το ψάρι

3.138 smile from ear to ear (expr) /smaɪl frəm ɪə tʊ ɪə/
smile very happily • *We smiled from ear to ear on hearing the good news.* ❖ γελάνε και τ'αυτιά του

3.139 leap (v) /liːp/
jump • *My dog leapt into my arms and licked my face.* ➣ leap (n) ❖ πηδώ

3.140 couch (n) /kaʊtʃ/
a long seat for two or more people • *She fell asleep on the couch.* ❖ καναπές ✎ Syn: sofa

3.141 stunned (adj) /stʌnd/
really shocked • *They were stunned when they realised they had won the lottery.* ➣ stun (v) ❖ σαστισμένος, άναυδος, κατάπληκτος

3.142 warmly (adv) /ˈwɔːmli/
in a friendly way • *She smiled at us warmly.* ➣ warm (adj), warmth (n) ❖ θερμά

3.143 desperately (adv) /ˈdespərətli/
very much • *Ella desperately wanted a child.* ➣ desperate (adj), despair (n) ❖ απεγνωσμένα

3.144 look forward to (expr) /lʊk ˈfɔːwəd tuː/
be excited and happy about sth that is going to happen • *Paula is looking forward to going to university.* ❖ ανυπομονώ

3.145 turn out (phr v) /tɜːn aʊt/
end in a particular way • *The day started out well, but turned out badly when he failed the audition.* ❖ καταλήγω

3.146 rude (adj) /ruːd/
impolite • *The rude man shut the door in my face.* ➣ rudeness (n), rudely (adv)
❖ αγενής

3.147 arrogant (adj) /ˈærəgənt/
behaving in a proud, unpleasant way • *That arrogant man thinks he is the best actor in Hollywood.* ➣ arrogance (n), arrogantly (adv)
❖ αλαζόνας

3.148 bitterly (adv) /ˈbɪtəli/
in a way which shows anger or disappointment • *Dawn was bitterly disappointed when she didn't get the role.*
➣ bitterness (n), bitter (adj)
❖ πικρά, οδυνηρά, βαριά

3.149 at last (expr) /ət laːst/
finally • *I waited for weeks but at last the letter arrived.* ❖ επιτέλους

3.150 not long afterwards (expr) /nɒt lɒŋ ˈaːftəwʊds/
a little later • *She arrived at four and, not long afterwards, they called her in for the audition.*
❖ λίγο αργότερα

3.151 out of the blue (expr) /aʊt əv ðə bluː/
unexpectedly • *We hadn't heard from Jack for years and then, out of the blue, he sent an email.*
❖ ξαφνικά

3.152 to make matters worse (expr) /tə meɪk ˈmætəz wɜːs/
as if that wasn't enough • *She couldn't see the stage and, to make matters worse, she had forgotten her glasses.*
❖ και σαν να μην έφτανε αυτό

3.153 nervous (adj) /ˈnɜːvəs/
worried • *He is always nervous before a date.*
➣ nervousness (n), nervously (adv)
❖ νευρικός, ανήσυχος, αμήχανος

3.154 meanwhile (adv) /ˈmiːnwaɪl/
while sth else is happening; in the time between two things happening
• *Ian was in his room studying. Meanwhile, his mum was preparing dinner.*
❖ εν τω μεταξύ

3.155 without warning (expr) /wɪðˈaʊt ˈwɔːnɪŋ/
unexpectedly • *It was a lovely day, but without warning it started to rain.*
❖ χωρίς προειδοποίηση

3.156 unexpectedly (adv) /ˌʌnɪkˈspektɪdli/
without warning • *They arrived unexpectedly.*
➣ expect (v), unexpected (adj)
❖ απρόσμενα, απροειδοποίητα

3.157 eventually (adv) /ɪˈventʃuəli/
at the end of a process or a long period of time • *Eventually, he agreed to come.*
❖ τελικά

Video: Confucianism in China page 42

3.158 Confucianism (n) /kənˈfjuːʃənɪzm/
Chinese ethical and moral philosophy based on the teachings of Confucius • *He is studying the teachings of Confucianism.*
❖ κομφουκιανισμός

3.159 quote (n) /kwəʊt/
words from a book, speech, etc. that you repeat because they are interesting or useful
• *The story begins with a quote from Shakespeare's 'Macbeth'.* ➣ quote (v)
❖ απόφθεγμα, γνωμικό

3.160 fool (n) /fuːl/
an idiot • *Only a fool would go out in the cold without a coat.* ➣ foolish (adj) ❖ ανόητος

3.161 warlord (n) /ˈwɔːlɔːd/
the leader of an unofficial military group
• *The warlords fought each other for years.*
❖ πολέμαρχος

3.162 respect (my) elders (expr) /rɪˈspekt (maɪ) ˈeldəz/
treat older people politely and admire them
• *You should respect your elders; they have more experience than you.* ❖ σέβομαι τους μεγάλους

3.163 dynasty /ˈdɪnəsti/
a family of kings and queens who have controlled a country for many years
• *The Shahi dynasty controlled India for centuries.*
❖ δυναστεία

3.164 foundation (n) /faʊnˈdeɪʃn/
basis • *Ancient Greek philosophy is at the foundation of modern European thought.*
❖ θεμέλιο

3.165 moral (adj) /ˈmɒrəl/
relating to ideas about what is right and wrong behaviour • *He is a very moral man who tries to do what is right.* ➣ morals (pl n), morality (n)
❖ ηθικός

3.166 retire (v) /rɪˈtaɪə/
stop working because you have reached a certain age • *In the UK, people will have to retire at the age of 67 instead of 65.* ➣ retirement (n), retired (adj)
❖ συνταξιοδοτούμαι

3.167 rule (v) /ruːl/
control a country or group of people • *King George III ruled for many years.* ➣ ruler, rule (n)
❖ κυβερνώ

3.168 restore (v) /rɪˈstɔː/
bring back • *After the war, peace was restored.*
❖ επαναφέρω, αποκαθιστώ

- **3.169 justice** (n) /ˈdʒʌstɪs/
  fairness • *A fair society treats everyone with justice.*
  ➢ just (adj) ❖ δικαιοσύνη

- **3.170 prosperity** (n) /prɒsˈperɪti/
  when people have money and the things they need for a good life • *Prosperity can only return if we manufacture and sell more goods.*
  ➢ prosper (v), prosperous (adj) ❖ ευημερία

- **3.171 decline** (v) /dɪˈklaɪn/
  become weaker • *The Roman Empire declined and eventually fell to the barbarians.*
  ➢ decline (n) ❖ παρακμάζω

- **3.172 policy** (n) /ˈpɒləsi/
  a way of doing sth that has been officially decided by a government • *The minister of education explained the new policy for secondary schools.*
  ❖ πολιτική

- **3.173 dutiful** (adj) /ˈdjuːtɪfʊl/
  doing what is expected of you • *He is very proud of his dutiful son who looks after him in his old age.*
  ➢ duty (n) ❖ υπάκουος, ευσυνείδητος

- **3.174 prosper** (v) /ˈprɒspə(r)/
  be successful • *His business continues to prosper.*
  ➢ prosperous (adj) ❖ ευημερώ, ανθώ

Vocabulary Exercises

A Choose the correct answers.

1 She turned ___ her best friend for advice.
   a to   b up to

2 He started ___ as an extra before he got a major role.
   a about   b out

3 The play came ___ for a lot of criticism.
   a down   b in

4 Did you ___ forward any good ideas?
   a put   b look

5 Woody Allen's movies always ___ up to my expectations.
   a live   b cater

6 Her neighbour looked ___ on her because she was poor.
   a up   b down

7 I thought the party would be boring, but it turned ___ to be a success.
   a around   b out

8 Why did the couple split ___?
   a up   b around

B Complete the table.

Adjective	Noun
1	victory
2	notoriety
3	influence
4	style
5	attraction
6	gift
7	qualification
8	accomplishment
9	scandal
10	privacy
11	duty
12	arrogance

C Read the definition and complete the words.

1. famous person: c _ _ _ _ _ _ _ _ _
2. well-known person: h _ _ _ _ _ _ _ _ _ n _ _ _
3. kill yourself: c _ _ _ _ _ _ s _ _ _ _ _ _ _
4. grave: b _ _ _ _ _ _ p _ _ _ _ _
5. socialising online: s _ _ _ _ _ _ n _ _ _ _ _ _ _ _ _ _
6. artificial: m _ _ -m _ _ _
7. astronaut of the Soviet Union: c _ _ _ _ _ _ _ _ _ _ _
8. beat: d _ _ _ _ _ _

D Complete the crossword.

Across

4. We are looking _____ to opening night with great anticipation.
8. To my _____, the singer who walked on stage was my cousin.
10. Stop teasing grandma and start respecting your _____.
11. Queen Elizabeth II's _____ is Prince Charles, her eldest son.

Down

1. Have you heard the _____ about the famous couple? They're splitting up.
2. Sandra smiled from ear to _____ when she saw me.
3. His favourite stringed _____ is the guitar.
5. No one knows where he is. He has _____ without a trace.
6. They employed him despite his criminal _____.
7. You have had _____ in your eyes since you were a little kid performing ballet shows.
9. He failed the audition and, to make matters _____, the other actors laughed at him.

3 Grammar

3.1 Past Perfect Simple

Κατάφαση	
I/he/she/it/we/you/they **had ('d)** work**ed**	
Άρνηση	
I/he/she/it/we/you/they **had not (hadn't)** work**ed**	
Ερώτηση	
Had I/he/she/it/we/you/they work**ed**?	
Σύντομες απαντήσεις	
Yes, I/he/she/it **had**.	No, I/he/she/it **hadn't**.
Yes, we/you/they **had**.	No, we/you/they **hadn't**.

Ορθογραφία:

look → look**ed**   move → mov**ed**   trip → tri**pped**   stu**dy** → stud**ied**   st**ay** → st**ayed**

Σημείωση: Κάποια ρήματα είναι ανώμαλα και δεν ακολουθούν αυτούς τους ορθογραφικούς κανόνες. Δες τη λίστα των ανωμάλων ρημάτων και των past participles τους στις σελ. 176-177 του Student's Book.

Χρησιμοποιούμε **Past Perfect Simple** για μια πράξη ή κατάσταση που τελείωσε πριν από κάποια άλλη πράξη, κατάσταση ή χρόνο στο παρελθόν.
→ She **had read** the play Antony and Cleopatra years before she saw the film.
→ By 1910, Cleopatra's story **had inspired** many writers.

Σημείωση: Κάποιες συνηθισμένες χρονικές εκφράσεις που χρησιμοποιούνται συχνά με τον Past Perfect Simple είναι before, after, when, already, for, for a long time, for ages, just, never, once, since 2006/February, yet, κλπ.
→ Valentina Tereshkova had made more than a hundred parachute jumps **before** she became a cosmonaut.

3.2 Past Perfect Continuous

Κατάφαση	
I/he/she/it/we/you/they **had ('d) been** work**ing**	
Άρνηση	
I/he/she/it/we/you/they **had not (hadn't) been** work**ing**	
Ερώτηση	
Had I/he/she/it/we/you/they **been** work**ing**?	
Σύντομες απαντήσεις	
Yes, I/he/she/it **had**.	No, I/he/she/it **hadn't**.
Yes, we/you/they **had**.	No, we/you/they **hadn't**.

Ορθογραφία:

us**e** → us**ing**   run → ru**nning**   cr**y** → cr**ying**

Χρησιμοποιούμε **Past Perfect Continuous** για:
πράξεις που ξεκίνησαν στο παρελθόν και ήταν ακόμα σε εξέλιξη όταν ξεκίνησε μια άλλη πράξη ή όταν έγινε κάτι.
→ The fans **had been waiting** all morning before the ticket office opened.
πράξεις που ήταν σε εξέλιξη στο παρελθόν και επηρέασαν μια μεταγενέστερη πράξη.
→ Joseph didn't finish his homework because he **had been watching** reality shows for hours.

Σημείωση: Κάποιες συνηθισμένες χρονικές εκφράσεις που χρησιμοποιούνται συχνά με Past Perfect Continuous είναι all day/night/week, before, for years, for a long time, for ages, since. Μπορούμε επίσης να χρησιμοποιήσουμε How long…? σε ερωτήσεις με Past Perfect Continuous και for (very) long σε ερωτήσεις και αρνητικές προτάσεις.
→ Archaeologists had been trying to find the tomb **for a long time**.
→ **How long** had Amelia Earhart been flying **before** her plane vanished?

3.3 Past Simple και Past Perfect (Simple και Continuous)

Όταν θέλουμε να δείξουμε με ποια σειρά έγιναν κάποιες πράξεις στο παρελθόν, χρησιμοποιούμε Past Perfect για την πράξη που συνέβη πρώτη στο παρελθόν και χρησιμοποιούμε Past Simple για τις επόμενες πράξεις στο παρελθόν.

→ *My father **had been taking** flying lessons for months before he **was** ready to fly alone.* (Πρώτα έκανε μαθήματα, και στη συνέχεια πέταξε μόνος του.)

Grammar Exercises

A Complete the sentences with the Past Perfect Simple or Past Perfect Continuous of the verbs in brackets.

1. They _____ (gossip) about her all morning when suddenly she walked into the room.
2. We _____ (just/find) a new sponsor when CosmoPhone gave us a better offer.
3. The fans _____ (wait) outside the cinema for the stars all afternoon.
4. _____ (you/mention) the problem to the lecturer before?
5. How long _____ (they/live) in Hollywood before you met them?
6. She _____ (not work) on an excavation before she joined this one.
7. Frangelica Jolly _____ (not get) any good reviews for her acting, but she continued to star in films.
8. It wasn't the first time their forces _____ (defeat) an enemy like this.

B Complete the sentences with the Past Simple or Past Perfect Simple/Continuous of the words below.

| barricade | circulate | guarantee | make | monitor | not reveal | not survive | steal |

1. Nobody had heard of him before he _____ a name for himself.
2. The robbers _____ the door before the police arrived.
3. The aviator had prepared properly, but sadly _____ the plane crash.
4. The government _____ pollution levels for years, but still hadn't done anything about them.
5. The newspaper _____ secrets about famous people before so this was a first.
6. The salesman who sold me the blu-ray player _____ it would last for years after I had paid for it.
7. They had already got a divorce before news of the split _____ in the papers.
8. They had put a lot of gold into the pyramid with the body of the pharaoh, but grave robbers _____ it years ago.

3 Grammar

C Complete the second sentence in each pair so that it has a similar meaning to the first sentence. Use the words in bold.

1 I saw the film after it became a blockbuster.
   When I saw the film it, _____ a blockbuster.   **ALREADY**

2 It was only midnight, but I had gone to bed three hours earlier.
   By the time it was midnight, I _____ three hours.   **FOR**

3 We had been listening to the song for ages before we realised how rude the lyrics were.
   We had been listening to the song _____ before we realised how rude the lyrics were.   **TIME**

4 We had dinner and then Julie called.
   We had already _____ Julie called.   **BEFORE**

5 When we got to the stadium, the 5,000m race was beginning.
   When we got to the stadium, they _____ the 5,000m race.   **JUST**

6 She was exhausted because she had been working since six o'clock in the morning.
   She _____ at six o'clock in the morning, so she was very tired.   **STARTED**

7 She had read the book when she was a teenager.
   She had _____ she was a teenager.   **NOT**

8 We had already watched the show when she got home.
   We had already watched the show _____ she got home.   **BY**

Use your English

Exam Task

For questions **1–10**, read the text below. Use the word given in capitals at the end of some of the lines to form a word that fits in the gap **in the same line**.

Some Like It Hot

The black and white movie *Some Like It Hot* is a wonderful classic and is film
(1) _____ at its best. Starring Tony Curtis, Jack Lemmon   **ENTERTAIN**
and the (2) _____ Marilyn Monroe, it is a great movie.   **GLAMOUR**
It surely must have been an (3) _____ to directors from the day   **INSPIRE**
of its release. Tony Curtis plays a poor (4) _____ disguised as a   **MUSIC**
woman in a woman's band, who having fallen for the band's singer – Monroe – then
disguises himself as a rich (5) _____ gentleman to win her heart.   **ARISTOCRAT**
The pretty singer becomes (6) _____ that she has found the man of   **CONVINCE**
her dreams and it doesn't take much for the female Curtis to make her join the gentleman
on a date. In the meantime, his companion, played by Lemmon, also disguised as a
female band member, is helping by distracting a real gentleman whose yacht
is the (7) _____ they want to use for the date. Lemmon lures the   **LOCATE**
real gentleman away so Curtis can gain (8) _____ to the yacht.   **ACCESSIBLE**
Chaos follows, creating comedy at its best. These (9) _____ actors   **GIFT**
give marvellous performances, and if you haven't seen *Some Like It Hot* yet, then add this
(10) _____ success to your list of must-sees.   **MASS**

4 City Living

Word Focus — page 44

4.1 slum (n) /slʌm/
a very poor area in a city, where people live in old dirty buildings • *Benji grew up in the slums of Cairo.* ❖ φτωχογειτονιά

4.2 discrimination (n) /dɪˌskrɪmɪˈneɪʃn/
when you treat sb or a group of people differently, usually in a worse way, than others • *We need laws that will help stop discrimination against the elderly.* ➣ discriminate (v) ❖ διάκριση, προκατάληψη

4.3 mugged (adj) /mʌgd/
attacked and robbed in a public place • *Amy was mugged in front of her house.* ➣ mug (v), mugger (n) ❖ (κάποιος) που του επιτέθηκαν/τον λήστεψαν (σε δημόσιο χώρο)

4.4 gritty (adj) /ˈgrɪti/
difficult, unpleasant or unattractive • *The documentary shows the gritty side of life in this city.* ❖ άσχημος, δυσάρεστος

Reading — pages 44–45

4.5 favela (n) /fæˈvelə/
a very poor area in Brazil, with small houses that are close together and in bad condition • *Erlen lives in a favela in Rio.* ❖ φτωχογειτονιά (στη Βραζιλία)

4.6 settlement (n) /ˈsetlmənt/
a place where people have come to live • *The family lived in a small settlement in the forest.* ➣ settle (v) ❖ οικισμός

4.7 cramped (adj) /kræmpt/
not having enough room to move freely • *The house is really small, so we're cramped.* ❖ στριμωγμένος

4.8 resident (n) /ˈrezɪdənt/
sb who lives in a particular place • *The residents of the village got cut off by snow last winter.* ➣ reside (v), residence (n) ❖ κάτοικος

4.9 middle-class (adj) /ˈmɪdl klɑːs/
connected with educated people who have good jobs and are neither very rich nor very poor • *He comes from a middle-class family.* ➣ middle class (n) ❖ που ανήκει στη μεσαία τάξη

4.10 urban (adj) /ˈɜːbən/
in or of a town or city • *More parks in urban areas would make towns more pleasant to live in.* ❖ αστικός

4.11 resources (n) /rɪˈsɔːsɪz/
sth that a person, organisation or country has and can use • *We have to make the best use of the resources we've got.* ❖ πόροι

4.12 disadvantaged person (n) /ˌdɪsədˈvɑːntɪdʒd ˈpɜːsn/
sb who does not have the things they need to succeed in life • *The organisation helps disadvantaged people find work.* ❖ άνθρωπος με κοινωνικά μειονεκτήματα/σε μειονεκτική (κοινωνική) θέση/στερημένος

4.13 fortunate (adj) /ˈfɔːtʃənət/
lucky • *I was fortunate enough to find a job that I liked.* ➣ fortune (n), fortunately (adv) ❖ τυχερός
✎ Opp: unfortunate

4.14 insecure (adj) /ˌɪnsɪˈkjʊə(r)/
not safe or protected • *Living in this neighbourhood, we often feel insecure.* ➣ insecurity (n) ❖ ανασφαλής, απροστάτευτος
✎ Opp: secure

4.15 depend on (phr v) /dɪˈpend ɒn/
If sth depends on sth else, it is changed or decided by that thing. • *Your future depends on how well you do in this exam.* ❖ εξαρτώμαι από

4.16 alley (n) /ˈæli/
a narrow street with walls on both sides • *The alley behind the shops was dark and scary at night.* ❖ στενό δρομάκι, σοκάκι

4.17 common sense (n) /ˈkɒmən sens/
when you are able to think and do the right thing and avoid mistakes • *It's common sense to keep matches away from children.* ❖ κοινή λογική

4.18 plus side (n) /plʌs saɪd/
the good things about sth; the advantages of sth • *On the plus side, you can spend more time with your family now.* ❖ θετική πλευρά

4.19 buzz (n) /bʌz/
a lot of activity, noise and excitement • *We could hear the buzz of the city from our hotel room.* ➣ buzz (v) ❖ οχλαγωγία, βουητό

4.20 universe (n) /ˈjuːnɪvɜːs/
the Earth and all the planets, stars and everything else in space • *It was an interesting documentary about how the universe began.* ❖ σύμπαν

4.21 pedestrian (n) /pəˈdestriəsn/
a person walking in the street • *Were any pedestrians injured in the accident?* ❖ πεζός

4.22 pastry shop (n) /ˈpeɪstri ʃɒp/
a shop that sells different kinds of small cakes • *Everything in that pastry shop is delicious!* ❖ ζαχαροπλαστείο

4.23 typical (adj) /ˈtɪpɪkl/
If sth is typical, it is a good example of a particular group or thing. • *This painting is typical of her work.* ❖ τυπικός, χαρακτηριστικός

4.24 on the run (expr) /ɒn ðə rʌn/
in a hurry; while doing sth else. • *He's busy, so he often eats on the run!* ❖ στο πόδι, βιαστικά

4.25 victim (n) /ˈvɪktɪm/
a person or thing that is hurt, killed or damaged by sb or sth • *Unfortunately, the victim died two hours after the attack.* ❖ θύμα

4.26 local council (n) /ˈləʊkl ˈkaʊnsl/
a group of people who are chosen to make rules and decide things in a particular town or area • *The local council has decided to build a sports centre.* ❖ τοπικό συμβούλιο

4.27 inhabitant (n) /ɪnˈhæbɪtənt/
sb who lives in a particular place • *This island has only three thousand inhabitants.* ➢ inhabit (v) ❖ κάτοικος

Vocabulary — page 46

4.28 flatmate (n) /ˈflætmeɪt/
sb who shares a flat with you • *I share a flat with a flatmate, so we pay half the rent each.* ❖ συγκάτοικος

4.29 landlord (n) /ˈlændlɔːd/
a man who rents a building, house, flat, etc to sb • *The landlord who owns our flat is not a very helpful man.* ❖ σπιτονοικοκύρης

4.30 landlady (n) /ˈlændleɪdi/
a woman who rents a building, house, flat, etc to sb • *The landlady showed us round the flat and told us how much rent she charged.* ❖ σπιτονοικοκυρά

4.31 lodger (n) /ˈlɒdʒə/
sb who pays rent to live in a room in sb's house • *Mrs Smith has two lodgers who live upstairs.* ❖ ένοικος

4.32 occupant (n) /ˈɒkjʊpənt/
sb who lives in a building, house, flat, etc • *The occupants had to leave the building when the fire broke out.* ➢ occupy (v) ❖ ένοικος, κάτοικος

4.33 squatter (n) /ˈskwɒtə/
sb who lives in a building illegally • *When they got back from their long holiday in the United States, they found that squatters were living in their house.* ➢ squat (v) ❖ καταπατητής

4.34 tenant (n) /ˈtenənt/
sb sho pays rent for the house, flat, etc they live in • *The landlord told the tenant that the rent was going up.* ❖ ενοικιαστής

4.35 rent (n) /rent/
money you pay to a landlord/landlady to live in a building, house, flat, etc • *The rent for this flat is 700 euros a month.* ➢ rent (v) ❖ ενοίκιο

4.36 commercial (adj) /kəˈmɜːʃl/
related to buying and selling things • *The major department stores are located in the commercial district of the town.* ➢ commercialise, (v) commerce (n) ❖ εμπορικός

4.37 industrial (adj) /ɪnˈdʌstrɪəl/
relating to the mass production of goods • *He works at a factory in the industrial park just outside town.* ➢ industry (n), industrialist (n) ❖ βιομηχανικός

4.38 inner-city (adj) /ˈɪnə-ˈsɪti/
near the centre of a large city, especially where the people are poor • *Inner-city areas are often dirty and have high crime rates.* ❖ στο κέντρο της πόλης

4.39 outskirts (pl n) /ˈaʊtskɜːts/
the edge of town • *He gets a train to the centre of town as he lives on the outskirts in a quiet area.* ❖ περίχωρα

4.40 residential (adj) /rezɪˈdenʃl/
where there are only houses and not factories or offices • *The residential area she lives in has many large houses.* ➢ residence, resident (n) ❖ κατοικημένος, αστική (περιοχή)

4.41 suburb (n) /ˈsʌbɜːb/
an area of a town or city where people live which is not in the town/city centre • *Kallithea is one of the largest suburbs of Athens.* ➢ suburbia (n), suburban (adj) ❖ προάστιο

4.42 majority (n) /məˈdʒɒrəti/
the largest part of a group of people or things • *The majority of students agree with me.* ❖ πλειοψηφία
✎ Opp: minority

4.43 avenue (n) /ˈævɪnjuː/
a wide road in a town or city, often with trees along it • *The avenue was wide and there were trees all along its length.* ❖ λεωφόρος

4.44 tree-lined (adj) /triː laɪnd/
with trees on both sides • *We drove along a tree-lined road.* ❖ με δέντρα και στις δύο πλευρές

4.45 pavement (n) /ˈpeɪvmənt/
a path at the side of a road for people to walk on • *We walked along the pavement and then stopped at the kerb before we crossed the road.* ❖ πεζοδρόμιο

4.46 parking meter (n) /ˈpɑːkɪŋ ˈmiːtə/
a machine at the side of a road in which you put money if you want to park your car next to it • *She put some coins in the parking meter and went shopping for two hours.* ❖ παρκόμετρο

4.47 approach (v) /əˈprəʊtʃ/
come near sb or sth • *As you approach the city centre, you'll see a park on your left.* ❖ πλησιάζω

4.48 junction (n) /ˈdʒʌŋkʃn/
a place where two or more roads meet • *There's a stop sign at the next junction so start slowing down now.* ❖ διασταύρωση

4.49 traffic light (n) /ˈtræfɪk laɪt/
a set of red, amber and green lights at junctions • *The traffic light is green so you can go.* ❖ φανάρι

4.50 **street sign** (n) /striːt saɪn/
a sign at the side of a road with symbols that give drivers information • *That street sign means 'No parking,' so you can't park here.*
❖ πινακίδα

4.51 **speed bump** (n) /spiːd bʌmp/
a part in a road which is built a little higher to make traffic go slowly • *There are speed bumps in the road outside this primary school, so drive slowly.*
❖ σαμαράκι περιορισμού ταχύτητας

4.52 **pedestrian area** (n) /pəˈdestriən ˈɜːriə/
a shopping area in a town where vehicles cannot go • *The city centre is a pedestrian area, so you can't drive there.* ❖ πεζόδρομος

4.53 **zebra crossing** (n) /ˈzebrə ˈkrɒsɪŋ/
white stripes on road where people can cross • *It's safer to cross the street at the zebra crossing.*
❖ διάβαση πεζών

4.54 **speed camera** (n) /spiːd ˈkæmrə/
a camera that takes photographs of cars that are travelling faster than the speed limit • *He was going over a hundred kilometres an hour and the speed camera got a photo of his licence plate.*
❖ κάμερα ελέγχου ταχύτητας

4.55 **speed limit** (n) /spiːd ˈlɪmɪt/
the fastest speed you are allowed to drive • *If you drive faster than the speed limit and you are caught, you have to pay a fine.* ❖ ανώτατο όριο ταχύτητας

Grammar page 47

4.56 **roof** (n) /ruːf/
the structure that covers or forms the top of a building • *Dad set up a new TV aerial on the roof.*
❖ ταράτσα, σκεπή

4.57 **move out** (phr v) /muːv aʊt/
leave the place you live in • *Her parents felt sad when she moved out to live in her own flat.*
❖ μετακομίζω, φεύγω

4.58 **ladder** (n) /ˈlædə(r)/
a thing that you climb up when you want to reach a high place • *He climbed up the ladder and got in through the window.* ❖ σκάλα

4.59 **estate agent** (n) /ɪˈsteɪt ˈeɪdʒənt/
a person whose job is to sell houses and land • *The estate agent showed us the house.*
❖ κτηματομεσίτης

4.60 **town hall** (n) /taʊn hɔːl/
a public building used for a town's local government • *I got a copy of my birth certificate at the town hall.* ❖ δημαρχείο

4.61 **collapse** (v) /kəˈlæps/
fall down suddenly • *The old house collapsed in the earthquake.* ❖ καταρρέω

Listening page 48

4.62 **dweller** (n) /ˈdwelə/
sb who lives in a particular place • *Few city dwellers have a garden.* ➢ dwell (v) ❖ κάτοικος

4.63 **citizen** (n) /ˈsɪtɪzən/
a legal inhabitant of a country • *After living in Canada for over ten years, James decided to become a citizen so that he could vote.*
➢ citizenship (n) ❖ πολίτης

4.64 **constant** (adj) /ˈkɒnstənt/
continual • *The constant noise in this flat is awful, it's even noisy at night!* ➢ constantly (adv)
❖ συνεχής

4.65 **level** (n) /ˈlevl/
amount • *There was a high level of anticipation in the stadium as the fans waited for the band to arrive.* ❖ επίπεδο

4.66 **rural** (adj) /ˈrʊərəl/
in or of the countryside • *She lives on a farm in the heart of rural England.* ❖ αγροτικός

4.67 **regulate** (v) /ˈregjuːleɪt/
control • *She takes medicine to regulate her blood pressure.* ➢ regulation (n) ❖ ρυθμίζω

4.68 **on a regular basis** (expr) /ɒn ə ˈregjələ(r) ˈbeɪsɪs/
often or at the same time each day, week, etc • *We meet on a regular basis.* ❖ τακτικά

4.69 **town planner** (n) /taʊn ˈplænə/
sb who studies the way towns work so that roads, houses, services etc can be provided effectively • *This pedestrian shopping area was designed by a town planner.* ➢ town planning (n)
❖ πολεοδόμος

4.70 **coast** (n) /kəʊst/
land next to the sea • *It's often windy here on the coast as nothing protects us from the sea.*
➢ coastal (adj) ❖ ακτή

4.71 **inland** (adj) /ˈɪnlənd/
far from the coast • *People prefer to spend their summer holidays on the coast rather than in inland areas.* ➢ inland (n) ❖ ενδοχώρα

4.72 **home town** (n) /həʊm taʊn/
the town where you were born and grew up • *He has a Welsh accent because his home town is Cardiff.* ❖ γενέτειρα

4.73 **mainly** (adv) /ˈmeɪnli/
mostly; more than anything else • *The club is popular with local residents, mainly teenagers.* ❖ κυρίως

4.74 **claim** (v) /kleɪm/
say sth is true • *Mum claims to be descended from royalty, but I don't think she is.* ➢ claim (n)
❖ ισχυρίζομαι

4.75 **salary** (n) /ˈsæləri/
money that you are paid every month by the organisation or person you work for • *His salary has gone down and now he can't pay the rent.*
❖ μηνιαίος μισθός

4.76 **low** (adj) /ˈləʊ/
below the usual or expected standard
• *Students with low marks had to do the exam again.* ❖ χαμηλός
✎ Opp: high

4.77 **standard of living** (n) /ˈstændəd əv ˈlɪvɪŋ/
the type of life a person has according to the amount of money they have • *The family's standard of living has dropped since both parents lost their jobs.* ❖ βιοτικό επίπεδο

4.78 **on the rise** (expr) /ɒn ðə raɪz/
If sth is on the rise, it is increasing. • *Police say that crime is on the rise.* ❖ σε άνοδο

4.79 **quality** (n) /ˈkwɒləti/
how good or bad sth is • *The quality of her work is amazing.* ❖ ποιότητα

4.80 **operate** (v) /ˈɒpəreɪt/
work • *The machine was not operating properly.*
➢ operation, operator (n) ❖ λειτουργώ

4.81 **mood swing** (n) /muːd swɪŋ/
change in how you feel • *Shelly has mood swings, so one minute she's happy and the next she's furious.* ❖ απότομη αλλαγή διάθεσης

4.82 **mental health** (n) /ˈmentl helθ/
the condition of your mind • *Her son suffered from mental health problems.* ❖ πνευματική υγεία, ψυχική υγεία

4.83 **health-care worker** (n) /helθ-keə ˈwɜːkə/
sb whose job is to look after sick people
• *A health-care worker visits Grandma once a day to help her take her medicine.*
❖ επαγγελματίας υγείας, νοσηλευτής

Speaking page 49

4.84 **I couldn't agree more.** (expr) /ˈaɪ ˈkʊdnt əˈɡriː mɔː/
used to show that you agree with sb completely
• *'We should wait.' 'I couldn't agree more.'*
❖ Συμφωνώ απόλυτα.

4.85 **entirely** (adv) /ɪnˈtaɪəli/
completely • *I entirely agree with you.*
❖ απόλυτα, τελείως

4.86 **up to a point** (expr) /ʌp tu ə pɔɪnt/
to some degree but not completely • *Yes, that's true, but only up to a point.* ❖ μέχρι ένα σημείο, όχι απόλυτα

4.87 **convinced** (adj) /kənˈvɪnst/
completely sure that sth is true • *I was convinced that she was right.* ➢ convince (v) ❖ πεπεισμένος

Grammar page 50

4.88 **accommodation** (n) /əˌkɒməˈdeɪʃn/
a place to stay or live • *Finding cheap accommodation in London won't be easy.*
❖ κατάλυμα, στέγαση

4.89 **laboratory** (n) /ləˈbɒrətri/
a special room where scientists work • *Do they do tests on animals in these laboratories?*
❖ (επιστημονικό) εργαστήριο

4.90 **carton** (n) /ˈkɑːtən/
a cardboard container • *You can buy a carton of orange juice at a kiosk if you get thirsty.*
❖ χάρτινη συσκευασία (για γάλα κλπ)

4.91 **loaf** (n) /ləʊf/
bread that has been baked in one piece • *Can I have a loaf of bread, please?* ❖ φραντζόλα

4.92 **distinctive** (adj) /dɪsˈtɪŋktɪv/
easily recognisable • *Santorini has very distinctive black sand on its beaches.* ❖ χαρακτηριστικός, ξεχωριστός

4.93 **estimate** (v) /ˈestɪmeɪt/
try to judge the size, cost etc of sth, without calculating it exactly • *It is estimated that there are around 1,000 homeless people living on the streets of this city.* ➢ estimate (n), estimation (n) ❖ υπολογίζω

4.94 **abandoned** (adj) /əˈbændənd/
no longer used by the people who own it
• *There are squatters living in that abandoned building.* ➢ abandon (v) ❖ εγκαταλειμμένος

4.95 **crumbling** (adj) /ˈkrʌmblɪŋ/
with pieces falling off • *The building looked terrible because of the crumbling walls inside and out.*
➢ crumble (v) ❖ που καταρρέει

4.96 **board up** (phr v) /bɔːd ʌp/
cover one or more windows or doors of a house with long flat pieces of wood • *They boarded up the door so no one could open it.*
❖ κλείνω/καλύπτω με σανίδες

4.97 **come to life** (expr) /kʌm tə laɪf/
become exciting, interesting or full of activity
• *The party came to life again when they arrived.*
❖ ζωντανεύω, γεμίζω ζωή

4.98 **canvas** (n) /ˈkænvəs/
a material or place you can paint on • *The wall was a canvas for graffiti artists.* ❖ καμβάς

4.99 **brighten up** (phr v) /ˈbraɪtn ʌp/
make sth more pleasant or enjoyable • *The pink curtains brightened up the room.* ❖ φωτίζω

4.100 **charm** (n) /tʃɑːm/
sth that makes people like a person or place • *The town still has its traditional charm.* ➢ charm (v), charming (adj) ❖ γοητεία

Use your English page 51

4.101 **hang out** (phr v) /hæŋ aʊt/
spend time with others socially • *She hangs out with her friends at the local café.* ❖ κάνω παρέα με κάποιον, συχνάζω κάπου

4.102 **move into** (phr v) /muːv ˈɪntuː/
start living in a place • *He has just moved into a larger flat so he has much more space for his stuff.*
❖ μετακομίζω, εγκαθίσταμαι

4.103 settle down (phr v) /ˈsetl daʊn/
start living a fixed and routine life • *'At last you are getting married and settling down,' said Grandma.*
❖ νοικοκυρεύομαι, αποκαθίσταμαι

4.104 ghost town (n) /ɡəʊst taʊn/
a town that used to have people in it, but now has very few or none • *After the war, many places became ghost towns because the residents had been killed.* ❖ πόλη-φάντασμα

4.105 talk of the town (expr) /tɔːk əv ðə taʊn/
sth or sb everyone is talking about • *John is the talk of the town in his new Mercedes; everybody is admiring it.* ❖ στο κέντρο της προσοχής

4.106 a night on the town (expr) /ə naɪt ɒn ðə taʊn/
a fun night out • *Janice had a night on the town with her friends to celebrate her birthday.*
❖ μια βραδιά γλεντιού

4.107 paint the town red (expr) /peɪnt ðə taʊn red/
go out and have a great time at night • *We always paint the town red at New Year.* ❖ ξεφαντώνω, το ρίχνω έξω

4.108 town hall (n) /taʊn hɔːl/
a public building used for a town's local government • *I got a copy of my birth certificate at the town hall.* ❖ δημαρχείο

4.109 pushing and shoving (expr) /ˈpʊʃɪŋ ənd ˈʃʌvɪŋ/
when people push each other to get sth
• *There was a lot of pushing and shoving on the first day of the sales.* ❖ σπρωξίματα

4.110 anxiety (n) /æŋˈzaɪəti/
a feeling of worry • *Try to control any anxiety you feel before exams.* ➢ anxious (adj)
❖ άγχος, ανησυχία

4.111 density (n) /ˈdensɪti/
how full sth is • *The population density of major cities is high.* ➢ dense (adj) ❖ πυκνότητα

4.112 square kilometre (n) /skweə(r) ˈkɪləmiːtə(r)/
the area equal to a square that is one kilometre on each side • *The island is four square kilometres in size.* ❖ τετραγωνικό χιλιόμετρο

4.113 peace and quiet (expr) /piːs ən ˈkwaɪət/
calm • *She went on holiday to a remote island to get some peace and quiet.* ❖ γαλήνη και ηρεμία

4.114 thrive (v) /ˈθraɪv/
grow; do well • *Jack thrives on city life and loves the noise and crowds.* ➢ thriving (adj)
❖ ακμάζω, ευημερώ

4.115 life (the) fast lane (expr) /laɪf ɪn ðə faːst leɪn/
an exciting, busy way of life that successful people usually have • *As a successful businesswoman, she's living life in the fast lane.*
❖ γρήγοροι ρυθμοί ζωής

4.116 take advantage (of) (expr) /teɪk ədˈvaːntɪdʒ (əv)/ make good use of sth • *You should take advantage of these special prices.* ❖ εκμεταλλεύομαι

4.117 come across (phr v) /kʌm əˈkrɒs/
meet or find sb or sth by chance • *I've never come across such a horrible person before!*
❖ συναντώ, γνωρίζω, βρίσκω

4.118 private (adj) /ˈpraɪvət/
for one person or group of people only and not for public use • *The hotel had its own private beach.* ❖ ιδιωτικός

4.119 individual (adj) /ˌɪndɪˈvɪdʒuəl/
for only one person or thing • *All our students get the individual attention they need.* ❖ ατομικός, μεμονωμένος

4.120 expansion (n) /ɪkˈspænʃn/
when sth increases in size, amount, etc • *They are discussing the expansion of their business.*
➢ expand (v) ❖ επέκταση

4.121 solid (adj) /ˈsɒlɪd/
hard, not in the form of a liquid or gas
• *When water freezes, it becomes solid.* ❖ στερεός

4.122 cement (n) /sɪˈment/
a powder that is mixed with sand and water to make concrete • *The workmen mixed the cement and then covered our yard with concrete.* ❖ τσιμέντο

People and housing

flatmate   landlady   occupant   tenant
landlord   lodger   squatter   resident

Writing: an article
pages 52–53

4.123 construction (n) /kənˈstrʌkʃn/
the process of building • *The construction of a new motorway can take years.* ➢ construct (v)
❖ κατασκευή
✎ NB: under construction = being built

4.124 challenge (n) /ˈtʃæləndʒ/
sth that tests strength, skill or ability • *Your first job will be a challenge because it is difficult.* ➢ challenge (v), challenging (adj) ❖ πρόκληση, δυσκολία

4.125 publish (v) /ˈpʌblɪʃ/ to print sth in a newspaper, magazine or book, etc • *Ken's story was published in the school magazine.* ➢ publisher
❖ δημοσιεύθω

4.126 function (v) /ˈfʌŋkʃn/
work; operate • *This cooker functions with gas.*
➢ function (n) ❖ λειτουργώ

4.127 electricity (n) /ɪlekˈtrɪsəti/
power that is carried by wires and is used to provide light and heat and to make machines work • *Turn off the TV to save electricity.*
➢ electric (adj) ❖ ηλεκτρική ενέργεια

4.128 petrol (n) /ˈpetrəl/
fuel used to power vehicles • *My old car ran on petrol but my new one is electric.* ❖ βενζίνη

4.129 **fossil fuel** (n) /ˈfɒsl ˈfjuːl/
a substance like coal or oil that was formed underground millions of years ago and is used to create energy • *We are dependent on fossil fuels to provide power for our modern lifestyles.*
❖ ορυκτό καύσιμο

4.130 **run out** (phr v) /rʌn aʊt/
finish; have nothing left • *We have run out of cement, so let's make some more.* ❖ ξεμένω

4.131 **come to a halt** (expr) /kʌm tu ə hɔːlt/
stop • *The car came to a halt outside our front door.*
❖ σταματώ

4.132 **cease** (v) /siːs/
stop • *Unless we start using sustainable energy, our way of life will cease to exist as we run out of power.*
❖ παύω

4.133 **invest (in)** (v) /ɪnˈvest (ɪn)/
put money, effort or time into sth to make a profit or gain an advantage • *This company invests in people and rewards hard-working employees.* ➢ investment (n) ❖ επενδύω (σε)

4.134 **alternative energy** (n) /ɔːlˈtɜːnətɪv ˈenədʒi/
a different source of energy from fossil fuel
• *Solar power is an alternative energy which companies can invest in here.* ❖ εναλλακτικές πηγές ενέργειας

Phrasal verbs
board up hang out settle down
brighten up move into run out
come across move out

4.135 **essential** (adj) /ɪˈsenʃl/
completely necessary • *Experience is essential for this job.* ❖ ουσιαστικός, απαραίτητος

Video: Urban Art page 54

4.136 **dimension** (n) /daɪˈmenʃn/
particular aspect • *Shrek gave film animation a whole new dimension because the humour appealed to adults.* ❖ διάσταση

4.137 **admire** (v) /ədˈmaɪə/
respect and like sb or sth • *The painting she admires the most is Da Vinci's Mona Lisa.*
➢ admirable (adj), admiration, admirer (n)
❖ θαυμάζω

4.138 **appreciate** (v) /əˈpriːʃieɪt/
understand how good sb or sth is • *I appreciate all your help. I couldn't have done everything by myself.*
➢ appreciation (n), appreciative (adj) ❖ εκτιμώ

4.139 **setting** (n) /ˈsetɪŋ/
the place where sth is or where sth happens
• *That big room was the perfect setting for our show.* ❖ χώρος, περιβάλλον

4.140 **fundamentally** (adv) /ˌfʌndəˈmentəli/
used when you are talking about the most important thing about sb or sth • *Fundamentally, he is a nice person, but he doesn't make friends easily.* ❖ ουσιαστικά, βασικά

4.141 **exploration** (n) /ˌekspləˈreɪʃn/
looking for and finding sth new • *One of the greatest achievements of space exploration was the moon landing of 1969.* ➢ explore (v), explorer (n)
❖ εξερεύνηση

4.142 **generation** (n) /dʒenəˈreɪʃn/
all the people who were born at about the same time • *The younger generation are not interested in politics.* ❖ γενιά

4.143 **innovative** (adj) /ˈɪnəvətɪv/
clever and new • *There are some innovative machines in this shop.* ➢ innovate (v), innovation (n) ❖ καινοτόμος

4.144 **bucket** (n) /ˈbʌkɪt/
a round container with handles for holding liquid
• *Fill this bucket with water and wash the windows.*
❖ κουβάς

4.145 **bold** (adj) /bəʊld/
colourful; bright • *I don't really like the bold colours in this painting; I prefer pastels.*
❖ ζωηρός

4.146 **uninhibited** (adj) /ˌʌnɪnˈhɪbɪtɪd/
confident or relaxed enough to do what you want to • *He paints in an uninhibited way and does not worry about what people will think.* ❖ αχαλίνωτος, χωρίς αναστολές, ασυγκράτητος
✎ Opp: inhibited

4.147 **inventive** (adj) /ɪnˈventɪv/
very good at thinking of new and original ideas
• *Whoever came up with the idea of the mobile phone must have been very inventive.* ➢ invent (v), invention (n) ❖ εφευρετικός
✎ Opp: uninventive

4.148 **deal** (n) /diːl/
agreement • *You will need a record deal if you want to make a career out of music.*
➢ deal (v) ❖ συμφωνία

Vocabulary Exercises

A Circle the correct words.

1 They couldn't pay the rent / tenant so the landlord asked them to move out.
2 The car has run out of electricity / petrol. How are we going to get home?
3 Can you hear the rain on the roof / ladder of the house?
4 Fossil fuels will one day cease / claim to exist.
5 A level / layer of ice covered the road making it dangerous to drive.
6 The population dimension / density of this city is well above average.
7 It is regulated / estimated that in fifty years summers will be much warmer.
8 Larissa is my home / ghost town, but I moved to Athens five years ago.
9 There are no houses in this industrial / residential area.
10 Birds seem to fluctuate / thrive in this area and their numbers are increasing.

B Match.

1 middle   a planner
2 parking   b class
3 traffic   c sense
4 street   d crossing
5 disadvantaged   e meter
6 zebra   f shop
7 speed   g limit
8 common   h person
9 pastry   i sign
10 town   j light

C Match.

1 Bill has just got married.   a Let's go out and paint the town red.
2 It's my birthday on Saturday.   b Please stop pushing and shoving.
3 I'm not surprised you were mugged.   c They're the talk of the town.
4 There are too many people in this queue.   d She loves life in the fast lane.
5 At first, he didn't like the coastal area.   e He needs to get away for some peace and quiet.
6 Kelly's on another business trip in New York.   f However, the sea air was beneficial.
7 Geoff looks tired and over-worked.   g He decided to settle down at long last.
8 I heard that Harry and Ginny have split up.   h Crime is on the rise in the neighbourhood.

D Circle the odd one out.

1 landlady	lodger	tenant
2 settlement	slum	favela
3 avenue	alley	roof
4 resident	pavement	occupant
5 outskirts	dweller	suburb
6 junction	traffic	function
7 squatter	ladder	bucket
8 urban	inner-city	rural
9 fossil fuel	expansion	petrol
10 run out	estimate	cease

4 Grammar

4.1 Future Simple

Κατάφαση
I/you/he/she/it/we/they **will** help
Άρνηση
I/you/he/she/it/we/they **will not (won't)** help
Ερώτηση
Will I/you/he/she/it/we/they help?
Σύντομες απαντήσεις
Yes, I/you/he/she/it/we/they **will**.
No, I/you/he/she/it/we/they **won't**.

Χρησιμοποιούμε **Future Simple**:
για αποφάσεις που παίρνουμε την ώρα που μιλάμε.
→ *I'm not busy, so I'**ll water** the plants on the roof.*
για προβλέψεις.
→ *Fossil fuels **will run out** soon.*
για υποσχέσεις.
→ *I promise I'**ll help** you park the car.*
για απειλές.
→ *If you don't pay the rent on time, I'**ll ask** you to leave the flat.*
για να μιλήσουμε για μελλοντικά γεγονότα.
→ *The architect **will come** at 8 am tomorrow.*
μετά από τα ρήματα *think, believe, expect, be sure*, κλπ, καθώς και με λέξεις όπως *probably, maybe*, κλπ.
→ *I'm sure more people **will be** interested in green roofs.*
για να προσφέρουμε να κάνουμε κάτι για κάποιον.
→ *I'**ll help** you insulate the roof.*
για να ζητήσουμε από κάποιον να κάνει κάτι.
→ ***Will** you **help** me find a new house in the suburbs?*

Σημείωση: Χρησιμοποιούμε *shall* με το *I* και το *we* σε ερωτήσεις και όταν θέλουμε να προτείνουμε ή να προσφέρουμε κάτι.
→ *Which art gallery **shall we** go to?*
→ ***Shall we** use public transport to go to the centre?*
→ ***Shall I** carry your luggage?*

4.2 Be Going To

Κατάφαση	Ερώτηση	
I **am ('m) going to** help	**Am** I **going to** help?	
he/she/it **is ('s) going to** help	**Is** he/she/it **going to** help?	
we/you/they **are ('re) going to** help	**Are** we/you/they **going to** help?	
Άρνηση	**Σύντομες απαντήσεις**	
I **am ('m) not going to** help	**Yes**, I **am**.	**No**, I'**m not**.
he/she/it **is not (isn't) going to** help	**Yes**, he/she/it **is**.	**No**, he/she/it **isn't**.
we/you/they **are not (aren't) going to** help	**Yes**, we/you/they **are**.	**No**, we/you/they **aren't**.

Χρησιμοποιούμε **be going to**:
για μελλοντικά σχέδια.
→ *My sister **is going to look for** a new flatmate.*
για προβλέψεις για το κοντινό μέλλον που στηρίζονται σε τωρινές καταστάσεις ή στοιχεία.
→ *There are no parking spaces! We **are going to be** late for work!*

Σημείωση: Κάποιες συνηθισμένες χρονικές εκφράσεις που χρησιμοποιούνται συχνά με Future Simple και το *be going to* είναι *this week/month/summer, tonight, this evening, tomorrow, tomorrow morning/afternoon/evening/night, next week/month/year, at the weekend, in June, in a few minutes/days/hours, on Friday, on Thursday morning*, κλπ.
→ *We are going to clean the drains **at the weekend**.*

4.3 Future Continuous

Κατάφαση
I/you/he/she/it/we/they **will be** help**ing**
Άρνηση
I/you/he/she/it/we/they **will not (won't) be** help**ing**
Ερώτηση
Will I/you/he/she/it/we/they **be** help**ing**?
Σύντομες απαντήσεις
Yes, I/you/he/she/it/we/they **will**. **No**, I/you/he/she/it/we/they **won't**.

Ορθογραφία:

imagin**e** → imagin**ing**   trave**l** → trave**lling**   cr**y** → cr**ying**

Χρησιμοποιούμε **Future Continuous**:

για πράξεις που θα βρίσκονται σε εξέλιξη σε συγκεκριμένη χρονική στιγμή στο μέλλον.
→ *We'**ll be talking** to the builders at nine o'clock tomorrow morning.*
για σχέδια και πράγματα που έχουμε κανονίσει για το μέλλον.
→ *My brother **will be attending** a conference on the environment in Paris next week.*

Σημείωση: Κάποιες συνηθισμένες χρονικές εκφράσεις που χρησιμοποιούνται συχνά με Future Continuous είναι *this time next week/month/summer, this time tomorrow morning/afternoon/night*, κλπ.
→ ***This time next week,*** *we'll be installing solar panels on the roof of our house.*

4.4 Future Perfect Simple

Κατάφαση
I/you/he/she/it/we/they **will have helped**
Άρνηση
I/you/he/she/it/we/they **will not (won't) have helped**
Ερώτηση
Will I/you/he/she/it/we/they **have helped**?
Σύντομες απαντήσεις
Yes, I/you/he/she/it/we/they **will**. **No**, I/you/he/she/it/we/they **won't**.

Ορθογραφία:

talk → talk**ed**   us**e** → us**ed**   trave**l** → trave**lled**   tr**y** → tr**ied**   pla**y** → pla**yed**

Σημείωση: Κάποια ρήματα είναι ανώμαλα και δεν ακολουθούν αυτούς τους ορθογραφικούς κανόνες. Δες τη λίστα των ανωμάλων ρημάτων στις σελίδες 176-177 του Student's Book.

Χρησιμοποιούμε **Future Perfect Simple**:
για μια πράξη που θα έχει ολοκληρωθεί ως ή πριν από μια συγκεκριμένη χρονική στιγμή στο μέλλον.
→ *They **will have repaired** the traffic lights by this evening.*
για να μιλήσουμε για τη διάρκεια που θα έχει διαρκέσει μια πράξη ως κάποια χρονική στιγμή στο μέλλον.
→ *By next week, **we will have lived** on this street for ten years.*

Σημείωση: Κάποιες συνηθισμένες χρονικές εκφράσεις που χρησιμοποιούνται συχνά με Future Perfect Simple είναι *by the end of this week/month/year, by this time tomorrow, by tomorrow evening/five o'clock/2015*, κλπ.
→ ***By the end of the year,*** *crime will have become much worse in this city.*

4 Grammar

Σημείωση: Άλλοι χρόνοι που περιγράφουν το μέλλοντα είναι Present Simple για προγράμματα/δρομολόγια, Present Continuous για σχέδια και ότι έχουμε κανονίσει για το μέλλον. Δες στο Grammar Reference 1.1 και 1.2.
→ *The lecture on environmental issues **begins** at 11 am.*
→ *My landlady **is installing** solar panels next weekend.*

4.5 Temporals

Όταν χρησιμοποιούμε **temporals** όπως *when, before, after, until, once, by the time*, κλπ για να μιλήσουμε για το μέλλοντα, τα χρησιμοποιούμε με Present Simple ή Present Perfect. Δε χρησιμοποιούμε Future με temporals.
→ ***After** I **read** the article on Wall Street, I'll give it to you.*
→ ***When** I'**m** thirty, I'll settle down.*

Χρησιμοποιούμε Present Perfect Simple για να τονίσουμε ότι η πρώτη πράξη έχει τελειώσει πριν αρχίσει η άλλη.
→ ***When** I **have found** a suitable building, I'll let you know.* (Πρώτα θα βρω το κατάλληλο κτίριο, και μετά θα σε ενημερώσω.)
→ ***After** we **have found** work in a rural area, we'll leave the city.* (Πρώτα θα βρούμε εργασία σε αγροτική περιοχή, και μετά θα φύγουμε από την πόλη.)

4.6 Countable Nouns

Τα περισσότερα ουσιαστικά είναι countable και έχουν ενικό και πληθυντικό τύπο.

car	→ cars		knife	→ knives
baby	→ babies		sheep	→ sheep
boy	→ boys		man	→ men
potato	→ potatoes		tooth	→ teeth

Συνήθως χρησιμοποιούμε *a* ή *an* με countable nouns ενικού αριθμού.
→ ***a** garden*   → ***an** alley*

Μπορούμε να χρησιμοποιήσουμε *some, any* ή έναν αριθμό (πχ *nine*) με countable nouns πληθυντικού αριθμού.
→ *We should plant **some** trees on the roof.*
→ *Are there **any** cars in the garage?*
→ *I have put **three** coins in the parking meter.*

Χρησιμοποιούμε ρήμα στον ενικό ή στον πληθυντικό με countable nouns, ανάλογα με το αν μιλάμε για ένα ή περισσότερα πράγματα.
→ ***A mural** often **improves** an old building.*
→ ***Murals** often **improve** an old building.*

Θυμήσου: Κάποια countable nouns δεν έχουν την κατάληξη –s στον πληθυντικό. Θυμήσου να χρησιμοποιήσεις ρήμα πληθυντικού αριθμού.
→ ***Men are** interested in new technology.*   → ***Women prefer** to live in quiet areas.*

4.7 Uncountable Nouns

Κάποια ουσιαστικά είναι uncountable, δηλαδή δεν έχουν πληθυντικό αριθμό.

advice	health	oil
business	history	progress
cheese	homework	research
chocolate	information	rubbish
equipment	knowledge	salt
food	luggage	scenery
fruit	mathematics	time
fun	milk	traffic
furniture	money	water
gasoline	music	weather

Δεν χρησιμοποιούμε *a* ή *an* με uncountable nouns. Μπορούμε να χρησιμοποιήσουμε *some* ή *any*.
→ He can give you **some** advice on graffiti art.
→ Was there **any** water in the drains after the rain last night?

Χρησιμοποιούμε πάντα ρήματα ενικού αριθμού με uncountable nouns.
→ Rubbish **is** a major problem in urban areas.
→ Traffic **is** becoming worse in large cities.

Θυμήσου: Κάποια uncountable nouns έχουν την κατάληξη –s. Θυμήσου να χρησιμοποιήσεις ρήμα ενικού αριθμού με αυτά.
→ Mathematics **was** my favourite subject when I was a student.
→ The news **is** not good.

Μπορούμε να χρησιμοποιήσουμε φράσεις που περιγράφουν ποσότητα με uncountable nouns για να πούμε τι ποσότητα έχουμε. Οι πιο συνηθισμένες από αυτές τις φράσεις είναι:

a bag of	a carton of	a loaf of
a bar of	a cup/glass of	a packet of
a bowl of	a jar of	a piece of
a can/tin of	a kilo of	a slice of

→ That's **an** expensive **piece of** luggage.
→ We need **a carton of milk** from the supermarket.

4.8 Quantifiers

Χρησιμοποιούμε *some* με uncountable nouns και με countable nouns πληθυντικού αριθμού, σε καταφατικές προτάσεις, και όταν ζητάμε ή προσφέρουμε κάτι.
→ I found **some exotic plants** for the garden.
→ Could I have **some milk** please?
→ Would you like **some pasta**?

Χρησιμοποιούμε *any* με uncountable nouns και με countable nouns πληθυντικού αριθμού σε αρνητικές προτάσεις και σε ερωτήσεις.
→ I don't have **any information** on the cost of a green roof.
→ Did you find **any coins** for the parking meter?

Χρησιμοποιούμε *a lot of/lots of* με uncountable nouns και με countable nouns πληθυντικού αριθμού, συνήθως στην κατάφαση.
→ Technology is making **a lot of progress** on environmental issues.
→ I've got **lots of magazines** on gardening.

Χρησιμοποιούμε *a little* με uncountable nouns, και *a few* με countable nouns πληθυντικού αριθμού, σε καταφατικές προτάσεις.
→ I need **a little time** before I make my decision.
→ There are **a few squatters** in the old building.

Χρησιμοποιούμε *much* με uncountable nouns και *many* με countable nouns πληθυντικού αριθμού σε αρνητικές προτάσεις και ερωτήσεις.
→ Do people who live in villages have **much stress**?
→ There aren't **many jobs** in rural areas.

4 Grammar

Grammar Exercises

A Choose the correct answers.

1 Mary has decided she ___ architecture at university.
   a is going to study   b will study   c will have studied

2 Be careful! That car ___.
   a won't stop   b isn't going to stop   c won't be stopping

3 We ___ a meeting at the town hall between eleven and twelve.
   a will be having   b will have had   c will have been having

4 ___ we go shopping at the new mall?
   a Are   b Do   c Shall

5 By this time next year, Dad ___ for thirty years.
   a will have been working   b will be working   c is going to be working

6 I think I ___ an umbrella with me. It looks like rain.
   a will be taking   b am going to take   c will take

7 In the future, we ___ alternative energy to power our cities.
   a will have used   b will have to use   c will have been using

8 The lodger ___ by Wednesday.
   a will have moved in   b shall move in   c will be moving in

B Complete the sentences with your own ideas.

1 Look out! That dog _____.
2 I have decided I _____.
3 By this time next year, I _____.
4 I predict that in the future _____.
5 It's a lovely day. I think I _____.
6 Don't worry about the dirty dishes. I _____.
7 Between two and three o'clock tomorrow, I _____.
8 By Sunday evening, I _____.

C Complete the sentences with the Present Simple form of the verbs in brackets.

1 There _____ some slices of bread in the packet but the bread _____ brown. (be)
2 That pasta _____ delicious and the bowls of soup _____ great too. (look)
3 The news _____ that maths _____ cancelled today! (be)
4 My new jeans _____ uncomfortable but this old pair of jeans _____ much better. (feel)
5 Traffic _____ our cities and factories _____ our countryside. (pollute)
6 Advice _____ useful if the information you give _____ clear. (not be)
7 Even a little noise _____ the baby and loud noises _____ Grandpa so please be quiet. (wake)
8 Inner-city areas _____ to be dangerous and people _____ to avoid them at night. (tend)

D Circle the correct words.

1 He usually has a bar / jar of chocolate during his lunch break.
2 The mayor shows few / little interest in this concrete jungle.
3 Is there much / many entertainment in this area?
4 I ate a whole packet / carton of pasta for supper.
5 There weren't much / many residents at the Neighbourhood Watch meeting.
6 He has some experiences / experience of living in town but too little to advise you.
7 Don't forget to brush your hair / hairs before the interview.
8 Is / Are there any room for another business in this office block?

Use your English

Exam Task

For questions **1–8**, complete the second sentence so that it has a similar meaning to the first sentence, using the word given. **Do not change the word given**. You must use between **two** and **five** words, including the word given.

1 By the end of the century, there will be no more fossil fuels.
   RUN
   Fossil fuels _____ by the end of the century.

2 He doesn't find architecture very interesting.
   LITTLE
   He has _____ in architecture.

3 We play tennis together every weekend.
   ON
   We play tennis together _____ basis.

4 I started working here at the end of April.
   HAVE
   By the end of June, I _____ here for two months.

5 I agree with you to some degree, but not completely.
   TO
   I agree with you _____ point

6 He socialises with his friends at the Internet café.
   OUT
   He _____ with his friends at the Internet café.

7 He enjoys physics more than any other subject.
   FAVOURITE
   Physics _____ subject.

8 There are not many entertaining things to do in this town.
   MUCH
   There _____ in this town.

5 Tied to Technology

page 57

5.1 **sophisticated** (adj) /səˈfɪstɪkeɪtɪd/
A sophisticated machine, system, etc is well design and often complicated. • *Computer programs are becoming more sophisticated all the time!* ❖ εξελιγμένος, πολύπλοκος

5.2 **range of movement** (expr) /reɪndʒ əv ˈmuːvmənt/
the way in which or how well sb can move a part of their body • *The operation gave his shoulder a greater range of movement.* ➢ ❖ εύρος κίνησης

Reading — page 58

5.3 **costly** (adj) /ˈkɒstli/
expensive • *NASA has stopped building space shuttles because it cannot pay for such a costly programme.* ➢ cost (v, n) ❖ δαπανηρός

5.4 **irrelevant** (adj) /ɪˈreləvənt/
not relating to a particular situation and therefore not important • *Many people think a knowledge of Latin is irrelevant in our modern world.* ➢ irrelevance (n) ❖ άσχετος
✎ Opp: relevant

5.5 **revolutionary** (adj) /revəˈluːʃənri/
bringing great change • *The Internet caused revolutionary changes in the way we communicate with each other.* ➢ revolution (n), revolutionise (v) ❖ επαναστατικός

5.6 **spectacular** (adj) /spekˈtækjʊlə/
impressive • *The take-off of the space shuttle was a spectacular sight.* ➢ spectacle (n) ❖ θεαματικός

5.7 **wasteful** (adj) /ˈweɪstfʊl/
using too much • *Don't be wasteful with water; turn the tap off while you brush your teeth.* ➢ waste (v, n) ❖ σπάταλος

Word Focus — page 58

5.8 **beam** (v) /biːm/
send • *The torch beamed a light through the darkness.* ➢ beam (n) ❖ ακτινοβολώ

5.9 **distort** (v) /dɪsˈtɔːt/
change the way sth looks so it becomes hard to recognise • *The old mirror distorted her reflection, so she looked strange.* ➢ distortion (n), distorted (adj) ❖ διαστρέφω, διαστρεβλώνω

5.10 **in earnest** (expr) /ɪn ˈɜːnɪst/
seriously; with energy and determination • *She started work on her report in earnest a week before it was due.* ❖ στα σοβαρά

5.11 **determination** (n) /dɪtɜːmɪˈneɪʃn/
a quality that makes you continue and not give up • *John showed a lot of determination when he began training every day for the marathon.* ➢ determined (adj) ❖ αποφασιστικότητα

5.12 **emit** (v) /ɪˈmɪt/
send out • *The fire alarm emitted a very loud noise and everyone ran out of the building.* ➢ emission (n) ❖ εκπέμπω

5.13 **pulse** (n) /pʌls/
an amount of sound that is produced by sth for a short time • *The radar emitted a pulse which showed where the submarine was.* ➢ pulse (v) ❖ παλμός, σφυγμός, δόνηση

Reading — pages 58–59

5.14 **revolutionise** (v) /revəˈluːʃənaɪz/
change sth completely • *Smartphones have revolutionised mobile phone technology.* ➢ revolution (n), revolutionary (adj) ❖ φέρνω επανάσταση

5.15 **thanks to** (expr) /θæŋks tuː/
because of • *Thanks to archaeologists we are always learning more about the ancient world.* ❖ χάρη στο

5.16 **point out** (phr v) /pɔɪnt aʊt/
draw attention to • *The teacher pointed out where we had made mistakes in our physics exam.* ❖ επισημαίνω

5.17 **atmosphere** (n) /ˈætməsfɪə/
layer of gas around a planet • *The Earth's atmosphere protects us from harmful rays from the sun.* ➢ atmospheric (adj) ❖ ατμόσφαιρα

5.18 **precise** (adj) /prɪˈsaɪs/
exact • *This microscope is precise and allows you to see great detail.* ➢ precision (n), precisely (adj) ❖ ακριβής ✎ Opp: imprecise

5.19 **in orbit** (expr) /ɪn ˈɔːbɪt/
circling the Earth • *There are many satellites in orbit around the Earth.* ❖ σε τροχιά

5.20 **rocket scientist** (n) /ˈrɒkɪt ˈsaɪəntɪst/
sb who designs rockets • *The rocket scientists wanted to design a more economical rocket.* ❖ επιστήμονας πυραύλων

5.21 **astrophysicist** (n) /ˌæstrəʊˈfɪzɪsɪst/
sb who studies astrophysics (the structure of the stars and the forces that influence them) • *The astrophysicist made an exciting new discovery about a distant galaxy.* ❖ αστροφυσικός

5.22 **initial** (adj) /ɪˈnɪʃl/
first • *Our initial idea was to see* Star Wars, *but the cinema was full.* ➢ initially (adv) ❖ αρχικός

5.23 **name sb/sth after sb/sth** (expr) /neɪm ˈsʌmbədi/ˈsʌmθɪŋ ˈɑːftə sʌmbədi/ˈsʌmθɪŋ/
give sb or sth the same name as another person or thing • *They have named many theatres after famous actors.* ❖ δίνω σε κάποιον /κάτι το όνομα κάποιου /κάτι

5.24 **service** (v) /ˈsɜːvɪs/
If sb services a machine, they examine it and keep it working well. • *It's important that someone services your car regularly.* ➢ service (n) ❖ κάνω σέρβις

5.25 **degrade** (v) /dɪˈɡreɪd/
decay; separate into smaller pieces • *A telescope that degrades in orbit will break into many pieces.* ➢ degradation (n) ❖ υποβαθμίζω, μειώνω, διασπώ

5.26 **successor** (n) /sʌkˈsesə/
a machine or person that takes the place of another one • *The DVD recorder was the successor of the VCR.* ➢ succeed (v) ❖ διάδοχος

5.27 **sonar mapping** (n) /ˈsəʊnə ˈmæpɪŋ/
creating a map using sound reflection • *Sonar mapping can be used to measure the depth of the sea.* ❖ χαρτογράφηση με σόναρ

5.28 **extraordinary** (adj) /ɪkˈstrɔːdnri/
surprising, unusual or impressive • *What an extraordinary idea!* ❖ εξαιρετικός, εκπληκτικός

5.29 **bat** (n) /bæt/
a mouse-like animal with wings • *The cave was full of bats hanging from the rock.* ❖ νυχτερίδα

5.30 **determine** (v) /dɪˈtɜːmɪn/
discover • *He determined his location by looking at the map.* ❖ υπολογίζω, προσδιορίζω, καθορίζω

5.31 **bounce** (v) /baʊns/
If light or sound bounces, it hits a surface and then moves quickly away from it. • *The bat could work out its location by bouncing sounds off the cave walls.* ➢ bounce (n) ❖ αντανακλώ, αναπηδώ

5.32 **echo** (n) /ˈekəʊ/
a sound that you hear again after a loud noise because it was made near sth such as a wall • *The echo of our voices in the empty room sounded strange.* ➢ echo (v) ❖ ηχώ, αντίλαλος

5.33 **structure** (n) /ˈstrʌktʃə(r)/
the way that sth is made • *The student was studying the structure of a bird's brain.* ❖ δομή

5.34 **loudspeaker** (n) /laʊdˈspiːkə/
a piece of equipment used to emit sound • *We found the music at the concert too loud because we were standing right next to a loudspeaker.* ❖ μεγάφωνο, ηχείο

5.35 **ping** (n) /pɪŋ/
a short, high-pitched noise • *He pressed the bell at hotel reception and it made a loud ping.* ➢ ping (v) ❖ ήχος κουδουνιού

5.36 **reflect** (v) /rɪˈflekt/
send back an image, light or sound off a surface • *She looked at her face reflected in the mirror.* ➢ reflection (n) ❖ αντανακλώ

5.37 **capture** (v) /ˈkæptʃə/
catch • *The robber was captured on the bank's video system.* ❖ καταγράφω, συλλαμβάνω, αιχμαλωτίζω

5.38 **fit (with)** (v) /fɪt wɪð/
equip (with) • *The tyres are fitted with chains so the car can drive on icy roads.* ❖ εξοπλίζω

5.39 **record** (v) /rɪˈkɔːd/
write down; keep a record of sth • *The black box recorded every movement of the plane.* ➢ record, recording (n) ❖ καταγράφω, καταχωρώ

5.40 **depth** (n) /depθ/
how deep sth is • *The depth of the sea here is over 50 metres.* ➢ deep (adj), deepen (v) ❖ βάθος

5.41 **plain** (n) /pleɪn/
a flat area of land • *The plains in Thessaly are used for farming because the flat land is fertile.* ❖ πεδιάδα

5.42 **geological feature** (n) /dʒiːəˈlɒdʒɪkl ˈfiːtʃə/
a particular quality of the land • *The cliffs of Santorini are a well-known geological feature.* ❖ γεωλογικό χαρακτηριστικό

5.43 **complicated** (adj) /ˈkɒmplɪkeɪtɪd/
not simple • *Our maths teacher set us two complicated problems which were too hard for me to solve.* ➢ complicate (v), complication (n) ❖ περίπλοκος

5.44 **detect** (v) /dɪˈtekt/
find • *The sonar equipment detected a large object on the ocean floor that turned out to be a ship.* ➢ detection, detective (n) ❖ ανιχνεύω

Space
astrophysicist   rocket scientist
atmosphere   universe
in orbit

Sound
echo   pulse   sonar
emit   record
ping   reflect

Vocabulary page 60

5.45 **proof** (n) /pruːf/
sth that shows sth to be true • *This photo of you at the party is proof that you were there.* ➢ prove (v) ❖ απόδειξη

5.46 **valid** (adj) /ˈvælɪd/
reasonable and generally accepted • *Her ideas were different but they were perfectly valid.* ❖ έγκυρος

5.47 **excursion** (n) /ɪkˈskɜːʃn/
a short trip that a group of people take to visit a place for pleasure • *The excursion to Sounion would have been better if the coach hadn't broken down.* ❖ εκδρομή

5.48 **lecture** (n) /ˈlektʃə/
a talk on a particular subject that sb gives to students in a university • *The students didn't understand a word of their first lecture on astrophysics.* ➢ lecture (v), lecturer (n) ❖ διάλεξη

5.49 **interactive** (adj) /ɪntərˈæktɪv/
An interactive computer program, game, etc allows you to communicate with it and reacts to your actions. • *I love playing interactive computer games with other people.* ➢ interact (v), interaction (n) ❖ διαδραστικός

5.50 **wind turbine** (n) /wɪnd ˈtɜːbaɪn/
a building with parts that turn around in the wind, used to produce electricity • *We use a wind turbine to heat water.* ❖ ανεμογεννήτρια

5.51 **originate** (v) /əˈrɪdʒɪneɪt/
come from • *The Olympic Games originated in Greece.* ➢ origin (n), original (n, adj) ❖ προέρχομαι

5.52 **generate** (v) /ˈdʒenəreɪt/
produce • *This power plant generates enough electricity for half the city.* ➢ generator (n) ❖ παράγω

5.53 **run out (of sth)** (phr v) /rʌn aʊt (ɒv ˈsʌmθɪŋ)/
have no more of sth • *We've run out of sugar. I'll go and get some.* ❖ ξεμένω (από), μου τελειώνει

5.54 **filthy** (adj) /ˈfɪlθi/
very dirty • *Wash your hands! They're filthy!* ➢ filth (n) ❖ βρομερός, βρόμικος

5.55 **answering machine** (n) /ˈɑːnsərɪŋ məˈʃiːn/
a machine connected to a phone that voice messages can be left on • *He left a message on her answering machine.* ❖ αυτόματος τηλεφωνητής

5.56 **cash machine** (n) /kæʃ məˈʃiːn/
a machine in or outside a bank from where you can get money with a plastic card • *I haven't got any money on me, so I'll stop at the cash machine to withdraw some.* ❖ ATM, αυτόματη ταμειακή μηχανή

5.57 **sewing machine** (n) /ˈsəʊwɪŋ məˈʃiːn/
a machine you can sew clothes with • *Mum made me a new skirt on her sewing machine.* ❖ ραπτομηχανή

5.58 **vending machine** (n) /ˈvendɪŋ məˈʃiːn/
a machine you can buy snacks and drinks from with coins • *Put your coins in that slot in the vending machine and then choose the snack you want.* ❖ μηχανή αυτόματων πωλήσεων

5.59 **count** (v) /kaʊnt/
add up and find the number • *Please count how many students are at the lecture.* ❖ μετρώ (αριθμούς)

5.60 **measure** (v) /ˈmeʒə/
find the size or quantity of sth using standard units • *Use a ruler to measure the length of the line.* ➢ measurement (n) ❖ μετρώ (διαστάσεις, ποσότητα, κλπ)

5.61 **release** (v) /rɪˈliːs/
let sth such as a gas, liquid, etc spread into the area around it • *Oil from the ship was released into the sea.* ➢ release (n) ❖ απελευθερώνω

5.62 **tool** (n) /tuːl/
an object used to make or repair things • *Dad can't fix your bike without his tools.* ❖ εργαλείο

5.63 **lose** (v) /luːz/
not know where sth is • *I've lost my notes; I can't find them anywhere.* ➢ loss (n) ❖ χάνω (ενα αντικείμενο)

5.64 **miss** (v) /mɪs/
not go somewhere or do sth • *He missed the chance to go on the museum trip because he was ill.* ❖ χάνω (μάθημα, το λεωφορείο, κλπ)

5.65 **price** (n) /praɪs/
the money you pay to buy sth • *The price of petrol is increasing all the time.* ➢ pricey (adj) ❖ τιμή

5.66 **cost** (n) /kɒst/
the money needed to buy, do or make sth • *The cost of building satellites must be astronomical.* ➢ cost (v), costly (adj) ❖ κόστος

5.67 **overwhelm** (v) /əʊvəˈwelm/
If sth overwhelms sb, it is too much or too difficult to deal with. • *The instructions for her new computer overwhelmed her and she had no idea what to do.* ➢ overwhelming (adj) ❖ κατακλύζω, καταβάλλω

5.68 **auditory** (adj) /ˈɔːdətri/
relating to your ability to hear • *The scientist wrote an article about the auditory areas of the brain.* ❖ ακουστικός

5.69 **stimulant** (n) /ˈstɪmjʊlənt/
sth that makes the mind or body more active • *Coffee wakes you up as it contains the stimulant caffeine.* ➢ stimulate (v), stimulation (n) ❖ τονωτικός, διεγερτικός

5.70 **aggressive** (adj) /əˈgresɪv/
angry and ready to attack • *She doesn't walk her new puppy in the park because there are some aggressive dogs there.* ➢ aggression (n) ❖ επιθετικός

5.71 **limitation** (n) /ˌlɪmɪˈteɪʃn/
a rule that does not allow sth to increase beyond a certain point • *There should be some limitations on the use of cars in the city.* ➢ limit (v, n) ❖ περιορισμός

5.72 **addict** (n) /ˈædɪkt/
sb who can't stop doing sth • *He is a video games addict and plays for hours every day.* ➢ addiction (n), addicted, addictive (adj) ❖ εξαρτημένος

5.73 **evident** (adj) /ˈevɪdənt/
clear • *It was evident from her sad expression that she had heard some bad news.* ➢ evidence (n), evidently (adv) ❖ φανερός

Phrasal verbs

hack into
hook up to
plug in
point out
run out
set off
set out
shut down
take on

Easily confused words

count – measure
lose – miss
price – cost

Grammar page 61

5.74 **update** (v) /ʌpˈdeɪt/
add the most recent information to something • *You need to update your computer's anti-virus program.* ➢ update (n) ❖ αναβαθμίζω

5.75 **virus protection** (n) /ˈvaɪrəs prəˈtekʃn/
a program that protects your computer from harmful programs or removes them before they can damage your computer • *If you had updated your virus protection, you wouldn't have lost all your work!* ❖ πρόγραμμα (υπολογιστή) για προστασία από ιούς

5.76 **film projector** (n) /fɪlm prəˈdʒektə/
a machine which projects pictures onto a screen • *Our school has a film projector which teachers use in class to show us documentaries.*
❖ προβολέας, προτζέκτορας

5.77 **external modem** (n) /eksˈtɜːnəl ˈməʊdəm/
a device that allows a computer to connect to the Internet • *This old computer connects to the Internet through that external modem over there.*
❖ εξωτερικό μόντεμ

5.78 **recharge** (v) /riːˈtʃɑːdʒ/
put power back in a battery • *Don't forget to recharge your phone.* ➢ rechargeable (adj)
❖ επαναφορτίζω

5.79 **digital camera** (n) /ˈdɪdʒɪtl ˈkæmrə/
a camera that produces digital images that can be stored on a computer • *He downloaded his holiday photos from his digital camera onto his laptop.*
❖ ψηφιακή φωτογραφική μηχανή

5.80 **faulty** (adj) /ˈfɔːlti/
not working properly; not made correctly • *The satellite is faulty, so the astronauts have to repair it.* ➢ fault (n) ❖ ελαττωματικός

5.81 **equation** (n) /ɪkˈweɪʒn/
a statement in mathematics that shows that two amounts are equal • *I've got five equations for maths homework.* ❖ εξίσωση

5.82 **forbidden** (adj) /fəˈbɪdən/
not allowed • *Eating and drinking on the Metro is forbidden, so please finish your sandwich before you get on the train.* ➢ forbid (v)
❖ απαγορευμένος, απαγορεύεται

5.83 **check-out** (n) /tʃek-aʊt/
the place in a supermarket where you pay for the things you want to buy • *He realised at the check-out that he had left his wallet at home.* ❖ ταμείο

Electrical equipment

answering machine
appliance
device
digital camera
external modem
film projector
sewing machine

Speaking page 63

5.84 **gadget** (n) /ˈɡædʒɪt/
a small, useful machine or tool • *It's a cool gadget you can use to cut bread into different shapes.*
❖ μικροσυσκευή, μικροεργαλείο

5.85 **device** (n) /dɪˈvaɪs/
a machine or tool that does a particular job
• *He invented a device which translates words into six other languages.* ❖ συσκευή

5.86 **reliant (on)** (adj) /rɪˈlaɪənt (ɒn)/
dependent on • *She lives alone, so she has become reliant on her dog for company.* ➢ rely (v)
❖ εξαρτημένος από

5.87 **remote** (adj) /rɪˈməʊt/
far away from where other people live • *They travelled to a remote island in the Indian Ocean.*
❖ απομακρυσμένος

Use your English page 65

5.88 **hack into** (phr v) /hæk ˈɪntuː/
illegally enter a computer system • *If someone hacks into your computer, they can steal your personal information.*
❖ αποκτώ πρόσβαση παράνομα

5.89 **hook up to** (phr v) /hʊk ʌp tuː/
connect to a machine • *You can hook your PSP up to the TV and play on a larger screen.* ❖ συνδέω

5.90 **plug in** (phr v) /plʌɡ ɪn/
connect a machine to an electricity supply
• *Plug in your laptop to charge the battery.*
❖ συνδέω, βάζω στην πρίζα
✎ Opp: unplug

5.91 **set off** (phr v) /set ɒf/
cause an alarm to ring • *Don't smoke in the hotel room; you'll set off the alarm.* ❖ ενεργοποιώ

5.92 **shut down** (phr v) /ʃʌt daʊn/
turn a computer off • *Please shut down your computers before you leave the office.* ❖ κλείνω
✎ Opp: start up

5.93 **electricity supply** (n) /ɪlek'trɪsəti sə'plaɪ/
a source of power • *We had no electricity supply for three hours during the blackout.* ❖ παροχή ηλεκτρικού ρεύματος

5.94 **idiot** (n) /'ɪdiət/
a stupid person; sb who does sth silly • *I was an idiot to leave the key in the door!* ❖ ανόητος
✎ Syn: fool

5.95 **appliance** (n) /ə'plaɪəns/
a piece of equipment used in people's homes • *Washing machines are time-saving appliances.* ❖ ηλεκτρική οικιακή συσκευή

5.96 **introverted** (adj) /'ɪntrəvɜːtɪd/
quiet and not enjoying spending time with other people • *She's always been shy and introverted.* ❖ εσωστρεφής

5.97 **stable** (adj) /'steɪbl/
unlikely to move, change or fall • *The patient's condition is stable.* ➢ stability (n) ❖ σταθερός

5.98 **divorce** (n) /dɪ'vɔːs/
the end of a marriage by law • *Jenny's parents are getting a divorce.* ➢ divorce (v) ❖ διαζύγιο

5.99 **operating system** (n) /'ɒpəreɪtɪŋ 'sɪstəm/
a set of programs on a computer that controls the way it works • *Which operating system do you use on your tablet?* ❖ λειτουργικό σύστημα

5.100 **artificial intelligence** (n) /ˌɑːtɪ'fɪʃl ɪn'telɪdʒəns/
the study of how to make computers copy human behaviour • *Is it true that artificial intelligence can be used to grade students' essays?* ❖ τεχνητή νοημοσύνη

5.101 **adapt** (v) /ə'dæpt/
change the way you do things because you are in a new situation • *Jim is finding it hard to adapt to his new school.* ❖ προσαρμόζομαι

5.102 **interact** (v) /ˌɪntər'ækt/
If two people interact, they communicate with each othe, do things together, etc. • *Jon interacts well with the other children in his class.* ➢ interactive (adj), interaction (n) ❖ συναναστρέφομαι

5.103 **take on** (phr v) /teɪk ɒn/
begin to have a certain appearance, quality, role, etc • *Mum's voice took on a more serious tone.* ❖ παίρνω, αναλαμβάνω

5.104 **screenplay** (n) /'skriːnpleɪ/
the words that are written for a film and the instructions for the actors • *The director was in his room, reading the screenplay for his new film.* ❖ σενάριο

5.105 **deserve** (v) /dɪ'zɜːv/
If you deserve sth, it is right that you should have it because of your behaviour or actions. • *She's good. She deserves to win.* ❖ αξίζω

5.106 **rely (on)** (v) /rɪ'laɪ (ɒn)/
need or depend on sb or sth • *She relies on her husband for money.* ❖ βασίζομαι σε

Writing: an essay (1)

pages 66–67

5.107 **column** (n) /'kɒləm/
a regular newspaper or magazine article on a particular subject or by a particular journalist • *She writes a column on technology for a well-known newspaper.* ❖ στήλη

5.108 **entitle** (v) /ɪn'taɪtl/
give a title to sth • *You should read this article entitled 'Are we alone in the universe?'* ➢ title (n) ❖ τιτλοφορώ

5.109 **aspect** (n) /'æspekt/
one of the parts or qualities of a situation, problem, idea, etc • *We need to think about the problem from every aspect.* ❖ πλευρά, άποψη

5.110 **depend (on)** (v) /dɪ'pend (ɒn)/
rely on • *People who don't buy a newspaper usually depend on the TV for news.* ❖ βασίζομαι

5.111 **current affairs** (pl n) /'kʌrənt ə'feəz/
important political or other events that are happening now • *It is important to keep informed about current affairs so you know what is happening in the world.* ❖ επικαιρότητα

5.112 **what's more** (expr) /wɒts mɔː/
in addition; used to add more information • *The pay is good. What's more, I really like the job.* ❖ επίσης, επιπλέον

5.113 **drawback** (n) /'drɔːbæk/
disadvantage • *I like it here. The only drawback is the weather.* ❖ μειονέκτημα, ελάττωμα

5.114 **consequently** (adv) /'kɒnsɪkwəntli/
as a result • *She lost her passport. Consequently, she couldn't get on the plane.* ➢ consequence (n) ❖ συνεπώς, έτσι

5.115 **socialise** (v) /'səʊʃəlaɪz/
spend time enjoying yourself with other people • *People usually socialise with those who are the same age as they are.* ➢ sociable, social (adj) ❖ κάνω παρέα, έχω κοινωνικές επαφές

5.116 **nevertheless** (adv) /ˌnevəðə'les/
however; but • *She had trained really hard. Nevertheless, she didn't win.* ❖ παρ'όλα αυτά

5.117 **thus** (adv) /ðʌs/
because of this; as a result of this • *He had lost his phone. Thus, it was impossible for him to call the police.* ❖ συνεπώς, έτσι

Video: Bionic Mountaineer page 68

5.118 prosthesis (n) /prɒsˈθiːsɪs/
an artificial body part • *He had a prosthesis fitted after he lost a leg in the war.* ➢ prosthetic (adj)
❖ τεχνητό μέλος, τεχνητό άκρο

5.119 artificial (adj) /ɑːtɪˈfɪʃl/
man-made • *She has an artificial arm because she lost her real arm in an accident.* ❖ τεχνητός

5.120 limb (n) /lɪm/
an arm or leg • *The athlete had strong limbs.*
❖ μέλος, άκρο

5.121 amputate (v) /ˈæmpjʊteɪt/
remove a damaged body part in an operation • *The climber's toes froze in the snow, so they had to be amputated.* ➢ amputation, amputee (n)
❖ ακρωτηριάζω

5.122 amputee (n) /æmpjuːˈtiː/
sb who has had a body part removed • *It is hard for amputees to learn to live without a limb.* ➢ amputate (v) ❖ ακρωτηριασμένος

5.123 attempt (v) /əˈtempt/
try to do sth difficult • *She attempted to break the world record.* ➢ attempt (n) ❖ επιχειρώ, προσπαθώ,

5.124 suffer (v) /ˈsʌfə/
feel pain • *The climber suffered in the cold for hours before he was rescued.* ➢ suffering (n) ❖ υποφέρω

5.125 wander (v) /ˈwɒndə/
walk in no particular direction • *We wandered around in the snowstorm with no idea where we were.* ❖ τριγυρίζω, περιφέρομαι

5.126 set out (to do sth) (phr v) /set aʊt (tə də ˈsʌmθɪŋ)/
start doing or working on sth in order to get a particular result • *They set out to build a house in the country.* ➢ ❖ ξεκινώ, σκοπεύω (να κάνω κάτι)

5.127 disoriented (adj) /dɪsˈɔːriəntɪd/
confused and lost • *They couldn't see anything in the fog and felt disoriented.*
❖ αποπροσανατολισμένος

5.128 expose (v) /ɪksˈpəʊz/
put sb in a situation where they are not protected from sth dangerous • *The winter weather exposed the villagers to the difficulties of cold and snow.* ➢ exposure (n) ❖ εκθέτω

5.129 the elements (pl n) /ðiː ˈelɪmənts/
the weather, especially bad weather • *The mountaineers faced the elements and managed to survive wind and snow.* ❖ στοιχεία της φύσης

5.130 frostbite (n) /ˈfrɒstbaɪt/
a condition where a body part becomes damaged because of cold • *The climber's fingers got frostbite in the freezing weather.* ➢ frostbitten (adj)
❖ κρυοπάγημα

5.131 sensation (n) /senˈseɪʃn/
a physical feeling • *I've got no sensation in my fingers because they are so cold.* ❖ αίσθηση

5.132 surgery (n) /ˈsɜːdʒəri/
an operation • *He had five surgeries on his leg.*
➢ surgeon (n), surgical (adj)
❖ χειρουργική επέμβαση

5.133 PhD (abbr) /piː eɪtʃ ˈdiː/
abbreviation for Doctor of Philosophy (a very high level university degree that involves doing research in a particular subject) • *She's got a PhD in chemistry.* ➢ ❖ διδακτορικό (πτυχίο)

5.134 rock face (n) /rɒk feɪs/
a very steep surface of rock on the side of a mountain • *It's amazing to see climbers go up high rock faces.* ❖ βράχος

5.135 astounding (adj) /əˈstaʊndɪŋ/
astonishing • *The amputee's ability to climb on prosthetic legs was truly astounding.* ➢ astound (v)
❖ καταπληκτικός, τρομερός, συγκλονιστικός

5.136 implement (v) /ˈɪmplɪment/
to make sth such as a law, idea or system start to work or be used • *Everyone liked the plan, but it was never implemented.* ❖ εφαρμόζω

Different adjective endings

astounding	irrelevant
complicated	revolutionary
costly	spectacular
initial	wasteful
interactive	

Vocabulary Exercises

A Match.

1. He was speaking in
2. We were rescued thanks
3. They pointed
4. We set out
5. His car has been fitted
6. They named the baby
7. Somebody hacked
8. Do you depend

a after his grandpa.
b earnest and meant every word.
c to design an environmentally-friendly house.
d on TV for entertainment?
e out that it was time to leave.
f into my laptop and stole my files.
g to George who went for help.
h with new wheels.

B Complete the sentences with these words.

affairs   camera   elements   face   features   machine   orbit   supply

1. There is no electricity _____ in this area so you will need a torch.
2. You can store thousands of photos on this digital _____ .
3. If I'm not at home, you can leave a message on my answering _____ .
4. This newspaper is very informative about current _____ .
5. You will have to face the _____ in the Himalayas.
6. The climber found it too hard to climb the rock _____ in the rain.
7. The satellite is now in _____ around the Earth.
8. There are many interesting geological _____ in this part of the world.

C Read the definition and complete the adjectives.

1. well designed and complicated: s _ _ _ _ _ _ _ _ _ _ _ _
2. exact: p _ _ _ _ _ _
3. confused and lost: d _ _ _ _ _ _ _ _ _ _
4. far away from where other people live: r _ _ _ _ _ _
5. not simple: c _ _ _ _ _ _ _ _ _ _
6. bringing great change: r _ _ _ _ _ _ _ _ _ _ _ _
7. first: i _ _ _ _ _ _
8. not allowed: f _ _ _ _ _ _ _ _
9. send out: e _ _ _
10. disadvantage: d _ _ _ _ _ _ _
11. angry and ready to attack: a _ _ _ _ _ _ _ _ _
12. as a result: c _ _ _ _ _ _ _ _ _ _ _

D Circle the odd one out.

1. device   calculator   limb
2. appliance   lecture   equipment
3. degrade   bounce   reflect
4. echo   proof   sonar
5. spectacular   astounding   irrelevant
6. capture   repair   record
7. update   measure   count
8. artificial   costly   wasteful

5 Grammar

5.1 Can & Could

Χρησιμοποιούμε **can** + bare infinitive (απαρέμφατο χωρίς *to*):
για να μιλήσουμε για γενική ικανότητα στο παρόν και στο μέλλον.
→ My grandfather **can send** messages on his mobile phone.
για να ζητήσουμε κάτι.
→ **Can** you **help** me find information on the Hubble Space Telescope?
για να δώσουμε την άδεια για κάτι.
→ Yes, you **can watch** the sports game on TV tonight.

Χρησιμοποιούμε **can't** + bare infinitive για να δείξουμε πως είμαστε σίγουροι ότι κάτι δεν ισχύει.
→ She **can't be** a lecturer, she's still a student!

Χρησιμοποιούμε **could** + bare infinitive:
για να μιλήσουμε για γενική ικανότητα στο παρελθόν. (αόριστος του *can*)
→ My sister **could type** on the computer when she was six.
για να μιλήσουμε για πιθανότητα.
→ You **could hurt** yourself if you carry the sewing machine alone.
για να ζητήσουμε κάτι ευγενικά.
→ **Could** you **help** me with my project on NASA?
για να προτείνουμε κάτι.
→ You **could find** information about prosthetics on the Internet.

5.2 May & Might

Χρησιμοποιούμε **may** + bare infinitive:
για να μιλήσουμε για πιθανότητα στο μέλλον.
→ We **may use** wind turbines to generate electricity in our village.
για να ζητήσουμε κάτι ευγενικά (με *I* και *we*).
→ **May** I **speak** to Professor Barnes?
για να δώσουμε την άδεια για κάτι με ευγενικό τρόπο.
→ Yes, you **may use** my scanner.

Χρησιμοποιούμε **might** + bare infinitive:
για να μιλήσουμε για πιθανότητα στο μέλλον.
→ She **might need** glasses soon.
σαν τον αόριστο του *may*.
→ Mum said she **might assemble** our new furniture herself.

5.3 Must

Χρησιμοποιούμε **must** + bare infinitive:
για να πούμε ότι κάτι είναι απαραίτητο.
→ We **must** always **wear** goggles when doing experiments.
για να μιλήσουμε για κάτι που είναι υποχρεωτικό.
→ You **must** unplug the machine when you've finished using it.
για να εκφράσουμε βεβαιότητα ότι κάτι ισχύει.
→ He **must be** the new astronomy professor.
για να προτείνουμε κάτι.
→ You really **must visit** the new science museum.

Χρησιμοποιούμε **mustn't** + bare infinitive για να μιλήσουμε για κάτι που δεν επιτρέπεται.
→ You **mustn't bring** your mobile phone to school. It's forbidden.

5.4 Should

για Χρησιμοποιούμε **should** + bare infinitive:
να δώσουμε συμβουλή.
→ You **should take** advantage of what modern technology has to offer.

5 Grammar

για να ζητήσουμε συμβουλή.
→ **Should** I **study** astrophysics?

Σημείωση: Μπορούμε να χρησιμοποιήσουμε και *ought to* για να δώσουμε μια συμβουλή, αλλά συνήθως δε χρησιμοποιείται στον ερωτηματικό τύπο.
→ Your sister **ought to answer** her e-mails more regularly.

5.5 Would

Χρησιμοποιούμε **would** + bare infinitive:
για πράξεις που κάναμε συχνά στο παρελθόν, αλλά δεν κάνουμε τώρα.
→ I **would watch** the news on TV, but now I prefer the Internet.
για να ζητήσουμε κάτι ευγενικά.
→ **Would** you **check** the answering machine for messages, please?

5.6 Needn't

Χρησιμοποιούμε **needn't** + bare infinitive για να πούμε ότι κάτι δεν είναι απαραίτητο.
→ You **needn't recharge** the batteries, I did it this morning.

Σημείωση: Μπορούμε να χρησιμοποιήσουμε το *need* σαν κανονικό ρήμα. Έχει καταφατικό, ερωτηματικό και αρνητικό τύπο, και χρησιμοποιείται συνήθως στον Present Simple και στον Past Simple. Ακολουθείται από full infinitive (απαρέμφατο με *to*).
→ They **need to service** the cash machine outside the bank.
→ You don't **need to have** any experience for that job. Training will be provided.
→ **Did** Anne **need to wear** glasses when she was a student?

5.7 Be able to

Χρησιμοποιούμε **be able to** για να μιλήσουμε:
για γενική ικανότητα.
→ We **are able to finish** the experiment without any help.
για συγκεκριμένη ικανότητα στο παρελθόν. (Δ εχρησιμοποιούμε *could* για συγκεκριμένη ικανότητα στο παρελθόν.)
→ She **was able to fix** the printer herself.

5.8 Have to

Χρησιμοποιούμε **have to**:
για να πούμε ότι κάτι είναι απαραίτητο.
→ You **have to be** careful when you use the telescope.
για να μιλήσουμε για υποχρέωση.
→ We **have to buy** tickets before we get on the bus.

5.9 Mustn't & Don't have to

Υπάρχει μια σημαντική διαφορά ανάμεσα στο **mustn't** και στο **don't have to**. Χρησιμοποιούμε **mustn't** για να πούμε ότι κάτι δεν επιτρέπεται, ενώ χρησιμοποιούμε **don't have to** για να πούμε ότι δεν υπάρχει υποχρέωση ή αναγκαιότητα.
→ You **mustn't enter** the science lab without protective gloves.
→ We **don't have to update** our anti-virus software. The technician said it's fine.

5.10 May/Might have

Χρησιμοποιούμε **may/might have** + past participle (παθητική μετοχή) για να πούμε ότι δεν είμαστε βέβαιοι για κάτι στο παρελθόν.
→ Irene **might have failed** her exams, but I'm not sure.

5.11 Should have

Χρησιμοποιούμε **should have** + past participle (παθητική μετοχή):
για να πούμε ότι κάτι που περιμέναμε δεν έγινε.
→ *The lecture **should have started** by now.*
για να ασκήσουμε κριτική στη συμπεριφορά μας ή στη συμπεριφορά κάποιου άλλου.
→ *I **should have explained** the dangers of the Internet to my daughter.*

5.12 Could have

Χρησιμοποιούμε **could have** + past participle:
για να πούμε ότι δεν είμαστε σίγουροι για κάτι στο παρελθόν.
→ *Alan **could have taken** your iPod. I don't remember.*
για να πούμε ότι κάτι ήταν πιθανό να γίνει στο παρελθόν, αλλά δεν έγινε.
→ *Sam **could have earned** a PhD in biochemistry, but he gave up in order to find work.*

5.13 Can't/Couldn't have

Χρησιμοποιούμε **can't/couldn't have** + past participle για να εκφράσουμε τη βεβαιότητα ότι κάτι δεν ισχύει για το παρελθόν.
→ *She **can't have repaired** the washing machine; she doesn't even know how to plug it in.*

5.14 Must have

Χρησιμοποιούμε **must have** + past participle για να εκφράσουμε τη βεβαιότητα ότι κάτι ισχύει για το παρελθόν.
→ *Making a scientific discovery **must have been** an incredible experience for Emma.*

5.15 Would have

Χρησιμοποιούμε **would have** + past participle για να πούμε ότι σκοπεύαμε να κάνουμε κάτι αλλά δεν το κάναμε.
→ *I **would have shown** you how the digital camera works, but I was away all week.*

5.16 Needn't have

Χρησιμοποιούμε **needn't have** + past participle για να πούμε ότι δεν ήταν απαραίτητο να κάνουμε κάτι, όμως το κάναμε.
→ *I **needn't have studied** so hard for the biology exam. It was so easy!*

Grammar Exercises

A Choose the correct answers.

1 That ___ be John at the door because he's out of town.
  a should
  b can't

2 Don't worry. I ___ service your car tomorrow after all.
  a will be able to
  b must

3 ___ you help me with my physics project?
  a May
  b Could

4 He ___ to do more research.
  a should
  b ought

5 You ___ write the report. I have already done it.
  a don't have to
  b mustn't

6 You ___ smoke in here because it is illegal to do so.
  a mustn't
  b couldn't

7 She ___ be late if her train is delayed.
  a must
  b might

8 That ___ be Theresa on the phone.
  a can
  b must

5 Grammar

B Put the words in the correct order.

1 out / you / go / revision / when / you / finish / your / may
_____

2 because / be / that / can't / Stuart / he's / lot / than / taller / that / a
_____

3 rain / she / get / walk / home / in / as / she / the / can / the / bus / needn't
_____

4 ought / our / teacher / to / the / explain / equations / clearly / more
_____

5 memory / I / to / buy / have / a / new / that / has / laptop / more
_____

6 of / you / many / shouldn't / really / so / Dr Patel's / miss / lectures
_____

7 must / Jack / be / in / his / sports / new / car / that
_____

8 the / could / I / you / for / trouble / time / ?
_____

C Complete the sentences with the correct positive or negative form of the verbs below.

| can/arrive   could/do   might/go away   must/lose |
| need/buy   ought to/go   should/speak   would/order |

1 I already have that DVD. You _____ it for me again.
2 If John had studied harder, he _____ much better in his exams.
3 My keys aren't here. Oh no! I _____ them!
4 That was rude. You _____ to him like that.
5 The plane landed an hour ago so he _____ through passport control by now.
6 Maria _____ at work because the trains are on strike.
7 It wasn't necessary for you to cook. I _____ a pizza.
8 I'm not sure but Sally _____ for the weekend.

D Complete the sentences with your own ideas.

1 I sent that message an hour ago. It must _____.
2 Mum has made supper. You don't _____.
3 George isn't here, so _____.
4 Your test marks aren't good. You _____.
5 If you had gone to university, you _____.
6 Smoking is forbidden so people _____.
7 He has an fast Internet connection, so he _____.
8 This is a wireless device, so you _____.

Use your English

Exam Task

For questions **1–10**, read the text below and decide which answer (**A, B, C** or **D**) best fits each gap.

Parental Control

If you are a parent and are unsure if you **(1)** ___ allow your child to have access to new technology, then parental control **(2)** ___ be the answer for you. Thanks **(3)** ___ parental control, you can protect your child when they are online by using content filters, usage controls, computer usage management controls and monitoring.

With content filters, kids **(4)** ___ access webpages which are considered inappropriate for their age groups. You **(5)** ___ worry about emails either as only people who have permission can send messages to your child's computer. Usage controls limit the time children can play on **(6)** ___ such as PSPs, for example, and also deny access to games which are inappropriate. Computer usage management tools are good for parents who depend **(7)** ___ computers to educate their children; these tools allow them to combine learning time and play time. Children **(8)** ___ to earn gaming time by completing educational material. Finally, you can monitor the whereabouts of your child so you always know their location.

Parental control **(9)** ___ enables parents to protect their children in a number of ways. One of these involves programs that are able to **(10)** ___ certain words on web pages and chat applications. It's a sad fact that dangers are out there, and it's a parent's duty to eliminate risks for their children.

1	A	should	B	ought	C	must	D	could
2	A	able	B	might	C	mustn't	D	can
3	A	on	B	with	C	to	D	into
4	A	can't	B	must	C	couldn't	D	can
5	A	needn't	B	mustn't	C	don't have	D	can't
6	A	surgeries	B	equations	C	appliances	D	devices
7	A	with	B	for	C	to	D	on
8	A	must	B	can	C	may	D	are able
9	A	software	B	equipment	C	calculator	D	pings
10	A	detect	B	reflect	C	distort	D	decrease

6 Fun, Fun, Fun!

page 69

6.1 **stunt** (n) /stʌnt/
sth dangerous or difficult that sb does to entertain people • *It's an excellent adventure film with exciting stunts.* ❖ ακροβατικό, κόλπο

6.2 **defy** (v) /dɪˈfaɪ/
happen or do sth in a way that is different from what has been decided, agreed, or what usually happens • *He was fired for defying the manager's orders.* ➢ ❖ αψηφώ

6.3 **gravity** (n) /ˈɡrævəti/
the force that causes sth to fall to the ground • *Is there gravity in space?* ❖ βαρύτητα

Reading
page 70

6.4 **amusement park** (n) /əˈmjuːzmənt paːk/
a fun fair • *Allou Fun Park is a great amusement park with lots of rides.* ❖ λούνα παρκ

Word Focus
page 70

6.5 **sharp** (adv) /ʃaːp/
punctually; exactly on time • *Be at the station at 10 am sharp or you will miss the train.* ❖ ακριβώς

6.6 **punctual** (adj) /ˈpʌŋktʃʊəl/
being on time • *You won't have to wait for him. He's always punctual.* ➢ punctuality (n), punctually (adv) ❖ στην ώρα

6.7 **shackled** (adj) /ˈʃækld/
bound with chains to sth • *He feels shackled to his desk as he can't even take a lunch break.* ➢ shackle (v), shackles (pl n) ❖ αλυσοδεμένος

6.8 **bound** (adj) /baʊnd/
tied • *She felt bound by her promise to marry him but wished she could say she had changed her mind.* ➢ bind (v) ❖ δεμένος, δεσμευμένος

6.9 **chain** (n) /tʃeɪn/
a line of metal rings that are joined together • *The poor dog was tied to a tree with a heavy chain.* ❖ αλυσίδα

6.10 **radical** (adj) /ˈrædɪkəl/
very new and different • *Her book explained her radical ideas, but I still don't agree with them.* ➢ radical (n), radically (adv) ❖ ριζοσπαστικός

Reading
pages 70–71

6.11 **animal shelter** (n) /ˈænɪml ˈʃeltə/
a place where lost and stray animals are cared for • *We adopted a stray cat from the animal shelter.* ❖ καταφύγιο ζώων

6.12 **ride** (n) /raɪd/
a large machine that people ride on for fun at a fair • *The best ride at the amusement park was the ghost train.* ❖ παιχνίδι σε λούνα παρκ

6.13 **attraction** (n) /əˈtrækʃn/
sth that makes sb go to a place because it's interesting • *The main attraction of the winter fair was the ice skating rink.* ➢ attract (v), attractive (adj) ❖ κάτι θεαματικό και ενδιαφέρον, ατραξιόν

6.14 **keep sb going** (expr) /kiːp ˈsʌmbədi ˈɡəʊɪŋ/
keep sb amused • *There's enough music on this CD to keep us going for hours.* ❖ με κρατάει απασχολημένο

6.15 **jaw-dropping** (adj) /ˈdʒɔː-ˌdrɒpɪŋ/
very surprising or shocking • *The jaw-dropping bungee jump he did from that bridge left me speechless.* ❖ απίστευτα καταπληκτικός, που σε αφήνει με το στόμα ανοιχτό

6.16 **awe** (n) /ɔː/
respect and amazement • *We watched in awe as the stuntman rode his motorbike over ten cars.* ➢ awesome (adj) ❖ δέος

6.17 **bumper car** (n) /ˈbʌmpə kaː/
a small car that you drive at a funfair and deliberately try to hit other cars • *As soon as they got to the fair they went on the bumper cars.* ❖ συγκρουόμενο

6.18 **rollercoaster** (n) /ˈrəʊləkəʊstə/
a track with steep slopes and curves that people ride on at amusement parks • *Don't eat before you go on the rollercoaster!* ❖ (καταδυόμενο) τρενάκι λούνα παρκ

6.19 **rafting** (n) /ˈræftɪŋ/
travelling on a raft, especially as a sport • *They went rafting on the river.* ➢ raft (n) ❖ ράφτινγκ

6.20 **worthy** (adj) /ˈwɜːði/
deserving • *Animal lovers say WWF is a worthy organisation that deserves our support.* ➢ worth (n) ❖ άξιος, αξιόλογος

6.21 **charity** (n) /ˈtʃærəti/
an organisation that raises money to help those in need • *S.O.S. is a charity that raises money for children.* ➢ charitable (adj) ❖ φιλανθρωπικό ίδρυμα

6.22 **concerned** (adj) /kənˈsɜːnd/
worried • *I'm concerned. I don't know where my child is.* ➢ concern (v, n) ❖ ανήσυχος
✎ Opp: unconcerned

6.23 **squander** (v) /ˈskwɒndə/
waste • *Dad says I squander too much time watching TV.* ❖ σπαταλώ

6.24 **hunch (over)** (v) /hʌntʃ (ˈəʊvə)/
sit with rounded shoulders • *Don't hunch over your books; sit up straight.* ❖ καμπουριάζω

6.25 **minority** (n) /maɪˈnɒrɪti/
the smaller part of a group • *Only a small minority of the people interviewed agree with the new law.*
❖ μειονότητα, μειοψηφία
✎ Opp: majority

6.26 **a fair bit** (expr) /ə feə(r) bɪt/
quite a lot; quite often • *I used to play this game a fair bit when it was new.* ❖ αρκετά, συχνά

6.27 **volunteer work** (n) /vɒlənˈtɪə wɜːk/
work sb offers to do without being paid for it
• *Why don't you do some volunteer work at the animal shelter?* ❖ εθελοντική εργασία

6.28 **indicate** (v) /ˈɪndɪkeɪt/
show • *The results of this survey indicate that teens prefer the cinema to the theatre.* ➢ indication (n), indicative (adj) ❖ υποδεικνύω, δίνω ένδειξη, δείχνω

6.29 **range** (n) /reɪndʒ/
a group of different things of the same type
• *There is a good range of rides at this amusement park, so it's great for all the family.*
❖ γκάμα, ποικιλία

6.30 **youth** (n) /juːθ/
young people • *There is a youth club for teenagers in our area.* ❖ νεολαία

6.31 **restless** (adj) /ˈrestləs/
easily bored • *Robert gets restless if he stays home all day.* ➢ rest (v, n) ❖ ανήσυχος

6.32 **degree** (n) /dɪˈɡriː/
a qualification from a university • *Yiannis is studying for a biology degree at Athens University.*
❖ πτυχίο

6.33 **sample** (v) /ˈsɑːmpl/
try • *He sampled many sports before he decided that tennis was his favourite.* ➢ sample (n) ❖ δοκιμάζω

6.34 **mature** (v) /məˈtjʊə/
start to behave sensibly, like an adult • *Bob matured at summer camp this year and is now more confident.* ➢ mature (adj) ❖ ωριμάζω

6.35 **engage (in)** (v) /ɪnˈɡeɪdʒ (ɪn)/
be involved in • *Teenage boys at this school engage in football and rugby.* ❖ ασχολούμαι, συμμετέχω

6.36 **lounge** (v) /laʊndʒ/
relax lazily • *We lounged around the house all day doing nothing.* ❖ κάθομαι, αράζω, χαζεύω

6.37 **worthwhile** (adj) /wɜːθˈwaɪl/
worth the time, effort or money spent on sth
• *If you want to do something worthwhile with your free time, why not join a yoga class and get fit?*
➢ ❖ αξίζει τον κόπο

6.38 **achievement** (n) /əˈtʃiːvmənt/
sth that sb succeeds in doing • *Learning to drive gave Greg a great sense of achievement.*
➢ achieve (v) ❖ επίτευγμα

6.39 **findings** (pl n) /ˈfaɪndɪŋz/
results • *The findings of the survey show that most teenagers prefer to go out than sit around at home.*
➢ find (v) ❖ ευρήματα

6.40 **reserve** (v) /rɪˈzɜːv/
arrange for a hotel room, a table at a restaurant, etc to be kept for you to use at a particular time in the future • *I'd like to reserve a table for four, please.*
➢ reservation (n) ❖ κάνω κράτηση, κλείνω

6.41 **6.41 settle down** (phr v) /ˈsetl daʊn/
become calm and quiet • *Come on, settle down, you two!* ❖ ησυχάζω

6.42 **bump into** (phr v) /bʌmp ˈɪntə/
meet sb by chance • *I bumped into Jack this morning.* ❖ συναντώ τυχαία

6.43 **colleague** (n) /ˈkɒliːɡ/
sb you work with • *Sam and Jo have been friends and colleagues for twelve years.* ❖ συνάδελφος

Amusement parks
attraction   ride
bumper car   rollercoaster

Vocabulary   page 72

6.44 **bowling alley** (n) /ˈboʊlɪŋ ˈæli/
a building where you go bowling • *They go to the bowling alley every Saturday.* ❖ σάλα μπόουλινγκ

6.45 **board** (n) /bɔːd/
a flat piece of wood or card that you play board games on • *Here's the board. Now let's play chess.*
❖ βάση επιτραπέζιου παιχνιδιού

6.46 **circuit** (n) /ˈsɜːkɪt/
a piece of ground for motorbikes, cars, etc to race around • *They're going to build a Formula One circuit here!* ❖ (αγωνιστική) πίστα

6.47 **course** (n) /kɔːs/
a place where a sport like golf is played • *He plays golf at the course in Glyfada.* ❖ γήπεδο (γκολφ)

6.48 **court** (n) /kɔːt/
a place where sports like tennis or basketball are played • *The tennis court was too wet to play on after the rain.* ❖ γήπεδο (τέννις ή καλαθοσφαίρισης)

6.49 **field** (n) /fiːld/
a area of land, often used for sports like football or rugby • *The football field was muddy after the rain.*
❖ γήπεδο (ποδοσφαίρου, ράγκμπη)

6.50 **pitch** (n) /pɪtʃ/
a place where a sport like football or cricket is played • *The grass on the new football pitch is top quality.* ❖ γήπεδο, αγωνιστικός χώρος (ποδοσφαίρου, κρίκετ, κλπ)

6.51 **ring** (n) /rɪŋ/
a small area surrounded by ropes where people box • *The boxer entered the ring to cheers from the crowd.* ❖ ρινγκ πυγμαχίας

6.52 **rink** (n) /rɪŋk/
a place where you go ice skating • *Let's go ice-skating at the rink this weekend.*
❖ παγοδρόμιο

6.53 **track** (n) /træk/
a circular course around which runners, cars etc race • *The cars raced round the track.* ❖ στίβος

6.54 **host** (v) /həʊst/
to provide the space and other things necessary for a special event • *Which country is going to host the next World Cup?* ➢ host (n)
❖ διοργανώνω, φιλοξενώ

6.55 **capable** (adj) /ˈkeɪpəbl/
having the ability or qualities necessary for sth • *Don't worry – she's capable of looking after herself.* ➢ capability (n) ❖ ικανός
✎ Opp: incapable

6.56 **spectator** (n) /spekˈteɪtə/
sb who watches a sport • *The spectators cheered when the players walked onto the pitch.* ➢ spectacle (n), spectacular (adj)
❖ θεατής (αθλητικού γεγονότος)

6.57 **seat** (v) /siːt/
hold, provide seats for • *How many people does the basketball stadium seat?* ➢ seat (n) ❖ χωράω

6.58 **award** (v) /əˈwɔːd/
give a prize • *They awarded Jean Dujardin an Oscar in 2012 for best performance by an actor in the film* The Artist. ➢ award (n)
❖ απονέμω βραβείο

6.59 **finish line** (n) /ˈfɪnɪʃ laɪn/
the line where a race ends • *Whoever crosses the finish line first is the winner.*
❖ γραμμή τερματισμού

6.60 **exhibit** (n) /ɪgˈzɪbɪt/
an object of interest in a museum • *Please do not touch the exhibits in the museum.* ➢ exhibit (v), exhibition (n) ❖ έκθεμα

6.61 **piece** (n) /piːs/
an object • *This golden mask is a priceless piece and the museum is very proud to display it.* ❖ κομμάτι

6.62 **stroll** (n) /strəʊl/
slow relaxed walk • *A stroll in the park is very relaxing.* ➢ stroll (v) ❖ περίπατος, βόλτα

6.63 **wander** (n) /ˈwɒndə/
a relaxed walk without destination or purpose • *As soon as I arrived in Paris, I went for a wander around the Latin Quarter.* ➢ wander (v)
❖ περίπατος, βόλτα

6.64 **seashore** (n) /ˈsiːʃɔː/
the land at the edge of the sea • *They walked along the seashore and breathed in the fresh sea air.*
❖ ακτή, παραλία

6.65 **deal** (v) /diːl/
give cards to players • *John dealt seven cards to each player.* ❖ μοιράζω την τράπουλα

6.66 **shuffle** (v) /ˈʃʌfl/
mix up cards • *He shuffled the cards before the next game of poker.* ❖ ανακατεύω την τράπουλα/τα χαρτιά

6.67 **grab** (v) /græb/
have or take sth quickly because you are busy or in a hurry • *Let's grab a sandwich before we go.*
❖ παίρνω/πιάνω κάτι στα γρήγορα

6.68 **a bite to eat** (expr) /ə baɪt tuː iːt/
a snack; a meal • *We got a bite to eat at Yummies on the way home.* ❖ κάτι να φάω

6.69 **browse** (v) /braʊz/
search for information on a computer or on the Internet • *We browsed the Internet for information on holidays in the Mediterranean.* ➢ browser (n)
❖ κάνω αναζήτηση στο διαδίκτυο

6.70 **hiking** (n) /ˈhaɪkɪŋ/
walking in the countryside • *They went hiking in the mountains.* ➢ hike (v, n) ❖ πεζοπορία

6.71 **path** (n) /paːθ/
a narrow strip of ground you walk along • *They walked along the path through the forest admiring the trees.* ❖ μονοπάτι

6.72 **compass** (n) /ˈkʌmpəs/
a device used to find directions (north, south, east, west) • *To find north, use your compass.*
❖ πυξίδα

6.73 **gear** (n) /gɪə/
equipment • *The gear I recommend for cycling is a helmet.* ❖ εξοπλισμός

6.74 **outing** (n) /ˈaʊtɪŋ/
a short journey for pleasure or education • *Our school is going on an outing to the Acropolis Museum tomorrow.* ❖ εκδρομή

6.75 **portable** (adj) /ˈpɔːtəbl/
that can be carried and moved to another place • *I have a portable television set which I sometimes watch in my bedroom.* ➢ portability (n)
❖ φορητός

6.76 **trekker** (n) /ˈtrekə/
sb who walks a long way as an adventure • *It took the trekkers eight hours to walk across the hills.* ➢ trek (v, n) ❖ πεζοπόρος

6.77 **geocaching** (n) /ˈdʒiːəʊˌkæʃɪŋ/
an activity where you look for hidden objects • *We spend our weekends geocaching and have found two hidden containers already.* ➢ geocache (n) ❖ αναζήτηση «κρυπτών» και αντικειμένων με χρήση GPS

6.78 **hide-and-seek** (expr) /haɪd-ənd-siːk/
a game in which one player shuts their eyes while the others hide, and then goes to look for them • *Kenny hid under the table in the game of hide-and-seek.* ❖ κρυφτό

6.79 **adventure seeker** (n) /ədˈventʃə ˈsiːkə/
a person who loves adventure • *This safari is for adventure seekers only!*
❖ κυνηγός περιπέτειας/συγκινήσεων

6.80 **container** (n) /kənˈteɪnə/
sth that you can put things in • *Put the biscuits in that container.* ➢ contain (v) ❖ δοχείο

6.81 **coordinates** (pl n) /kəʊˈɔːdɪnəts/
a set of numbers which give the exact position of a point on a map • *He put the set of coordinates into the GPS which then showed him where to find the geocache.* ❖ συντεταγμένες

6.82 **load** (v) /ləʊd/
put a program into a computer • *You can load these songs onto your MP3 player in just a few minutes.* ❖ φορτώνω

Sport venues
bowling alley, field, rink
course, pitch, track
court, ring

Grammar — page 73

6.83 **feel up to** (phr v) /fiːl ʌp tuː/
have the strength, energy etc to do sth • *I don't feel up to going out as I'm so tired.* ❖ μπορώ, αντέχω, έχω διάθεση

6.84 **flame** (n) /fleɪm/
bright burning gas that you see when sth is on fire • *The flames in the fire burned orange and blue.* ❖ φλόγα

6.85 **maintain** (v) /meɪnˈteɪn/
keep • *The police maintained order during the demonstration and there was no trouble.* ➢ maintenance (n) ❖ διατηρώ

6.86 **Olympic Torch Relay** (n) /əˈlɪmpɪk tɔːtʃ rɪˈleɪ/
an event during which the Olympic Flame is carried from Olympia, Greece, to the place where the Olympic Games are going to be held • *The 2004 Olympic Torch Relay was the first to start and end in Greece.* ❖ Τελετή Ολυμπιακής Φλόγας

6.87 **mirror** (n) /ˈmɪrə/
a piece of glass which you can see your reflection in • *She is so vain that she looks at herself in the mirror all the time.* ➢ mirror (v) ❖ καθρέφτης

6.88 **host city** (n) /həʊst ˈsɪti/
a country that provides the necessary space, equipment etc for a special event • *Athens was the host city for the 2004 Olympic Games.* ❖ διοργανώτρια πόλη

Listening — page 74

6.89 **boiling** (adj) /ˈbɔɪlɪŋ/
very hot • *It's boiling in here! Open the window.* ❖ πάρα πολύ ζεστός

6.90 **proceed** (v) /prəˈsiːd/
move in a particular direction • *Would passengers on flight 301 to Rome please proceed to Gate 32?* ❖ μεταβαίνω, πηγαίνω

6.91 **miss out (on sth)** (phr v) /mɪs aʊt (ɒn ˈsʌmθɪŋ)/
lose an opportunity to do or have sth • *Get your tickets now! Don't miss out on all the fun!* ❖ χάνω (ευκαιρία)

6.92 **discount** (n) /ˈdɪskaʊnt/
a reduction in the price of sth • *There is a discount on clothes at this shop – they're 30% cheaper this week.* ❖ έκπτωση

6.93 **annually** (adv) /ˈænjuəli/
once a year • *The festival is held annually in February.* ❖ ετησίως

6.94 **catalogue** (n) /ˈkætəlɒg/
a book with information in it • *I browsed the catalogue to see if there were any nice clothes in it that I could buy.* ❖ κατάλογος

6.95 **venue** (n) /ˈvenjuː/
a place where an event takes place • *The Olympic Stadium is the perfect venue for track and field events.* ❖ τόπος, τοποθεσία

6.96 **troupe** (n) /truːp/
a group of singers, actors, dancers etc who work together • *The dance troupe will perform at the Badminton Theatre in March.* ❖ θίασος

Sport
finish line, spectator
host city, tournament

Pastimes
hide-and-seek, stroll
hiking, trekker
outing

Speaking — page 75

6.97 **theme park** (n) /θiːm pɑːk/
an amusement park with a theme, eg Disneyland • *They visited a Wild West theme park when they went to the USA.* ❖ λούνα παρκ, θεματικό πάρκο

6.98 **aqua park** (n) /ˈækwə pɑːk/
an amusement park with water slides, swimming pools and rides with flowing water • *The kids had an amazing time at the aqua park.* ❖ υδάτινο πάρκο

Grammar — page 76

6.99 **tournament** (n) /ˈtɔːnəmənt/
a set of games where you must win to carry on to the next game • *There is one more match in this tournament: the final!* ❖ τουρνουά

6.100 kick-off (n) /ˈkɪk-ɒf/
the time when a football game starts • *The kick-off for the match between Arsenal and Barcelona is at nine.* ➢ kick off (phr v) ❖ ξεκίνημα, έναρξη

Use your English page 77

6.101 get together (phr v) /ɡet təˈɡeðə/
meet • *She gets together with her friends every Saturday and they usually watch a DVD.* ➢ get-together (n) ❖ συναντιέμαι, βρίσκομαι

6.102 run into (phr v) /rʌn ˈɪntuː/
meet by chance • *I ran into Gerry at the shops, so we stopped for a coffee.* ❖ συναντώ τυχαία

6.103 show up (phr v) /ʃəʊ ʌp/
appear; arrive • *What time did Kim turn up at the party?* ❖ εμφανίζομαι

6.104 sit around (phr v) /sɪt əˈraʊnd/
spend a lot of time sitting and doing nothing very useful • *The weather was horrible so instead of going out we sat around and watched TV.* ❖ αράζω, τεμπελιάζω

6.105 sit back (phr v) /sɪt bæk/
get into a comfortable position and relax • *We sat back and enjoyed the film at the cinema.* ❖ κάθομαι αναπαυτικά

6.106 sleep in (phr v) /sliːp ɪn/
let yourself sleep later than usual in the morning • *Teenagers often go to bed late, so they sleep in the next morning.* ❖ κοιμάμαι μέχρι αργά

6.107 turn down (phr v) /tɜːn daʊn/
reject; refuse • *They offered her a job, but she turned it down.* ❖ απορρίπτω

6.108 head out (phr v) /hed aʊt/
go out • *Let's head out early so there isn't much traffic.* ❖ φεύγω

Writing: a report pages 78–79

6.109 screen (v) /skriːn/
show a film • *The film will be screened at 7 pm and 10 pm at this cinema.* ➢ screen (n) ❖ προβάλλω

6.110 part-time (adv) /pɑːt-taɪm/
working a few days or hours per week • *He works part-time at a restaurant, three days a week.* ❖ μερικής απασχόλησης ✎ Opp: full-time

6.111 screening (n) /ˈskriːnɪŋ/
the act of showing a film or television programme • *What are the screening times for 'The Hole' at the Odeon Cinema today?* ➢ screen (v, n) ❖ προβολή

6.112 relevant (adj) /ˈreləvənt/
relating to the subject being discussed • *In the film, the woman's marriage wasn't relevant to the main story, and it could have been left out.* ➢ relevance (n) ❖ σχετικός, σημαντικός ✎ Opp: irrelevant

6.113 commitment (n) /kəˈmɪtmənt/
a thing that you must do • *He made a commitment to help out at the animal shelter every weekend.* ❖ υποχρέωση

6.114 supervisor (n) /ˈsuːpəvaɪz/
sb who is in charge of an activity or person and makes sure that things are done correctly • *The department supervisor praised the employees for their hard work.* ➢ supervision (n), supervise (v) ❖ επιτηρητής

6.115 on display (expr) /ɒn dɪsˈpleɪ/
on show for the public to see • *A famous painting by Picasso is on display at the National Gallery.* ❖ σε έκθεση

6.116 entrance fee (n) /ˈentrəns fiː/
the money you pay to enter (an exhibition) • *The entrance fee for the museum was 10 euros.* ❖ τιμή εισόδου

Verbs connected to leisure

browse	load	shuffle
deal	screen	take part
host	seat	

Video: Canyaking Adventure page 80

6.117 canyon (n) /ˈkænjən/
a long narrow valley with steep sides • *The most famous canyon must surely be the Grand Canyon in North America.* ❖ φαράγγι

6.118 descent (n) /dɪˈsent/
movement from a higher to lower level • *The descent from the mountain took the climbers four hours.* ➢ descend (v) ❖ κατάβαση, κάθοδος ✎ Opp: ascent

6.119 hybrid (n) /ˈhaɪbrɪd/
a combination of (usually) two things • *This car is a hybrid, so it runs on petrol and electricity.* ❖ υβρίδιο

6.120 steep (adj) /stiːp/
rising or falling quickly • *We couldn't ride our bikes because the road was so steep.* ➢ steeply (adv) ❖ απότομος (με κλίση), απόκρημνος

6.121 trust (n) /trʌst/
a strong belief in the goodness of sb or sth • *'My guide dog has my complete trust,' said the blind man.* ➢ trust (v), trustworthy (adj) ❖ εμπιστοσύνη ✎ Opp: distrust, mistrust

6.122 waterfall (n) /ˈwɔːtəfɔːl/
water running over a cliff or mountain • *A beautiful waterfall flowed over the rock face into a lake below.* ❖ καταρράκτης

6.123 consult (v) /kənˈsʌlt/
ask for expert advice • *We consulted a financial expert on how to invest our money.*
➢ consultation, consultant (n) ❖ συμβουλεύομαι

6.124 terrain (n) /təˈreɪn/
a particular type of land • *We drove across the rocky terrain in a jeep.* ❖ έδαφος

6.125 pay off (phr v) /peɪ ˈɒf/
have successful results • *Our preparations paid off and the party was a success.*
❖ φέρνω αποτέλεσμα, αποδίδω

6.126 effortless (adj) /ˈefətləs/
done well or successfully with little or no effort • *He's amazing. He makes playing the violin seem effortless.* ➢ effort (n) ❖ ξεκούραστος, εύκολος

6.127 vertical (adj) /ˈvɜːtɪkl/
straight up • *The waterfall was a vertical mass of water falling into the river below.* ➢ vertically (adv)
❖ κάθετος

6.128 ultimate (adj) /ˈʌltɪmət/
Sb's ultimate aim is their most important aim.
• *His ultimate goal is to climb Mount Everest.*
➢ ultimately (adv) ❖ τελικός, υπέρτατος

6.129 objective (n) /əbˈdʒektɪv/
aim • *The objective of this course is to teach you how to direct a short film.* ❖ σκοπός, στόχος

6.130 consist of (phr v) /kənˈsɪst ɒv/
be formed from two or more things, parts or people • *The team consists of three girls and two boys.* ❖ αποτελούμαι από

6.131 lower (v) /ˈləʊə/
move sth down • *They lowered the bucket into the well to collect water.* ➢ low (adj) ❖ χαμηλώνω
✎ Opp: raise

6.132 peak (n) /piːk/
the top of a mountain • *They started their climb on Friday and reached the peak on Sunday.* ❖ κορυφή

6.133 inspect (v) /ɪnˈspekt/
examine sth carefully to make sure that it is safe, correct or working properly • *After the fire, the building was inspected for damage.* ❖ εξετάζω, επιθεωρώ

6.134 accomplish (v) /əˈkʌmplɪʃ/
succeed in doing sth • *She accomplished everything she wanted to do.*
➢ accomplishment (n) ❖ εκπληρώ, πετυχαίνω

Teenagers
mature	teen
radical	youth
restless	

Phrasal verbs
feel up to	show up
get together	sit around
head out	sit back
pay off	sleep in
run into	turn down

Vocabulary Exercises

A Match.

1	amusement	☐	a	shelter
2	animal	☐	b	work
3	bumper	☐	c	alley
4	volunteer	☐	d	coaster
5	host	☐	e	car
6	roller	☐	f	fee
7	bowling	☐	g	city
8	entrance	☐	h	park

B Complete the table.

Noun	Adjective
relevance	1
2	awesome
radical	3
4	charitable
concern	5
6	trustworthy
rest	7
8	attractive

C Complete the sentences with these phrasal verbs.

feel up to   get together   head out   pay off   run into   show up   sit back   turn down

1 I've got a cold so I don't _____ going out tonight.
2 Let's _____ now so we get to the theatre on time.
3 I'm sure his hard work will _____ and he will get good exam results.
4 Do you think Sandra will _____ my offer of help or accept it?
5 That new TV series starts in a few minutes so let's _____ and see if it's any good.
6 Charles didn't _____ at the match so he must have been busy.
7 We didn't expect to _____ Jack at the mall so it was quite a surprise to see him there.
8 We always _____ on Sunday at our grandparents' house for a family meal.

D Choose the correct answers.

1 I'm hungry. Let's __ a bite to eat before we go to the cinema.
   a grab   b defy   c lower
2 The football __ was very muddy after the heavy rain.
   a court   b course   c pitch
3 The rollercoaster is her favourite __ at the amusement park.
   a ride   b terrain   c piece
4 You should __ another doctor for a second opinion.
   a squander   b consult   c deal
5 The boxers entered the __ and faced each other aggressively.
   a track   b rink   c ring
6 He donated a large sum of money to a __ charity of his choice.
   a portable   b worthy   c comprehensive
7 Please __ the cards well so I know you are not cheating.
   a shuffle   b screen   c maintain
8 The teenagers were __ in the living room, watching TV.
   a hunching   b sampling   c lounging
9 She wants to get a(n) __ in maths from university.
   a degree   b achievement   c collection
10 Which city will __ the next Winter Olympics?
   a seat   b host   c browse
11 What is your __ objective in life?
   a steep   b ultimate   c shackled
12 The __ all cheered when the player scored a goal.
   a supervisors   b trekkers   c spectators

6 Grammar

6.1 Gerunds

Το gerund (γερούνδιο) σχηματίζεται με το ρήμα και την κατάληξη –ing. Χρησιμοποιούμε το gerund:
σαν ουσιαστικό.
→ **Dancing** is something a lot of teens enjoy.
μετά από πρόθεση.
→ I am thinking about **volunteering** at the local charity.
μετά από το ρήμα go όταν μιλάμε για δραστηριότητες.
→ My parents go **bowling** with their friends every Friday.

Χρησιμοποιούμε επίσης gerund μετά από κάποια ρήματα και φράσεις.

admit	enjoy	involve	practise
avoid	fancy	it's no good	prefer
be used to	feel like	it's no use	prevent
can't help	finish	it's (not) worth	regret
can't stand	forgive	keep	risk
deny	hate	like	spend time
dislike	have difficulty	love	suggest
(don't) mind	imagine	miss	

→ I avoid **shopping** in malls. They're too crowded.
→ A lot of teens dislike **sitting** around the house all day.

6.2 Infinitives

	Active / Ενεργητική	**Passive** / Παθητική
Present (παρόν)	(to) give	(to) be given
Perfect (παρελθόν)	(to) have given	(to) have been given

→ They will **provide** the golf balls for the tournament.
→ The golf balls will **be provided** for the tournament.
→ He should **have sold** that bicycle.
→ That bicycle should **have been** sold.

6.3 Full Infinitives

Σχηματίζουμε full infinitives με το και το ρήμα. Χρησιμοποιούμε full infinitives:
για να εξηγήσουμε το σκοπό μιας πράξης.
→ I bought the map **to go** hiking.
μετά από επίθετα όπως afraid, scared, happy, glad, pleased, sad, κλπ.
→ Were you afraid **to try** bungee jumping?
μετά από τις λέξεις too και enough.
→ It's too hot **to go** jogging today.
→ It's not cool enough **to go** jogging today.

Χρησιμοποιούμε επίσης full infinitives (απαρέμφατα με to) μετά από συγκεκριμένα ρήματα και φράσεις.

afford	decide	manage	promise
agree	expect	need	refuse
allow	fail	offer	seem
appear	forget	persuade	start
ask	hope	plan	want
begin	invite	prepare	would like
choose	learn	pretend	

→ My brother offered **to walk** the dog tonight.
→ We agreed **to discuss** our school trip at the next meeting.

6.4 Bare Infinitives

Χρησιμοποιούμε bare infinitives (απαρέμφατα χωρίς to) μετά από:
modal verbs
→ Otto shouldn't **squander** his time on computer games.

6 Grammar

had better για να δώσουμε συμβουλή.
→ *You'd better **take** a torch and a compass on the trip.*
would rather για να μιλήσουμε για προτίμηση. Συχνά χρησιμοποιούμε τη λέξη than.
→ *I'd rather **go** to the gym than stay home.*

Σημείωση:
1. Χρησιμοποιούμε *let* + αντικείμενο + bare infinitive όταν θέλουμε να πούμε ότι επιτρέπουμε σε κάποιον να κάνει κάτι. Χρησιμοποιείται μόνο στην ενεργητική φωνή. Στην παθητική μπορούμε να χρησιμοποιήσουμε το ρήμα *to be allowed to*.
   → *Mum let us **go** on the rollercoaster ride.*
   → *We were allowed **to go** on the rollercoaster ride.*
2. Χρησιμοποιούμε *make* + αντικείμενο + bare infinitive στην ενεργητική φωνή (active voice) όταν θέλουμε να πούμε ότι αναγκάζουμε κάποιον να κάνει κάτι, αλλά στην παθητική φωνή (passive voice) χρησιμοποιούμε full infinitive (*to* + απαρέμφατο).
   → *The coach made us **carry** the equipment inside.*
   → *We were made **to carry** the equipment inside by the coach.*

6.5 Gerund ή Infinitive;

Ορισμένα ρήματα ακολουθούνται από γερούνδιο ή *to* + απαρέμφατο χωρίς να αλλάζει η σημασία τους. Τέτοια ρήματα είναι *begin, bother, continue, hate, like, love,* και *start*.
→ *The students continued **talking/to talk** about the new animal shelter.*
→ *I like **shuffling/to shuffle** the cards when we play UNO.*
→ *Henry started **socialising/to socialise** when he went to college.*

Υπάρχουν άλλα ρήματα που ακολουθούνται από γερούνδιο ή απαρέμφατο, αλλά αλλάζει η σημασία τους. Τα πιο συνηθισμένα από αυτά είναι *go on, forget, regret, remember, stop* και *try*.
→ *Gabriel went on **chatting** online although it was late.* (Συνέχισε να το κάνει.)
→ *Gabriel went on **to chat** online although it was late.* (Έκανε κάτι, το σταμάτησε, και συνέχισε με κάτι διαφορετικό.)
→ *I forgot **giving** you the GPS.* (Δεν θυμόμουνα ότι σου το έδωσα.)
→ *I forgot **to give** you the GPS.* (Δεν θυμήθηκα να σου το δώσω, ξέχασα να το κάνω, δεν σου το έδωσα.)
→ *I regret **not visiting** the new art gallery.* (Δεν πήγα, αλλά τώρα θα ήθελα να είχα πάει.)
→ *We regret **to announce** that the art gallery will be closed on Sunday.* (Λυπούμαστε που πρέπει να ανακοινώσουμε αυτό το δυσάρεστο.)
→ *My father remembers **seeing** Mohamed Ali in the boxing ring.* (Τον έχει δει, και θυμάται αυτό το γεγονός, έχει ανάμνηση.)
→ *She remembered **to bring** her hiking boots on the camping trip.* (Πρώτα θυμήθηκε πως πρέπει να τις φέρει, και μετά τις έφερε.)
→ *The kids stopped **driving** the bumper cars because they were bored.* (Σταμάτησαν, δεν το κάνουν πια.)
→ *They stopped **to ask** about the new volunteer project.* (Διέκοψαν αυτό που έκαναν ώστε να κάνουν κάτι άλλο.)
→ *Try **drinking** some warm milk before bedtime. It will help you go to sleep.* (Δοκίμασε λίγο ζεστό γάλα πριν πας για ύπνο. Ίσως να σε βοηθήσει να κοιμηθείς.)
→ *Try **to relax**. I know it's not easy.* (Προσπάθησε να χαλαρώσεις. Ξέρω πως δεν είναιν εύκολο να το κάνεις.)

6.6 Indirect Questions

Μπορούμε να εισάγουμε μια ερώτηση έμμεσα, δηλαδή χρησιμοποιώντας πλάγιους ερωτηματικούς τύπους. Στις έμμεσες ερωτήσεις, χρησιμοποιούμε τη σειρά των λέξεων που θα είχαμε σε μια καταφατική πρόταση, και στο τέλος της πρότασης συχνά χρησιμοποιούμε τελεία και όχι ερωτηματικό. Οι έμμεσες ερωτήσεις θεωρούνται πιο ευγενικές από τις άμεσες.
→ ***I'd like to know** when the baseball game starts.*
→ ***Could you tell me** how much the tickets for the water park cost?*

Ερωτήσεις των οποίων η απάντηση είναι ναι ή όχι, πρέπει να έχουν τη λέξη *if* ή *whether*.
→ *Do you know **if** the festival begins on Friday?*
→ *I don't suppose you know **whether** they sell nachos at the snack bar.*

6.7 Question Tags

Question tags είναι οι σύντομες ερωτήσεις στο τέλος μιας καταφατικής ή αρνητικής πρότασης. Σχηματίζονται με modal ή auxiliary verb + προσωπική αντωνυμία (personal pronoun).

Συνήθως χρησιμοποιούμε καταφατικό question tag μετά από αρνητική πρόταση, και αρνητικό question tag μετά από καταφατική πρόταση.
→ Ben has become a youth worker, **hasn't he**?
→ Most young people aren't against volunteer work, **are they**?

Όταν μια καταφατική πρόταση περιέχει ρήμα στον Present Simple ή στον Past Simple, χρησιμοποιούμε do/does, don't/doesn't και did/didn't στο question tag.
→ The amusement park provides all-day passes, **doesn't it**?
→ Rosa watched the African dance troupes, **didn't she**?

Χρησιμοποιούμε question tags:
όταν περιμένουμε πως κάποιος θα συμφωνήσει μαζί μας.
→ It was a great game, **wasn't it**?
για να επιβεβαιώσουμε ότι αυτό που λέμε είναι σωστό.
→ You got your degree in 2011, **didn't you**?

Θυμήσου: Κάποια question tags είναι ανώμαλα. Πρόσεξε πώς σχηματίζονται τα παρακάτω question tags.
→ I am right, **aren't I**?
→ Everyone is at the beach, **aren't they**?
→ Let's discuss how we can help at the shelter, **shall we**?
→ Don't go shopping again today, **will you**?
→ Use the GPS when you drive abroad, **won't you**?
→ This/That is the best programme, **isn't it**?
→ These/Those are the theatre tickets, **aren't they**?

6.8 Negative Questions

Οι αρνητικές ερωτήσεις χρησιμοποιούνται:
σε επιφωνήματα.
→ Wow! **Wasn't** that a great game?
για να δείξουμε έκπληξη ή αμφιβολία.
→ **Isn't** your sister coming with us?
→ **Why doesn't** she answer the phone?
όταν περιμένουμε ο άλλος να συμφωνήσει μαζί μας.
→ **Don't** you love eating hot dogs at football games?

Grammar Exercises

A Circle the correct words.

1 He suggested to get / **getting** a part-time job at the supermarket.
2 She'd rather **eat** / to eat at home than at a restaurant.
3 Did you remember **to do** / doing your homework or have you forgotten again?
4 Train / **Training** hard for a big match is tiring.
5 It's not worth **going** / go to the theme park as it's pouring with rain.
6 She didn't study hard enough **to earn** / earning a place at university.
7 The delight of win / **winning** the award was overwhelming.
8 Do you feel up to cook / **cooking** supper with me?
9 She stopped to drink / **drinking** coffee three months ago and hasn't had a single cup since.
10 We might **leave** / to leave after the interval if this film doesn't improve.

6 Grammar

B Complete the sentences with the words below.

can intend remember running stopped stops to watching

1 He _____ driving when he turned eighty and now takes the bus.
2 Do you _____ visiting Grandma every week when we were young?
3 She was too late _____ catch the train, so she had to wait for the next one.
4 Most babies _____ stand up when they are one.
5 _____ TV all day is a waste of time!
6 We _____ to award this trophy to the best athlete.
7 John started _____ a mile a day to try to get fit.
8 She always _____ to visit me when she's in town.

C Rewrite the direct questions as indirect questions.

1 Where is the library?
  Could you _____?
2 What's the time?
  I wonder if _____.
3 When does the match kick off?
  I don't suppose _____.
4 How many people does the stadium seat?
  Do _____?
5 Where is the nearest taxi rank?
  Would you _____?
6 Has the golf course opened yet?
  I would like _____.
7 Why are you here?
  Could _____?
8 What did you enjoy about the film?
  I'd _____.

D Circle the correct words.

1 Let's get a bite to eat, **will / shall** we?
2 Behave yourself at the party, **won't / aren't** you?
3 I'm awful at driving bumper cars, **am / aren't** I?
4 The main events had already started, **hadn't / didn't** they?
5 Don't forget your compass, **will / are** you?
6 Everyone found the exhibition extremely interesting, didn't **they / he**?
7 **Didn't / Weren't** you go climbing last weekend?
8 Amazing! **Isn't / Hasn't** that waterfall beautiful?

Use your English

Exam Task

For questions **1–12**, read the text below and think of the word which best fits each gap. Use only **one** word in each gap.

Teens

Teens are often unjustly labelled as lazy kids who **(1)** _____ rather sit around at home than take **(2)** _____ in some exciting activity. If this is your view, then stop for a moment **(3)** _____ think again and re-evaluate. Youth activities are usually the most extreme and challenging of all and many young people are engaged **(4)** _____ exciting pastimes which their parents wouldn't dream of **(5)** _____. One day their children are innocently playing hide **(6)** _____ seek and the next they feel **(7)** _____ to doing a bungee jump!

Research indicates **(8)** _____ teens tend to experience little fear and are attracted to thrilling activities. Many adults surely remember **(9)** _____ rid of energy on the school playing field and enjoying an adrenaline rush. Only, nowadays more daring pastimes are available to teenagers, aren't **(10)** _____? Bungee jumping, snowboarding, skateboarding, climbing and parachuting to name but a few are enjoyed by teenage boys and girls alike.

Teen daring is not limited to sport, however. Teens today know they had **(11)** _____ try hard to succeed academically. More and more teens are going on to further education than ever before. So the next time you see your teenagers hunched **(12)** _____ a computer, don't assume they are browsing aimlessly. They could be looking for an extreme sport to try or which university to apply to.

7 Right or Wrong?

page 83

7.1 **occupy** (v) /ˈɒkjʊpaɪ/
fill a space, area or amount of time • *Reading occupies most of her free time.* ❖ καταλαμβάνω

7.2 **protest** (n) /ˈprəʊtest/
sth you do that shows publicly that you do not agree with sth • *They took part in street protests against the war.* ➢ protest (v), protester (n) ❖ διαμαρτυρία

7.3 **financial** (adj) /faɪˈnænʃl/
relating to money • *They're having serious financial problems.* ❖ οικονομικός

Reading page 84

7.4 **punish** (v) /ˈpʌnɪʃ/
make sb suffer for sth wrong they have done • *The criminal was punished and sent to prison for two years.* ➢ punishment (n) ❖ τιμωρώ

7.5 **arson** (n) /ˈɑːsən/
the act of setting fire intentionally to a building, a forest, etc • *The police believe the fire was not an accident but arson.* ➢ arsonist (n) ❖ εμπρησμός

7.6 **burglary** (n) /ˈbɜːɡləri/
breaking into a building a stealing from it • *All the money in the house was stolen during the burglary.* ➢ burgle (v), burglar (n) ❖ διάρρηξη

7.7 **computer hacking** (n) /kəmˌpjuːtə ˈhækɪŋ/
illegally accessing a computer • *Computer hacking is a serious problem as personal information can be stolen from your computer.* ❖ ηλεκτρονική πειρατεία, κλοπή

7.8 **illegal parking** (n) /ɪˈliːɡəl ˈpɑːkɪŋ/
parking where you are not allowed to • *Illegal parking will be fined, so please park in the car park instead.* ❖ παράνομη στάθμευση

7.9 **kidnapping** (n) /ˈkɪdnæpɪŋ/
taking sb somewhere by force in order to get money for returning them • *The kidnapping of the star's child ended well and the child was returned to his parents.* ➢ kidnap (v), kidnapper (n) ❖ απαγωγή

7.10 **pickpocketing** (n) /ˈpɪkpɒkɪtɪŋ/
stealing from people's pockets • *Pickpocketing is common in crowded places like buses.* ➢ pickpocket (n) ❖ κλοπή (από πορτοφόλι)

7.11 **robbery** (n) /ˈrɒbəri/
stealing from a bank or shop • *The robbery was carried out by two masked men.* ➢ rob (v), robber (n) ❖ ληστεία

7.12 **vandalism** (n) /ˈvændəlɪzm/
the crime of deliberately damaging things • *There was a lot of vandalism after the match and many shops were damaged.* ➢ vandalise (v), vandal (n) ❖ βανδαλισμός

7.13 **offence** (n) /əˈfens/
a crime • *Burglary is a serious offence.* ➢ offend (v), offender (n) ❖ αδίκημα

7.14 **try** (v) /traɪ/
judge a person in a court • *The kidnappers were caught and then tried in court.* ➢ trial (n) ❖ δικάζω

Word Focus page 84

7.15 **juvenile** (adj) /ˈdʒuːvənaɪl/
concerning people under eighteen • *Many teenagers are getting caught up in juvenile crime.* ➢ juvenile (n) ❖ ανήλικος

7.16 **inadequate** (adj) /ɪnˈædɪkwət/
not (good) enough • *The system is often inadequate and cannot provide help for young lawbreakers.* ➢ inadequacy (n), inadequately (adv) ❖ ανεπαρκής
✎ Opp: adequate

7.17 **ineffective** (adj) /ɪnɪˈfektɪv/
without achieving what sth is intended to achieve • *Sending teens to prison is an ineffective punishment as there they often become worse criminals.* ➢ ineffectiveness (n), ineffectively (adv) ❖ αναποτελεσματικός
✎ Opp: effective

7.18 **jury** (n) /ˈdʒʊəri/
a group of people who listen to the facts of a trial in a court and decide if sb is guilty or not guilty • *The jury decided that the accused man was not guilty.* ❖ ένορκοι

7.19 **trial** (n) /ˈtraɪəl/
a formal meeting in court to decide if sb is guilty of a crime • *He attended the trial of the armed robber who had broken into his shop.* ➢ try (v) ❖ δίκη

7.20 **court** (n) /kɔːt/
a place where legal matters are decided by judge and jury • *In court the judge told everyone to remain silent.* ❖ δικαστήριο

7.21 **refer** (v) /rɪˈfɜː/
direct sb somewhere for help • *The couple was referred to a marriage counsellor for advice.* ➢ referral (n) ❖ παραπέμπω

7.22 **municipal** (adj) /mjuːˈnɪsɪpəl/
belonging to a city or town • *There were many people walking in the municipal gardens.* ➢ municipality (n) ❖ αστικός, δημοτικός

7.23 guardian (n) /ˈgɑːdɪən/
sb legally responsible for a person under eighteen
• *When her parents died, her aunt became her guardian and looked after her until she turned 18.*
➣ guard (v) ❖ κηδεμόνας

Reading pages 84–85

7.24 rise (n) /raɪz/
when the number, amount or level of sth goes up
• *There's been a 15% rise in the price of oil.* ➣ rise (v)
❖ αύξηση, άνοδος
✎ Syn: increase

7.25 alternative (n) /ɔːlˈtɜːnətɪv/
sth you can choose to do, use, etc instead of sth else • *You've got two alternatives: pay in cash or by credit card.* ➣ alternative (adj)
❖ εναλλακτική λύση, (αντίστοιχη) επιλογή

7.26 peer (n) /pɪə/
sb who is the same age as you • *He is a friendly boy and he is popular with his peers.*
❖ συνομήλικος
✎ Also: peer group; peer pressure

7.27 offender (n) /əˈfendə/
sb who commits a crime • *Offenders will be arrested and tried for their crimes.* ➣ offend (v), offence (n) ❖ παραβάτης

7.28 hearing (n) /ˈhɪərɪŋ/
a meeting of a court to find out the facts about a case • *The court hearing is at nine tomorrow morning.* ➣ hear (v) ❖ ακρόαση

7.29 courtroom (n) /ˈkɔːtruːm/
a room where a judge or group of people decide if sb is guilty or not guilty • *The victim's mother was not allowed in the courtroom.*
❖ αίθουσα δικαστηρίου

7.30 defendant (n) /dɪˈfendənt/
sb accused of a crime who is being tried in court
• *The defendant pleaded not guilty to the offence.*
➣ defend (v), defence (n)
❖ εναγόμενος (κατηγορούμενος)

7.31 on a voluntary basis (expr) /ɒn ə ˈvɒləntri ˈbeɪsɪs/
If you do sth on a voluntary basis, you do it because you want to, not because you have to.
• *She works here on a voluntary basis – she needs the experience.* ❖ εθελοντικά, σε εθελοντική βάση

7.32 criminal act (n) /ˈkrɪmɪnəl ækt/
a crime • *Shoplifting is a criminal act and you will be arrested if you are caught.*
❖ εγκληματική πράξη

7.33 judge (v) /dʒʌdʒ/
give an opinion about sb after thinking about all the information you know about them • *I can't judge if she is guilty or not.* ➣ judge (n), judgement (v) ❖ κρίνω, δικάζω

7.34 sentence (v) /ˈsentəns/
punish and send to prison • *The hooligans were sentenced to thirty hours of community service.*
➣ sentence (n) ❖ καταδικάζω

7.35 prosecution (n) /prɒsɪˈkjuːʃn/
the lawyers who try to prove sb is guilty • *The prosecution had proof that the defendant was at the scene of the crime.* ➣ prosecute (v)
❖ ποινική δίωξη

7.36 defence (n) /dɪˈfens/
the lawyers who try to prove sb is innocent
• *The defence said that their client was not guilty because he had been abroad when the crime was committed.* ➣ defend (v), defendant (n)
❖ υπεράσπιση

7.37 fine (n) /faɪn/
the money sb has to pay as punishment
• *The defendant had to pay a fine for speeding.*
➣ fine (v) ❖ πρόστιμο

7.38 devote (v) /dɪˈvəʊt/
use most of your time, effort etc in order to do sth • *He devoted a month to his project on teenage crime.* ➣ devotion (n) ❖ αφιερώνω

7.39 case (n) /keɪs/
a crime which is being investigated • *The judge told the jury not to discuss the case outside the court.* ❖ υπόθεση

7.40 victim (n) /ˈvɪktɪm/
sb who is hurt or killed • *The victim of the violent attack had to go to hospital.* ❖ θύμα

7.41 long-lasting (adj) /lɒŋ ˈlɑːstɪŋ/
continuing for a long time • *Love is the key to a long-lasting relationship.* ❖ μακροχρόνιος

7.42 eligible (adj) /ˈelɪdʒəbl/
qualified or able to do sth • *He will be eligible to vote when he turns eighteen.* ➣ eligibility (n)
❖ επιλέξιμος
✎ Opp: ineligible

7.43 proceedings (pl n) /prəˈsiːdɪŋz/
when sb uses a court of law to deal with a legal case • *The proceedings lasted all morning.*
❖ διαδικασία

7.44 plead guilty (expr) /pliːd ˈgɪlti/
admit you have committed a crime • *The armed robber pleaded guilty and was sent to prison.*
❖ ομολογώ την ενοχή μου (στο δικαστήριο)
✎ Opp: plead not guilty

7.45 theft (n) /θeft/
stealing • *There has been a theft; somebody has stolen my wallet.* ➣ thief (n) ❖ κλοπή

7.46 gang (n) /gæŋ/
a group of young people who spend time together and who are often involved in crime
• *There was a gang of teenage boys on the street corner who looked as if they wanted a fight.*
❖ συμμορία

7.47 weapon (n) /ˈwepən/
an object like a knife or gun used to hurt or kill
• *The gang used large sticks as weapons.* ❖ όπλο

7.48 procedure (n) /prəˈsiːdʒə/
a way of doing sth • *The judge explained the procedure of a trial to the jury.* ❖ διαδικασία

7.49 community service (expr) /kəˈmjuːnəti ˈsɜːvɪs/
unpaid work that sb does to help other people as punishment for a crime • *The man had to do community service cleaning the park.*
❖ κάνω κοινωφελή εργασία (αντί για φυλάκιση)

7.50 fire department (n) /ˈfaɪə(r) dɪˈpɑːtmənt/
an organisation of people whose job is to stop fires • *Help! Call the fire department!*
❖ πυροσβεστικό σώμα

7.51 old people's home (n) /əʊld ˈpiːplz həʊm/
a place where old people live and are cared for • *Sarah's grandmother has been in an old people's home for three years.*
❖ οίκος ευγηρίας, γηροκομείο

7.52 misdemeanour (n) /mɪsdəˈmiːnə/
a bad action that is not very serious • *You won't go to prison for a misdemeanour like parking illegally.*
❖ πλημμέλημα

7.53 jury duty (n) /ˈdʒʊəri ˈdjuːti/
legal requirement to be a jury member • *He was called up for jury duty and was away from work for a week.* ❖ παρουσιάζομαι ως ένορκος

7.54 subsequent (adj) /ˈsʌbsɪkwənt/
following • *The first trial was for robbery and the subsequent one for arson.* ❖ επόμενος

7.55 attendance (n) /əˈtendəns/
being present at an event • *Attendance at the meeting was higher than expected.* ➢ attend (v)
❖ παρακολούθηση, συμμετοχή

7.56 anger management (n) /ˈæŋɡə ˈmænɪdʒmənt/
learning to recognise you are becoming angry and take action to calm down and deal with the situation positively • *The boxer had to attend anger management classes to control his temper outside the ring.* ❖ έλεγχο θυμό

7.57 issue (n) /ˈɪʃuː/
a subject or problem that people talk or argue about • *They talked about pollution and other environmental issues.* ❖ ζήτημα, θέμα

7.58 authority (n) /ɔːˈθɒrɪti/
the power you have because of your official position • *You must respect the authority of the court and only speak when you are allowed to.*
❖ εξουσία

7.59 approval (n) /əˈpruːvəl/
when you have a positive opinion of sb or sth • *The approval of his friends made him feel good.* ➢ approve (v) ❖ έγκριση

7.60 disapproval (n) /dɪsəˈpruːvəl/
when you have a negative opinion of sb or sth • *My parents' disapproval of my bad behaviour made me feel a bit guilty.* ➢ disapprove (v)
❖ αποδοκιμασία

7.61 count (for) (v) /kaʊnt (fɔː)/
be important • *My opinion doesn't count for anything at the office!* ❖ έχω αξία, μετράω

7.62 conventional (adj) /kənˈvenʃənəl/
normal, typical • *A conventional roof does not have grass on it.* ➢ convention (n)
❖ συμβατικός
📎 Opp: unconventional

7.63 judicial system (n) /dʒuːˈdɪʃl/
system of laws and courts • *The judicial system is supposed to protect society from criminals.*
❖ δικαστικό σύστημα

7.64 consequence (n) /ˈkɒnsɪkwens/
a result of sth • *The consequence of your crime is a prison sentence.* ➢ consequently (adj)
❖ συνέπεια

7.65 clean record (expr) /kliːn ˈrekɔːd/
If you have a clean record, the police do not have a record of any crimes connected with you.
• *He could not have a clean record, having spent a year in prison for theft.* ❖ καθαρό μητρώο

7.66 gain (v) /ɡeɪn/
get sth that you want or need • *You will gain useful experience from that job.* ❖ αποκτώ, κερδίζω

7.67 self-esteem (n) /self-əˈstiːm/
confidence in yourself • *The approval of her friends and family increased her self-esteem.*
❖ αυτοεκτίμηση

7.68 reoffend (v) /riːɒˈfend/
commit a crime again • *Many people who are sent to prison reoffend when they are released and find themselves back in court.*
❖ ξαναπαραβαίνω

7.69 deny (v) /dɪˈnaɪ/
say sth isn't true • *Julie denied that she had stolen my earrings, but I'm sure I saw her wearing them.*
➢ denial (n) ❖ αρνούμαι

7.70 pass (a) sentence (on sb) (expr) /pɑːs (ə) ˈsentəns (ɒn ˈsʌmbədi)/
officially decide how a criminal will be punished and say what the punishment will be • *The judge will pass sentence on Jones this afternoon.*
❖ επιβάλλω ποινή (σε κάποιον)

7.71 punishment (n) /ˈpʌnɪʃmənt/
sth you do to sb because they have done sth wrong • *'I think tougher punishments will reduce crime,' said the woman.* ❖ τιμωρία

7.72 lawyer (n) /ˈlɔɪə/
sb who represents people in court • *The man had a good lawyer who convinced the jury he was not guilty.* ➢ law (n) ❖ δικηγόρος

7.73 judge (n) /dʒʌdʒ/
sb who decides a punishment in court • *The judge sentenced the defendant to five weeks' community service.* ➢ judge (v), judgement (n) ❖ δικαστής

7.74 clerk (n) /klɑːk/
an official in charge of the records of a court • *The judge asked the clerk to find the record of the case.* ❖ δικαστικός υπάλληλος

7.75 witness (n) /ˈwɪtnɪs/
sb who sees a crime or event • *There were three witnesses and they were all asked to give details in court.* ➣ witness (v) ❖ μάρτυρας

People in court

clerk	lawyer
defendant	prosecution
defence	victim
judge	witness
jury	

Vocabulary
page 86

7.76 speeding (n) /ˈspiːdɪŋ/
driving faster than the law allows • *He was stopped by police for speeding along the motorway.* ➣ speed (v, n) ❖ παράβαση της νόμιμης ταχύτητας

7.77 commit (v) /kəˈmɪt/
do (sth bad) • *The crime that he committed was burglary.* ❖ διαπράττω

7.78 harsh (adj) /hɑːʃ/
severe, cruel or unkind • *I think the punishment was harsh and unfair.* ❖ σκληρός, αυστηρός

7.79 verdict (n) /ˈvɜːdɪkt/
a decision made in a court about whether sb is guilty of a crime • *The jury returned a verdict of not guilty and the man was free.* ❖ ετυμηγορία

7.80 hostage (n) /ˈhɒstɪdʒ/
sb kept as a prisoner by an enemy or a criminal so that others will do what they demand • *The armed robber held six people hostage in the bank.* ❖ όμηρος

7.81 statement (n) /ˈsteɪtmənt/
sth that sb says or writes officially • *The witness made a statement to the police about what she had seen.* ➣ state (v) ❖ δήλωση

7.82 confess (v) /kənˈfes/
admit to sth bad • *The man confessed to killing his neighbour.* ➣ confession (n) ❖ ομολογώ

7.83 the accused (n) /ðiː əˈkjuːzd/
sb who has been charged with a crime • *The accused stood up in court and pleaded not guilty.* ➣ accuse (v) ❖ ο κατηγορούμενος

7.84 accuse (v) /əˈkjuːz/
say sb has done sth wrong • *The woman was accused of robbing a bank, but she denied any involvement in the crime.* ❖ κατηγορώ

7.85 dismiss (v) /dɪsˈmɪs/
If a judge dismisses a court case, he or she stops it from continuing. • *The judge dismissed the case because of lack of evidence.* ➣ dismissal (n) ❖ απορρίπτω

7.86 suspect (n) /ˈsʌspekt/
sb police think committed a crime • *She was the main suspect because her fingerprints had been found on the weapon.* ➣ suspect (v), suspicion (n), suspicious (adj) ❖ ύποπτος

7.87 undercover (adv) /ˌʌndəˈkʌvə/
done secretly in order to catch criminals or find out information • *The police officers worked undercover and managed to find out what the criminals were planning.* ➣ undercover (adj) ❖ μυστικά

7.88 plain clothes (n) /pleɪn kləʊðz/
ordinary clothes, not a police uniform • *The police officer was in plain clothes so the criminal didn't notice him.* ❖ πολιτικά

7.89 hardened criminal (n) /ˈhɑːdənd ˈkrɪmɪnəl/
a criminal who is not likely to change and obey the law • *He is a hardened criminal and will always lead a life of crime.* ❖ σκληρός εγκληματίας

7.90 hold up (phr v) /həʊld ˈʌp/
rob • *The men held up the shop and stole five hundred euros.* ❖ ληστεύω

7.91 loaded (adj) /ˈləʊdɪd/
with bullets • *Be careful because that is a loaded gun.* ➣ load (v) ❖ γεμάτος

7.92 deadly (adj) /ˈdedli/
able to kill • *Even a small knife can be a deadly weapon and can kill somebody.* ➣ death (n), dead (adj) ❖ θανάσιμος

7.93 suspect (v) /səˈspekt/
think that sth is true or likely to happen, but not be certain • *I began to suspect that he was lying.* ➣ suspicion (n), suspicious (adj) ❖ υποψιάζομαι

7.94 wheel (n) /wiːl/
the round object that you use to control a car, bus, etc. and make it move in a particular direction • *Keep your eyes on the road and your hands on the wheel!* ❖ τιμόνι

Crime and criminals

arson	offence
burglary	offender
computer hacking	pickpocketing
criminal act	speeding
culprit	robbery
gang	theft
hardened criminal	vandalism
kidnapping	

Phrasal verbs

do away with	own up
get away with	put away
give yourself up	see through
hold up	

Grammar
page 87

7.95 demolish (v) /dɪˈmɒlɪʃ/
completely destroy a building so that it falls down • *The old factory will be demolished next year.*
➢ demoliton (n) ❖ κατεδαφίζω

7.96 demonstrator (n) /ˈdemənstreɪtə(r)/
sb who takes part in a public event organised to protest against or support sb or sth • *Several of the demonstrators were arrested.*
➢ demonstrate (v), demonstration (n)
❖ διαδηλωτής

7.97 arrest (v) /əˈrest/
If the police arrest sb, the person is taken to a police station because the police think they have committed a crime. • *He was arrested for looting during the riot.* ➢ arrest (n) ❖ συλλαμβάνω

7.98 spray (v) /spreɪ/
force liquid out of a container and cover sb or sth with it • *I caught him spraying red paint on my car!*
➢ spray (n) ❖ ψεκάζω

7.99 water cannon (n) /ˈwɔːtə(r) ˈkænən/
a piece of equipment that sends out a large amount of water, used by the police to control large groups of people • *Police used water cannons to stop the demonstrators from entering the building.* ❖ εκτοξευτήρας νερού

7.100 object (v) /əbˈdʒekt/
not like, agree with or approve of sth • *Many local people objected to the mayor's plan.*
➢ objection (n) ❖ αντιτίθεμαι, αποδοκιμάζω

7.101 security camera (n) /sɪˈkjʊərəti ˈkæmrə/
a camera that records people to prevent and detect crime • *The shoplifter was caught on the security camera, so it was possible to identify her.*
❖ κάμερα ασφαλείας

7.102 officer (n) /ˈɒfɪsə/
a policeman or policewoman • *The hooligan was arrested by an officer for vandalising a street sign.*
❖ αξιωματικός

7.103 question (v) /ˈkwestʃən/
ask sb questions in order to get information about sth • *The suspect was questioned at the police station about where he was on the night of the murder.* ➢ question (n) ❖ εξετάζω

7.104 innocent bystander (expr) /ˈɪnəsənt ˈbaɪstændə(r)/
sb who is at the scene of a crime or accident and may get hurt or killed although they are not directly involved in the event • *An innocent bystander was hit by a bullet as the two gangs shot at each other.* (n) ❖ αθώος παριστάμενος

7.105 hijack (v) /ˈhaɪdʒæk/
take control of a plane, ship, etc using violence
• *The plane was hijacked by three men who said they had a bomb.* ➢ hijacker (n) ❖ κάνω αεροπειρατεία

7.106 ransom (n) /ˈrænsəm/
money paid to kidnappers • *The kidnappers demanded a ransom of one hundred thousand dollars.* ❖ λύτρα

7.107 raging (adj) /ˈreɪdʒɪŋ/
very powerful • *The ship was caught in a raging storm.* ❖ έντονος, μαινόμενος

7.108 investigate (v) /ɪnˈvestɪgeɪt/
try to find out the truth about sth like a crime, accident, etc • *The case was investigated and evidence that the man was guilty was found.*
➢ investigation, investigator (n) ❖ ερευνώ

7.109 uncover (v) /ʌnˈkʌvə/
discover sth • *The police have uncovered evidence that the man was involved in the murder.*
❖ αποκαλύπτω, ξεσκεπάζω

7.110 bank (n) /bæŋk/
the land along the sides of a river • *He had a small house on the bank of the Hudson River.* ❖ όχθη

7.111 victimless (adj) /ˈvɪktɪmləs/
A victimless crime is one where no people are harmed. • *Twenty-five years in prison for a victimless crime is a bit too harsh, I think.*
❖ χωρίς θύματα

7.112 make a getaway (expr) /meɪk ə ˈgetəweɪ/
escape from a crime scene • *The armed robbers made a getaway in a blue van.* ❖ ξεφεύγω

Listening
page 88

7.113 ecstatic (adj) /ekˈstætɪk/
extremely happy and excited • *He was ecstatic about winning the competition.* ❖ εκστασιασμένος

7.114 exhausted (adj) /ɪgˈzɔːstɪd/
very tired • *The police officer was exhausted after running after the robbers.* ➢ exhaust (v), exhaustion (n) ❖ εξαντλημένος

7.115 indifferent (adj) /ɪnˈdɪfərənt/
not at all interested in sth • *He was indifferent to the news because he wasn't interested in current affairs.* ➢ indifference (n) ❖ αδιάφορος

7.116 sympathetic (adj) /sɪmpəˈθetɪk/
feeling sorry about sb's problems • *The judge was sympathetic towards the victim who had been attacked.* ➢ sympathise (v), sympathy (n)
❖ συμπονετικός
✏ Opp: unsympathetic

7.117 bring to justice (expr) /brɪŋ tʊ ˈdʒʌstɪs/
arrest sb and try them for a crime • *The criminals were caught and brought to justice.*
❖ απονέμω δικαιοσύνη

7.118 confused (adj) /kənˈfjuːzd/
unable to understand sth or think clearly
• *Sorry, I'm a bit confused. What do I have to do?*
➢ confuse (v), confusion (n)
❖ μπερδεμένος, σαστισμένος

7.119 **culprit** (n) /ˈkʌlprɪt/
sb guilty of doing sth wrong • *The city centre was vandalised, but the culprits were never brought to justice.* ❖ ένοχος

7.120 **adolescent** (n) /ædəˈlesənt/
a teenager • *Adolescents under eighteen must be accompanied in court by a parent or guardian.* ➢ adolescence (n) ❖ έφηβος

7.121 **fit** (v) /fɪt/
be suitable for or similar to sth • *He fits the description of the man seen leaving the building.* ❖ αρμόζω, ταιριάζω

7.122 **deter** (v) /dɪˈtɜː/
stop sb doing sth by making them realise it will have bad results • *Long prison sentences are supposed to deter people from committing crimes.* ➢ deterrent (n) ❖ αποτρέπω

7.123 **crime-prevention** (n) /kraɪm-prɪˈvenʃn/
stop crime from happening • *More police on the streets is an effective crime-prevention method.* ❖ πρόληψη του εγκλήματος

7.124 **verdict** (n) /ˈvɜːdɪkt/
a decision in a court about whether sb is guilty or not • *The jury returned a verdict of 'guilty'.* ❖ ετυμηγορία

7.125 **removal** (n) /rɪˈmuːvəl/
the act of taking sb or sth away from a place • *The students were helping with the removal of graffiti from the school walls.* ➢ remove (v) ❖ αφαίρεση

Speaking page 89

7.126 **forensic scientist** (n) /fəˈrensɪk ˈsaɪəntɪst/
a person whose job it is to use scientific methods to solve crimes • *According to the forensic scientist, Smith's DNA was found on the glass.* ➢ forensic science (n) ❖ εγκληματολόγος

Grammar page 90

7.127 **burglar alarm** (n) /ˈbɜːɡlər əˈlɑːm/
a piece of equipment that makes a loud noise when sb tries to enter a building by force • *When the man broke the window, the burglar alarm went off.* ❖ συναγερμός

7.128 **vacate** (v) /vəˈkeɪt/
leave a building, room, seat, etc • *Hotel guests must vacate their rooms by 12 p.m.* ❖ εκκενώνω, εγκαταλείπω

7.129 **the authorities** (pl n) /ðiː ɔːˈθɒrɪtɪz/
people or organisations in charge of a particular country or area • *The vandals are wanted by the authorities.* ❖ οι αρχές

7.130 **deport** (v) /dɪˈpɔːt/
make sb leave a country and return to the country they came from • *'All illegal immigrants will be deported,' said the government minister.* ➢ deportation (n) ❖ απελαύνω

Use your English page 91

7.131 **do away with** (phr v) /duː əˈweɪ wɪð/
kill; get rid of • *The murderers did away with the witness and her body was never found.* ❖ σκοτώνω, ξεφορτώνομαι

7.132 **get away with** (phr v) /ɡet əˈweɪ wɪð/
not get caught for doing sth wrong • *The bank robbers got away their crime and were never caught.* ❖ παραμείνω ατιμώρητος

7.133 **give yourself up** (phr v) /ɡɪv jəˈself ʌp/
surrender to the police • *He knew the police would catch him, so he gave himself up.* ❖ παραδίδομαι

7.134 **own up** (phr v) /əʊn ʌp/
confess • *Tim owned up to eating all the biscuits.* ❖ ομολογώ

7.135 **put away** (phr v) /pʊt əˈweɪ/
put sb in prison • *The murderer was put away for life.* ❖ φυλακίζω

7.136 **see through** (phr v) /siː θruː/
realise sb is lying • *There's no point lying to Dad as he will see through your lies.* ❖ αντιλαμβάνομαι

7.137 **surrender** (v) /səˈrendə(r)/
stop fighting; stop avoiding the police because you know you cannot win • *After hiding for three days, the man surrendered to the police.* ❖ παραδίνομαι

7.138 **against the law** (expr) /əˈɡenst ðə lɔː/
illegal • *It is against the law for children to buy alcoholic drinks.* ❖ παράνομο, είναι ενάντια στο νόμο

7.139 **lethal** (adj) /ˈliːθəl/
causing death • *That enormous knife is a lethal weapon.* ❖ θανάσιμος

7.140 **self-defence** (n) /self-dɪˈfens/
protecting yourself • *She hit the mugger in self-defence and managed to break his nose.* ❖ αυτοάμυνα

7.141 **release** (v) /rɪˈliːs/
let sb go free • *When are they going to release him from prison?* ➢ release (n) ❖ απελευθερώνω

Writing: a formal letter pages 92–93

7.142 **get tough** (expr) /ɡet tʌf/
become stricter • *The police are getting tough and arresting people who demonstrate.* ❖ γίνομαι σκληρός

7.143 **consider** (v) /kənˈsɪdə(r)/
think carefully about sth • *I'm considering buying a new car.* ➢ consideration (n) ❖ σκέφτομαι, αναλογίζομαι

7.144 **proposal** (n) /prəˈpəʊzl/
an official suggestion or plan • *The manager's proposal to shorten the coffee breaks was not accepted.* ➢ propose (v) ❖ πρόταση

7.145 **gathering place** (n) /ˈɡæðərɪŋ ˈpleɪs/
a place where people often come together in a group • *The park has become a gathering place for people of all ages.* ❖ τόπος/σημείο συγκέντρωσης

7.146 **curfew** (n) /ˈkɜːfjuː/
a law which says that people must stay indoors after a particular time at • *Make sure you're back before curfew!* ❖ απαγόρευση κυκλοφορίας

7.147 **recipient** (n) /rɪˈsɪpiənt/
a person who receives sth • *Write the name of the recipient on the left-hand side of the envelope.* ➢ receive (v) ❖ παραλήπτης

7.148 **incident** (n) /ˈɪnsɪdənt/
sth that happens, especially sth bad or unusual • *Have you told the police about the incident?* ❖ περιστατικό, γεγονός

Video: Capoeira: The Fighting Dance — page 94

7.149 **abolishment** (n) /əˈbɒlɪʃmənt/
when a law or a system is officially ended • *The abolishment of smoking in public places aimed to improve public health.* ➢ abolish (v) ❖ κατάργηση
✎ Syn: abolition

7.150 **foster home** (n) /ˈfɒstə həʊm/
a home where a child is raised by sb who is not their natural parent • *John grew up in a foster home and has never met his real parents.*
❖ ανάδοχη οικογένεια

7.151 **mentor** (n) /ˈmentɔː/
sb who gives help and advice over a period of time • *He's a friend and mentor and he gives me a lot of advice and support.* ❖ μέντορας

7.152 **martial art** (n) /ˈmɑːʃl ɑːt/
style of fighting like karate, kung fu and tae kwon do • *People who do martial arts have to be fit and strong.* ❖ πολεμική τέχνη

7.153 **raise** (v) /reɪz/
look after a child or animal until it can take care of itself • *Her parents died when she was four and she was raised by her aunt.* ❖ μεγαλώνω, ανατρέφω

7.154 **adoptive parent** (expr) /əˈdɒptɪv ˈpeərənt/
sb who has legally adopted a child • *Lee was raised by his adoptive parents after losing his family in the war.* ❖ εξ υιοθεσίας γονέας

7.155 **slavery** (n) /ˈsleɪvəri/
the system of owning people and making them work for you for no money • *Slavery is a terrible thing. It takes away people's freedom and dignity.* ➢ enslave (v), slave (n) ❖ σκλαβιά

7.156 **soul** (n) /səʊl/
the part of a person that contains their thoughts, feelings and character • *Yoga is good for the body and soul.* ❖ ψυχή, πνεύμα

7.157 **homeless** (adj) /ˈhəʊmləs/
not having a home • *The homeless man slept in a shop doorway at night.* ❖ άστεγος

7.158 **oppose** (v) /əˈpəʊz/
disagree with sth such as a plan or idea and try to stop it • *Many local residents opposed the new law.* ➢ opposed (adj), opposing (adj), opposition (n)
❖ αντιτίθεμαι

Vocabulary Exercises

A Match.

1. The woman was guilty, but she was not sent to prison.
2. She's working undercover.
3. The murderer has committed another crime.
4. Your early release is because of good behaviour.
5. The boy joined a gang but he wasn't really a criminal.
6. The burglars made a quick getaway with all his possessions.
7. They have been in prison many times.
8. I'm warning you that you mustn't smoke in here.

a. Dropping litter is not a serious crime.
b. She had to do community service instead.
c. It was the second time his house had been broken into.
d. It's against the law.
e. He just wanted to be accepted by his peers.
f. They are hardened criminals.
g. This is the third person he has done away with.
h. So she has to be in plain clothes.

B Circle the odd one out.

1 defendant — judge — trial
2 arson — shoplifting — misdemeanour
3 suspect — culprit — the accused
4 evidence — clue — ransom
5 try — prosecute — put away
6 loaded — lethal — deadly
7 lawyer — victim — guardian
8 inadequate — indifferent — ineffective

C Read the definition and complete the words.

1 people who listen to the facts of a trial in a court: j _ _ _
2 a crime: o _ _ _ _ _ _ _
3 lawyers who try to prove somebody is innocent: d _ _ _ _ _ _ _
4 make somebody suffer because they have done something wrong: p _ _ _ _ _ _
5 commit a crime again: r _ _ _ _ _ _ _ _
6 admit that you have committed a crime: c _ _ _ _ _ _
7 arrest and try: b _ _ _ _ to j _ _ _ _ _ _
8 say somebody has committed a crime: a _ _ _ _ _

D Complete the crossword.

Across

3 _____ is a problem in most inner-city areas. Gangs of youths destroy things.
5 She has shown good behaviour in prison, so she is _____ for an early release.
7 _____ bystanders were hurt when the robbers started firing at the police.
9 _____ is one of the most common crimes in areas where there are a lot of tourists.
10 Perhaps _____ crime is on the rise because young people are bored.

Down

1 The woman _____ shoplifting. She claimed she had just forgotten to pay for the lipstick.
2 Ten years in prison is a _____ punishment for a misdemeanour.
4 She earns very little money. In fact, she has _____ problems.
6 The jury returned a _____ of not guilty.
8 The police think the murder _____ was a heavy object.

7 Grammar

7.1 Passive Voice: Tenses

Χρησιμοποιούμε passive voice (παθητική φωνή) όταν:
η πράξη είναι πιο σημαντική από αυτόν ή αυτό που ευθύνεται γι' αυτήν (the agent/ποιητικό αίτιο).
→ Zoe's car **was stolen** last night.
δε γνωρίζουμε το ποιητικό αίτιο (the agent), ή δεν είναι σημαντικό, ή εννοείται.
→ Three men **were arrested** for the robbery.

Σημείωση: Όταν είναι σημαντικό να αναφέρουμε το ποιητικό αίτιο (the agent) στην παθητική πρόταση, χρησιμοποιούμε τη λέξη *by*. Όταν θέλουμε να αναφέρουμε το εργαλείο ή το υλικό σε μία παθητική πρόταση, χρησιμοποιούμε τη λέξη *with*.
→ A fire **destroyed** the courthouse. → The burglar **was hit** over the head **with** an umbrella.
→ The courthouse **was destroyed by** fire. → Airports **are fitted with** security cameras.

Σχηματίζουμε passive voice με το ρήμα *be* και past participle (παθητική μετοχή). Πρόσεξε πώς οι ενεργητικοί τύποι του ρήματος (active verbs) μετατρέπονται σε παθητικούς τύπους ρήματος (passive verbs).

Tense	Active	Passive
Present Simple	drive/drives	am/are/is driven
Present Continuous	am/are/is driving	am/are/is being driven
Past Simple	drove	was/were driven
Past Continuous	was/were driving	was/were being driven
Present Perfect Simple	have/has driven	have/has been driven
Past Perfect Simple	had driven	had been driven
Future Simple	will drive	will be driven

Σημείωση: Δεν υπάρχει παθητικός τύπος για τους χρόνους Future Continuous, Present Perfect Continuous και Past Perfect Continuous.

Μετατρέπουμε μια ενεργητική πρόταση σε παθητική με τον παρακάτω τρόπο:
Το αντικείμενο του ρήματος της ενεργητικής πρότασης γίνεται υποκείμενο του ρήματος της παθητικής πρότασης. Το ρήμα *be* χρησιμοποιείται στον ίδιο χρόνο με το κύριο ρήμα της ενεργητικής πρότασης, μαζί με την παθητική μετοχή (past participle) του κυρίου ρήματος της ενεργητικής πρότασης.
→ They **found** the stolen goods. → The stolen goods **were found**.
Σε αυτό το παράδειγμα, δε γνωρίζουμε ή δεν είναι σημαντικό ποιος βρήκε τα κλεμμένα αντικείμενα,
και έτσι αυτή η πληροφορία δεν αναφέρεται στην παθητική πρόταση.

Σημείωση: Όταν θέλουμε να μετατρέψουμε μια πρόταση με δύο αντικείμενα στην παθητική φωνή, τότε το ένα γίνεται υποκείμενο της παθητικής πρότασης και το άλλο παραμένει αντικείμενο. Ποιο από τα δύο αντικείμενα θα επιλέξουμε εξαρτάται από το τι θέλουμε να τονίσουμε. Αν το προσωπικό αντικείμενο (personal object) παραμένει αντικείμενο στην παθητική πρόταση, θα πρέπει να χρησιμοποιήσουμε και την κατάλληλη πρόθεση (*to*, *for*, κλπ).
→ He **sent** Anita a letter of apology. → A letter of apology **was sent to** Anita.
→ Anita **was sent** a letter of apology.

7.2 The Passive Voice: Gerunds, Infinitives & Modal Verbs

Verb Form	Active	Passive
Gerund	driving	being driven
Bare Infinitive	drive	be driven
Full Infinitive	to drive	to be driven
Modal	can drive	can be driven

→ The man admitted **being given** the stolen paintings.
→ Pablo should **be released** from prison for good behaviour very soon.
→ The juvenile offender agreed **to be judged** by his peers.
→ Young offenders **can be told** to do community service.

Συχνά χρησιμοποιούμε ρήματα όπως *believe, consider, know, expect, say, suppose* και *think* στην παθητική φωνή. Μπορούν να χρησιμοποιηθούν σε απρόσωπη ή σε προσωπική σύνταξη. (impersonal or personal structure).

Η απρόσωπη παθητική σύνταξη (impersonal passive structure) σχηματίζεται με *it* + παθητικό ρήμα (passive verb) + *that* + πρόταση.
→ **Most people believe that** computer hacking is a serious crime.
→ **It is believed that** computer hacking is a serious crime.

Η προσωπική σύνταξη σχηματίζεται με ουσιαστικό + παθητικό ρήμα (passive verb) + απαρέμφατο με *to* (full infinitive).
→ **A lot of people say** that teen courts **are** a positive measure.
→ Teen courts **are said to be** a positive measure.

7.3 Causative

Χρησιμοποιούμε causative:
για να πούμε ότι κάποιος έχει κανονίσει να κάνει κάποιος άλλος κάτι για λογαριασμό του.
→ We **are having the school walls cleaned** right now.
για να πούμε ότι κάτι δυσάρεστο συνέβη σε κάποιον.
→ Leon **had his nose broken** in last week's demonstration.

Σχηματίζουμε causative με το ρήμα *have* + αντικείμενο + past participle (παθητική μετοχή). Μπορεί να χρησιμοποιηθεί σε πολλούς χρόνους. Όταν θέλουμε να αναφέρουμε το ποιητικό αίτιο (agent), χρησιμοποιούμε τη λέξη *by*.
→ They **had a new security alarm installed**.
→ My grandparents **are going to have a new security door put in**.
→ They **are having the fire investigated** by a private detective.

Σημείωση: Μπορούμε επίσης να χρησιμοποιήσουμε *get* + αντικείμενο + past participle. Αυτή η σύνταξη έχει λιγότερο επίσημο ύφος. Όταν όμως περιγράφουμε δυσάρεστα γεγονότα, πρέπει να χρησιμοποιήσουμε το ρήμα *have*.
→ You should **get the fine paid** as soon as possible.   → She **had her wallet stolen** at the cinema yesterday.

Grammar Exercises

A Complete the sentences with the correct passive form of the verb in brackets.

1 The smugglers _____ (arrest) yesterday.
2 Oh no! That man _____ (mug) by a gang of teenagers.
3 _____ (the students/punish) yet for cheating?
4 The case _____ (not investigate) by anyone at the moment.
5 Demonstrations _____ (can/hold) with official permission only.
6 Police promise that the robbers _____ (catch) soon.
7 An extensive search for the kidnapped boy _____ (carry out) when he was found.
8 It _____ (now/believe) that the culprits were hungry homeless people.

B Rewrite the sentences in the passive voice.

1 They must inform the authorities.

2 They will try the criminals in May.

3 I object to you telling me where to sit.

4 Someone broke into his house.

5 Many people think that the sentence was unfair.

6 They have uncovered more evidence.

7 Did they steal all the laptops?

8 Nobody should break the law.

7 Grammar

C Put the words in the correct order.

1 have / we / our / had / insured / possessions
_____

2 the / suspect / officer / had / the / searched
_____

3 checked / the / was / having / the / files / all / boss
_____

4 going / she / is / to / fitted / have / her / with / alarm / an / car
_____

5 have / they / yet / had / his / record / criminal / checked / not
_____

6 the / had / witness / statement / her / taken
_____

7 have / did / you / account / your / hacked / ?
_____

8 should / the / had / stealing / him / for / arrested / school / have
_____

Use your English

Exam Task

For questions **1–8**, read the text below. Use the word given in capitals at the end of some of the lines to form a word that fits in the gap **in the same line.**

Rioting and Looting

In the UK, from the age of sixteen you are **(1)** _____ responsible for   **LEGAL**
yourself, so you cannot turn to your parent or **(2)** _____ if you are   **GUARD**
arrested for committing a crime. You would think the threat of prison would deter
youngsters from breaking the law, but sadly this is not always the case, especially
during riots. Many find **(3)** _____ a way of releasing anger.   **VIOLENT**
(4) _____ is common and it is believed that some young people   **VANDALISE**
destroy other people's property purely to gain the **(5)** _____ of their   **APPROVE**
peers. Furthermore, there is less fear of **(6)** _____ as there is less   **PUNISH**
chance of being caught by the police.

However, many **(7)** _____ go a step further. They smash shop windows   **OFFEND**
and steal all the goods they can carry. This is looting, which is just another form of
(8) _____, and is a very serious crime indeed.   **ROB**

8 Environmental Affairs

page 95

8.1 affair (n) /əˈfeə/
a situation or subject that is being considered • *You shouldn't ask so many questions about other people's affairs!* ❖ ζήτημα, υπόθεση

Reading   page 96

8.2 power (v) /ˈpaʊə/
supply power to a vehicle or machine • *This car is powered by a special engine.* ➢ power (n), powerful (adj) ❖ τροφοδοτώ (με ενέργεια)

8.3 tornado (n) /tɔːˈneɪdəʊ/
a violent windstorm which rotates very fast • *The spinning tornado destroyed all the houses along the street.* ❖ σίφουνας, ανεμοστρόβιλος

8.4 spin (v) /spɪn/
turn round quickly • *The dancer was spinning in circles.* ❖ στριφογυρίζω, περιστρέφομαι

Word Focus   page 96

8.5 rotation (n) /rəʊˈteɪʃn/
going round in a circle • *Night and day are a result of Earth's rotation.* ➢ rotate (v) ❖ περιστροφή

8.6 gust (n) /ɡʌst/
a sudden strong movement of wind or rain • *Strong gusts of wind made it hard to walk along the seafront.* ❖ φύσημα

Reading   pages 96–97

8.7 carve (v) /kaːv/
cut into • *Rivers carve rock over millions of years and create valleys.* ➢ carving (n) ❖ χαράζω

8.8 whip up (phr v) /wɪp ʌp/
create; cause • *The teacher whipped up enthusiasm for the excursion by telling the students they would see some interesting things.* ❖ δημιουργώ

8.9 tear (v) /teə/
go very fast • *The dog tore across the park after the ball.* ❖ περνώ σαν αστραπή, τρέχω σαν αστραπή, σπεύδω

8.10 airborne (adj) /ˈeəbɔːn/
in the air • *When the plane was airborne, we could see the land below.* ❖ στον αέρα, σε πτήση

8.11 unevenly (adv) /ʌnˈiːvənli/
not regularly • *The food was heated unevenly in the microwave oven, so some of it was hot and some cold.* ➢ uneven (adj) ❖ ανομοιόμορφα

8.12 breezy (adj) /ˈbriːzi/
a little windy • *It was a breezy day–perfect for flying a kite.* ➢ breeze (n) ❖ με αεράκι

8.13 hoist (v) /hɔɪst/
pull sth heavy up, eg sails • *They hoisted the sails when it got breezy and the yacht moved smoothly over the water.* ❖ υψώνω

8.14 pattern (n) /ˈpætən/
the regular way in which sth happens or is done • *Meteorologists study weather patterns in order to forecast future weather.* ❖ μορφή, σχήμα, μοτίβο

8.15 Equator (n) /ɪˈkweɪtə/
an imaginary line around the middle of the Earth • *Greece lies north of the Equator in the northern hemisphere.* ➢ equatorial (adj) ❖ ισημερινός

8.16 harness (v) /ˈhaːnɪs/
control and use the power of sth • *We can harness the wind to generate electricity.* ➢ harness (n) ❖ χρησιμοποιώ, δαμάζω

8.17 crop (n) /krɒp/
a kind of plant grown on a farm for eating • *This farm's main crop is potatoes.* ❖ σοδειά

8.18 steel (n) /stiːl/
a strong metal often used in buildings and bridges • *These knives are made of steel.* ❖ ατσάλι

8.19 storey (n) /ˈstɔːri/
a floor or level of a building • *I live on the third floor of a block of flats.* ❖ όροφος

8.20 top (with) (v) /tɒp (wɪð)/
put on the top • *This building is topped with a roof garden.* ❖ καλύπτω (με), σκεπάζω (με)

8.21 blade (n) /bleɪd/
a flat piece of metal or wood on a windmill • *The blades of the windmill turned slowly in the breeze.* ❖ πτερύγιο

8.22 generator (n) /ˈdʒenəreɪtə/
a machine that produces electricity • *Hospitals have generators which can produce electricity if there is a blackout.* ➢ generate (v) ❖ γεννήτρια

8.23 account for (phr v) /əˈkaʊnt fɔː/
be the reason for sth • *The high temperatures and heavy rain account for the thick vegetation in this area.* ❖ είναι αιτία, εξηγώ

8.24 tube (n) /tjuːb/
a hollow cylinder • *Please buy me a tube of toothpaste from the supermarket.* ❖ σωλήνας

8.25 upright (adj) /ˈʌpraɪt/
standing up • *After being ill in bed for so long, it was difficult for him to stand upright.* ❖ όρθιος

8.26 hurricane (n) /ˈhʌrɪkən/
a strong storm • *Hurricanes can destroy large coastal areas if they reach the shore.* ❖ τυφώνας

8.27 **mass** (n) /mæs/
a large amount of sth • *A mass of dark clouds started to gather in the sky before the storm.* ❖ μάζα

8.28 **moist** (adj) /mɔɪst/
slightly wet • *We could tell it was going to rain soon because of the moist air.* ➢ moisture (n) ❖ υγρός

8.29 **uproot** (v) /ˌʌpˈruːt/
pull a tree, plant, etc out of the ground • *The storm uprooted several large trees.* ❖ ξεριζώνω

8.30 **strike** (v) /straɪk/
hit sb or sth • *She fell and struck her head on the table.* ❖ χτυπάω

8.31 **lightning** (n) /ˈlaɪtnɪŋ/
a sudden bright light in the sky during a storm • *The tree was struck by lightning.* ❖ αστραπή, κεραυνός

Weather words
tornado   breezy
twister   thunderstorm
hurricane gust

Vocabulary — page 98

8.32 **torrential** (adj) /təˈrenʃl/
very heavy (rain) • *The torrential rain caused the rivers to flood.* ➢ torrent (n) ❖ καταρρακτώδης

8.33 **rainfall** (n) /ˈreɪnfɔːl/
the amount of rain that falls on an area in a particular period of time • *The crops are dying in the fields because of the very low rainfall.* ❖ βροχόπτωση

8.34 **moisture** (n) /ˈmɔɪstʃə/
small amounts of water in the air, a substance, etc • *There is always a lot of moisture in the air in the mornings.* ➢ moist (adj) ❖ υγρασία

8.35 **coastal** (adj) /ˈkəʊstl/
next to the sea • *We live in a coastal area near a fishing village.* ➢ coast (n) ❖ παράκτιος

8.36 **ecosystem** (n) /ˈiːkəʊˌsɪstəm/
all the plants and animals that live in the same place and their relationship • *The ecosystem of this lake has been destroyed by pollution.* ❖ οικοσύστημα

8.37 **evaporation** (n) /ɪˌvæpəˈreɪʃn/
when a liquid changes into a gas • *The simplest method of getting salt is through the evaporation of salt water.* ➢ evaporate (v) ❖ εξάτμιση

8.38 **natural resource** (n) /ˈnætrl rɪˈzɔːs/
things like coal, oil, water, trees, etc that can be used by people • *Our way of life depends on natural resources like oil and natural gas.* ❖ φυσικός πόρος

8.39 **draught** (n) /drɑːft/
a cold current of air • *Please close the door as there is a draught in the room.* ➢ draughty (adj) ❖ ρεύμα (αέρα)

8.40 **drought** (n) /draʊt/
a long period of time without rain • *The crops all died because of the drought.* ❖ ξηρασία

8.41 **gradual** (adj) /ˈgrædʒuəl/
happening slowly over a period of time • *The gradual increase in temperatures on Earth will change our climate.* ❖ σταδιακός

8.42 **emission** (n) /ɪˈmɪʃn/
the act of sending out light, heat, gas etc • *The emission of fumes from cars causes a lot of pollution.* ➢ emit (v) ❖ εκπομπή

8.43 **omission** (n) /əˈmɪʃn/
when you do not include or do not do sth • *The omission of the conclusion in your essay makes it incomplete.* ➢ omit (v) ❖ παράλειψη

8.44 **trap** (v) /træp/
prevent sth from getting away • *Smoke was trapped in the room and we couldn't open the window to let it out.* ➢ trap (n) ❖ παγιδεύω

8.45 **carbon dioxide** (n) /ˈkɑːbən daɪˈɒksaɪd/
a kind of gas • *We breathe in oxygen and breathe out carbon dioxide.* ❖ διοξείδιο του άνθρακα

8.46 **methane** (n) /ˈmiːθeɪn/
a gas often used as fuel • *Natural gas consists mainly of methane.* ❖ μεθάνιο

8.47 **greenhouse gas** (n) /ˈgriːnhaʊs gæs/
a gas that traps heat and causes the greenhouse effect • *Carbon dioxide is the main greenhouse gas and its emissions are increasing.* ❖ αέριο του θερμοκηπίου

8.48 **fumes** (pl n) /fjuːmz/
unpleasant smoke • *The fumes from the old car smelt horrible.* ❖ αναθυμιάσεις, αέρια, καυσαέρια

8.49 **blanket** (n) /ˈblæŋkɪt/
a thick covering of sth • *When we woke up, there was a blanket of snow on the ground.* ❖ στρώμα

8.50 **remains** (pl n) /rɪˈmeɪnz/
the body of a person or animal after it has died • *The remains of animals were excavated at the site.* ❖ λείψανα

8.51 **oil** (n) /ɔɪl/
the thick liquid found underground from which petrol is produced • *People drill for oil in the desert and under the sea.* ❖ πετρέλαιο

8.52 **natural gas** (n) /ˈnætʃrʊl gæs/
gas found underground • *Natural gas is used to heat many houses.* ❖ φυσικό αέριο

8.53 **coal** (n) /kəʊl/
black solid rock found underground and burnt as fuel • *They put more coal on the fire because they were freezing.* ❖ άνθρακας, κάρβουνο

8.54 **renewable** (adj) /rɪˈnjuːəbl/
that will never run out • *Wind power is renewable energy.* ➢ renew (v) ❖ ανανεώσιμος

8.55 **usable** (adj) /ˈjuːsəbl/
that can be used • *Those batteries aren't usable. They're dead.* ➢ use (v) ❖ χρησιμοποιήσιμος

8.56 **conserve** (v) /kənˈsɜːv/
use as little water, energy etc as possible so as not to waste it • *We need to conserve water because there is not enough of it.* ➢ conservation, conservationist (n) ❖ προστατεύω

8.57 **consume** (v) /kənˈsjuːm/
use up • *If we consume all the fossil fuels, we will have to find alternative sources of energy.* ➢ consumption (n) ❖ καταναλώνω

8.58 **crude oil** (n) /kruːd ɔɪl/
oil in its natural state • *Crude oil cannot be used for fuel. It has to be refined first.* ❖ αργό πετρέλαιο

8.59 **raw** (adj) /rɔː/
uncooked • *Do you like raw fish or do you prefer it cooked?* ❖ ωμός

8.60 **deforestation** (n) /ˌdiːfɒrɪsˈteɪʃn/
destruction of the forests • *The deforestation of the Amazon will be a disaster for the whole world.* ❖ αποψίλωση των δασών

8.61 **erosion** (n) /ɪˈrəʊʒn/
the process by which rock or soil is gradually destroyed by wind or water • *The erosion of the hillsides means that trees can't grow there any more.* ➢ erode (v) ❖ διάβρωση

8.62 **current** (n) /ˈkʌrənt/
a continuous movement of water in the sea or a river • *A strong current swept the swimmer far from the shore.* ❖ ρεύμα

8.63 **delta** (n) /ˈdeltə/
an area of land near the sea where a river splits into many smaller rivers • *A lot of water birds live in the river delta.* ❖ δέλτα

8.64 **downpour** (n) /ˈdaʊnpɔː/
heavy rainfall • *We got completely soaked in the downpour.* ❖ νεροποντή

8.65 **habitat** (n) /ˈhæbɪtæt/
the natural place where an animal or plant lives • *This spider's natural habitat is the desert.* ❖ φυσικό περιβάλλον

8.66 **soaking wet** (expr) /ˈsəʊkɪŋ wet/
completely wet • *I didn't have an umbrella, so I arrived home soaking wet.* ❖ μούσκεμα, βρεγμένος μέχρι το κόκαλο

8.67 **grassy** (adj) /ˈɡrɑːsi/
covered with grass • *They cycled down a grassy hillside.* ➢ grass (n) ❖ χορταριασμένος, καλυμμένος με χόρτα

8.68 **sweep** (v) /swiːp/
force sb or sth to move in a particular direction • *The little boat was swept out to sea in the storm.* ❖ παρασύρω

8.69 **flow** (v) /fləʊ/
move continuously • *The river flowed out to sea.* ➢ flow (n) ❖ ρέω

8.70 **irrigation** (n) /ˌɪrɪˈɡeɪʃn/
supply land or crops with water • *Proper irrigation is essential as crops need water to grow.* ➢ irrigate (v) ❖ άρδευση

Phrasal verbs

account for	turn into
block out	wear away
blow over	whip up
breathe out	wipe out
freeze over	

Environmental problems

global warming	deforestation
drought	erosion
fumes	radiation
greenhouse gas	

Grammar — page 99

8.71 **reactor** (n) /rɪˈæktə(r)/
a large machine used for producing nuclear energy • *The Chernobyl reactor exploded in 1986.* ❖ (πυρηνικός) αντιδραστήρας

8.72 **species** (n) /ˈspiːʃiːz/
a group of animals or plants that are the same and can produce young animals or plants together • *There are over 400 species of shark.* ❖ είδος
✎ Plural: species

8.73 **recycled** (adj) /riːˈsaɪkld/
used again • *This book is made from recycled paper.* ➢ recycling (n), recycle (v) ❖ ανακυκλωμένος

8.74 **turn into** (phr v) /tɜːn ˈɪntə/
become sth different or make sb or sth do this • *In six months, the little puppy turned into a big, scary dog.* ❖ γίνομαι, αλλάζω (σε κάτι)

8.75 **reduce** (v) /rɪˈdjuːs/
make sth smaller or less • *They reduced the price of the T-shirt from £20 to £15.* ➢ reduction (n) ❖ μειώνω

8.76 **fancy** (adj) /ˈfænsi/
expensive and fashionable • *Mia took us to a fancy restaurant on her birthday.* ❖ φανταχτερός, φαντεζί

8.77 **explosion** (n) /ɪksˈpləʊʒn/
a blast of energy (often from a bomb)
• *There was a loud explosion when the gas heater blew up.* ➢ explode (v), explosive (n, adj) ❖ έκρηξη

8.78 **humid** (adj) /ˈhjuːmɪd/
wet; damp • *The day was hot and humid and in the evening it rained heavily.* ➢ humidity (n) ❖ υγρός

8.79 **restricted** (adj) /rɪˈstrɪktɪd/
If sth is restricted, it can only be used by people with special permission because it is secret or dangerous. • *This is a restricted area – you can't enter.* ➢ restrict (v), restriction (n)
❖ απαγορευμένος, περιορισμένος

8.80 **billionaire** (n) /ˈbɪljəˌneə/
sb who has a billion dollars, pounds or euros in money • *The richest people in the world are billionaires.* ➢ billion (n) ❖ δισεκατομμυριούχος

8.81 **shellfish** (n) /ˈʃelˌfɪʃ/
an edible sea creature with a shell • *I love eating shellfish, especially prawns and mussels.*
❖ οστρακοειδή

8.82 **nasty** (adj) /ˈnɑːsti/
painful, dangerous or serious • *He had a nasty cut on his foot.* ❖ άσχημος, σοβαρός

8.83 **rash** (n) /ræʃ/
red inflammation on the skin • *His skin was red and the doctor said it was an allergic rash.*
❖ εξάνθημα

Rubbish
scrap   recycling bin
recycled   household waste

Listening — page 100

8.84 **admit** (v) /ədˈmɪt/
agree that you did sth bad or that sth bad is true
• *The meteorologist admitted that they had not forecast the weather correctly.* ❖ παραδέχομαι

8.85 **complain** (v) /kəmˈpleɪn/
say you are not happy about sth • *We complained that there was no heating in the hotel.*
➢ complaint (n) ❖ παραπονούμαι

8.86 **enquire** (v) /ɪnˈkwaɪə/
ask • *We enquired at the station about train times.*
➢ enquiry (n) ❖ ρωτώ

8.87 **inform** (v) /ɪnˈfɔːm/
tell sb sth • *Our teacher informed us that she would be giving us a test.* ➢ information (n)
❖ ενημερώνω

8.88 **predict** (v) /prɪˈdɪkt/
say what will happen in the future
• *Meteorologists predict that the weather will be fine this weekend.* ➢ prediction (n), predictable (adj)
❖ προβλέπω

8.89 **seek permission** (expr) /siːk pəˈmɪʃn/
ask to do sth • *You will have to seek permission from the city council if you want to hold a concert in the square.* ❖ ζητώ άδεια

8.90 **recycling bin** (n) /riːˈsaɪklɪŋ bɪn/
a container for materials that can be recycled, such as glass, paper and aluminium • *I take my empty glass bottles to the recycling bin outside the supermarket.* ❖ κάδος ανακύκλωσης

8.91 **genetically modified food** (expr) /dʒəˈnetɪkli ˈmɒdɪfaɪd fuːd/
food that has had its DNA changed by genetic engineering • *Do you think genetically modified food might affect our health?*
❖ γενετικά τροποποιημένα τρόφιμα

8.92 **organic** (adj) /ɔːˈɡænɪk/
grown without chemicals • *Organic food is supposed to be good for your health.*
➢ organically (adv) ❖ βιολογικός

8.93 **stuff** (n) /stʌf/
used to talk about a substance, material, group of objects, etc when you do not know what they are called or when the name is not important • *What's that black stuff on your shirt?*
❖ πράγμα(τα)

8.94 **photovoltaic panel** (n) /ˌfəʊtəʊvɒlˈteɪɪk ˈpænəl/
a panel which makes electricity from the sun
• *Photovoltaic panels on your roof can power your home.* ❖ φωτοβολταϊκός συλλέκτης

8.95 **discourage** (v) /dɪsˈkʌrɪdʒ/
make sb lose confidence or enthusiasm about sth • *The terrible weather discouraged us from going to the beach for the day.*
➢ discouragement (n) ❖ αποθαρρύνω
✎ Opp: encourage

8.96 **prohibit** (v) /prəˈhɪbɪt/
say that an action is illegal or not allowed
• *Swimming is prohibited here. There are sharks in the water.* ❖ απαγορεύω

8.97 **express doubt** (expr) /ɪksˈpres daʊt/
say you are not sure about sth • *He expressed doubt about the weather forecast for rain as the sun was shining in the sky.* ❖ εκφράζω αμφιβολία

8.98 **criticise** (v) /ˈkrɪtɪsaɪz/
point out the negative things about sb or sth
• *The boss criticised his employees for not writing thorough reports.* ➢ criticism (n), critical (adj)
❖ επικρίνω, κάνω κριτική

8.99 **environmentally-friendly** (adj) /ɪnˌvaɪərəˈmentəli-ˈfrendli/
things that are environmentally friendly do not harm the environment • *Environmentally-friendly packaging which can be recycled is used in many supermarkets nowadays.*
❖ φιλικός προς το περιβάλλον

Speaking — page 101

8.100 plot (n) /plɒt/
a small piece of land used for building or growing things on • *I made this salad with tomatoes from my own vegetable plot.* ❖ μικρό κομμάτι γης

Grammar — page 102

8.101 litter (v) /ˈlɪtə(r)/
drop rubbish on the ground in a public place • *There was a sign on the beach that said 'Please do not litter'.* ❖ ρυπαίνω

8.102 endangered (adj) /ɪnˈdeɪndʒəd/
that may soon no longer exist • *The giant panda is an endangered species.* ❖ υπό εξαφάνιση

8.103 extinct (adj) /ɪkˈstɪŋkt/
no longer alive • *Dinosaurs became extinct about 65 million years ago.* ➢ extinction (n) ❖ εξαφανισμένο (είδος)

8.104 household waste (n) /ˈhaʊshəʊld weɪst/
rubbish from sb's house • *Household waste can be divided into regular rubbish and material for recycling.* ❖ οικιακά απόβλητα

8.105 acid rain (n) /ˈæsɪd reɪn/
polluted rain • *The pollution from the factory rose into the clouds and then created acid rain which destroyed the forests.* ❖ όξινη βροχή

8.106 torrential (adj) /təˈrenʃl/
very heavy (rain) • *The torrential rain caused the rivers to flood.* ➢ torrent (n) ❖ καταρρακτώδης

Use your English — page 103

8.107 block out (phr v) /blɒk aʊt/
stop light from coming in • *She shaded her eyes to try to block out the bright sun.* ❖ μπλοκάρω, εμποδίζω

8.108 blow over (phr v) /bləʊ ˈəʊvə/
go away without serious effect • *The storm soon blew over and the sun came out again.* ❖ περνώ, κοπάζω, ξεθυμαίνω

8.109 burst into flames (expr) /bɜːst ˈɪntə fleɪmz/
suddenly start to burn with large flames • *The plane crashed and burst into flames.* ❖ τυλίγομαι στις φλόγες

8.110 freeze over (phr v) /friːz ˈəʊvə/
when the surface of water turns to ice • *Last winter the pond in our garden froze over.* ❖ παγώνω

8.111 wear away (phr v) /weə əˈweɪ/
become gradually smaller and smoother • *The cliffs have been worn away by the sea.* ❖ διαβρώνω

8.112 wipe out (phr v) /waɪp aʊt/
destroy completely • *Many species have been wiped out by hunters.* ❖ εξαφανίζω

8.113 smooth (adj) /smuːð/
without sudden movements or changes • *The plane made a smooth landing.* ❖ ομαλός, ήρεμος

8.114 catch fire (expr) /kætʃ faɪə/
start to burn • *The wooden house caught fire when it was struck by lightning.* ❖ πιάνω φωτιά

8.115 patch (n) /pætʃ/
a small area • *There were patches of dry grass on the football pitch.* ❖ κομμάτι γης

8.116 pessimistic (adj) /pesɪˈmɪstɪk/
believing bad things will happen • *He is pessimistic about the future of the planet and says people will destroy it.* ➢ pessimism (n) ❖ απαισιόδοξος
✎ Opp: optimistic

8.117 keen (adj) /kiːn/
liking or interested in sth • *She is keen on geography and hopes to study it at university.* ❖ μου αρέσει πολυ

8.118 weaken (v) /ˈwiːkən/
lose strength • *Luckily the hurricane weakened before it reached the coast.* ➢ weakness (n), weak (adj) ❖ εξασθενίζω
✎ Opp: strengthen

8.119 large-scale (adj) /ˈlɑːdʒ skeɪl/
using or involving a lot of people, things, effort, etc • *After a large-scale investigation, 197 people were arrested.* ❖ εκτεταμένος, μεγάλης κλίμακας

8.120 meteorological (adj) /miːtɪərəˈlɒdʒɪkl/
to do with the weather • *Meteorological studies help us to understand weather patterns.* ➢ meteorology, meteorologist (n) ❖ μετεωρολογικός

Useful verbs

admit	enquire
complain	inform
criticise	predict
discourage	prohibit

Writing: an essay (2) — pages 104–105

8.121 destination (n) /ˌdestɪˈneɪʃn/
the place where sb or sth is going • *After a twelve-hour drive, we reached our destination.* ❖ προορισμός

8.122 dump (v) /dʌmp/
get rid of sth that you do not want • *They dumped their old car near the beach.* ❖ πετώ, ξεφορτώνομαι

8.123 unpleasant (adj) /ʌnˈpleznt/
not nice or enjoyable • *Seeing her was an unpleasant surprise.* ❖ δυσάρεστος, άσχημος

8.124 **exhaust fumes** (pl n) /ɪgˈzɔːst fjuːmz/
gases produced when an engine is working
• *Exhaust fumes from cars are responsible for the pollution.* ❖ καυσαέρια (της εξάτμισης)

Video: Global warming   page 106

8.125 **global warming** (n) /ˈgləʊbl ˈwɔːmɪŋ/
the rise in the Earth's temperature • *Global warming will cause the ice caps to melt and sea levels to rise.* ❖ υπερθέρμανση του πλανήτη

8.126 **greenhouse effect** (n) /ˈgriːnhaʊs ɪˈfekt/
the gradual rise in the Earth's temperature caused by high levels of gases in the atmosphere
• *The greenhouse effect is making the ice caps melt and sea levels rise.* ❖ φαινόμενο του θερμοκηπίου

8.127 **power plant** (n) /ˈpaʊə plaːnt/
a building or group of buildings where electricity is produced • *The blackout was due to a fire at the power plant.* ❖ ηλεκτροπαραγωγικός σταθμός, εργοστάσιο παραγωγής ηλεκτρικής ενέργειας
✎ Syn: power station

8.128 **breathe out** (phr v) /briːð aʊt/
let air out of your lungs • *When the danger passed, she breathed out in relief.* ❖ εκπνέω
✎ Opp: breathe in

8.129 **chemical reaction** (n) /ˈkemɪkl rɪˈækʃn/
a chemical change produced when two or more substances are mixed • *A chemical reaction causes the liquid to change colour.* ❖ χημική αντίδραση

8.130 **melt** (v) /melt/
If heat melts sth, it becomes liquid. • *The child's ice cream melted in the hot sun.* ❖ λιώνω

8.131 **shrink** (v) /ʃrɪŋk/
become smaller • *If you wash that woollen pullover in hot water, it will shrink.* ❖ μπαίνω, μαζεύω

8.132 **Industrial Revolution** (n) /ɪnˈdʌstrɪəl revəˈluːʃn/
the period in the eighteenth and nineteenth centuries when many machines were invented and the first factories were built • *Trains became a common form of transport thanks to the Industrial Revolution.* ❖ βιομηχανική επανάσταση

8.133 **decrease** (v) /dɪˈkriːs/
become or make sth smaller or less • *The price of oil decreased by 2% last year.* ➣ decrease (n)
❖ μειώνω, μειών ομαι
✎ Opp: increase

8.134 **slight** (adj) /slaɪt/
small; not important or serious • *I'm afraid we've got a slight problem.* ❖ μικρός, ασήμαντος

8.135 **floe** (n) /fləʊ/
an area of ice floating in the sea • *From their ship, they saw a group of penguins on a floe.*
❖ ογκόπαγος, κομμάτι πάγου που επιπλέει σε θάλασσα

Vocabulary Exercises

A Complete the table.

Nouns	Adjectives
breeze	1
moisture	2
meteorology	3
torrent	4
extinction	5
coast	6
pessimism	7
recycling	8

B Choose the correct answers.

1 The ___ killed off all the crops as we had no irrigation.
  a drought   b draught   c vehicle

2 A strong ___ of wind blew the old tree over.
  a cycle   b gust   c mass

3 This river ___ into a wide delta before reaching the sea.
  a adapts   b flows   c harnesses

4 Rain and wind cause ___ .
  a erosion   b emission   c column

5 The ___ weather made the day feel hotter than it was.
  a keen   b torrential   c humid

6 The office block had ten ___ and he worked on the top one.
  a storeys   b masses   c blades

7 The trees were uprooted by a(n) ___ .
  a tornado   b irrigation   c blanket

8 The neighbours ___ about our recycling bins outside their house.
  a banned   b complained   c admitted

C Match. Then write the words.

1 natural   oil
2 crude   fall
3 greenhouse   fumes
4 rain   fish
5 global   panel
6 natural   effect
7 exhaust   dioxide
8 photovoltaic   warming
9 shell   gas
10 carbon   resource

D Choose the correct answers.

1 If an aircraft is airborne, it
  a has taken off.
  b has landed.

2 When the day is breezy, there is
  a a little wind.
  b a little rain.

3 Somebody who is put off
  a feels discouraged.
  b feels encouraged.

4 If you are sitting in a draught, you feel
  a very hot.
  b a current of cold air.

5 If you conserve water, you
  a use a lot of it.
  b don't waste it.

6 Somebody who seeks permission
  a refuses to give it.
  b asks for it.

7 In a downpour, everything will
  a get soaked.
  b melt.

8 Trouble that blows over
  a becomes worse.
  b goes away.

8 Grammar

8.1 Zero Conditional

If clause	Main clause
Present Simple	Present Simple

Χρησιμοποιούμε το **zero conditional** για να μιλήσουμε για μια πράξη ή κατάσταση που πάντα έχει το ίδιο αποτέλεσμα. Στη θέση του *if* μπορούμε να χρησιμοποιήσουμε το *when*.
→ *If you heat ice, it melts.*
→ *When you heat ice, it melts.*

8.2 First Conditional

If clause	Main clause
Present tense	*will* + bare infinitive

Χρησιμοποιούμε το **first conditional** για να μιλήσουμε για μια πράξη ή μια κατάσταση που θα έχει κάποιο αποτέλεσμα στο μέλλον.
→ *If we **don't drive** our cars so much, the air in our cities **will improve**.*
→ *If they **are conserving** water, it **will last** longer.*

Μπορούμε να χρησιμοποιήσουμε *can, could, may* ή *might* στην κύρια πρόταση στη θέση του *will*. Μπορούμε επίσης να χρησιμοποιήσουμε προστακτική (imperative).
→ *If schools want students to recycle, they **could** put more bins in the yard.*
→ *If you want to conserve electricity, **turn off** your PC at night.*

8.3 Second Conditional

If clause	Main clause
Past tense	*would* + bare infinitive

Χρησιμοποιούμε το **second conditional** για να κάνουμε μια υπόθεση:
που είναι μάλλον απίθανη στο μέλλον.
→ *If I **had** the money, I **would buy** a hybrid car.*
που είναι αδύνατη στο παρόν ή στο μέλλον, ή φανταστική.
→ *If I **were** the mayor, I **would ban** all cars from the city centre.*

Μπορούμε να χρησιμοποιήσουμε το second conditional για να δώσουμε συμβουλή.
→ *If I **were you**, I **wouldn't buy** genetically modified food.*

Μπορούμε να χρησιμοποιήσουμε *could* ή *might* στην κύρια πρόταση στη θέση του *would*.
→ *If we improved irrigation, we **could** produce better crops.*
→ *If you wanted information on solar panels, Tina **might** be able to help you.*

Σημείωση: Συνήθως χρησιμοποιούμε *were* για όλα τα πρόσωπα σε προτάσεις του second conditional.
→ *If she **were** more careful, her water bill **wouldn't be** so high.*

8.4 Third Conditional

If clause	Main clause
Past Perfect	*would* + *have* + past participle

Χρησιμοποιούμε το **third conditional** για να μιλήσουμε για πράξεις που συνέβησαν ή που δεν συνέβησαν στο παρελθόν, και κάνουμε υποθέσεις για το πώς τα πράγματα θα μπορούσαν να ήταν διαφορετικά.
→ *If it **had been** really windy last weekend, we **would've gone** windsurfing.* (Όμως δεν φυσούσε δυνατός αέρας, και έτσι δεν πήγαμε.)

Μπορούμε να χρησιμοποιήσουμε *could* ή *might* στην κύρια πρόταση στη θέση του *would*.
→ *I **could** have avoided the traffic jam if I had taken the train instead of the car.*

8.5 Mixed Conditionals

If clause	Main clause
Past Perfect	*would* + bare infinitive

Έχουμε **mixed conditional**, όταν τα δύο μέρη της υποθετικής πρότασης αναφέρονται σε διαφορετικό χρόνο. Χρησιμοποιούμε mixed conditional για να εκφράσουμε το αποτέλεσμα που έχει στο παρόν ένα υποθετικό γεγονός ή κατάσταση του παρελθόντος.
→ *If you **had installed** solar panels, your bills **would be** much lower.*

8.6 Conditionals χωρίς *if*

Μπορούμε να χρησιμοποιήσουμε *provided/providing that on condition that*, και *as long as* στη θέση του *if* σε προτάσεις του first conditional.

→ ***Provided that** the weather is good, we can go sailing.*
→ *I'll let you use my kite, **on condition that** you are careful with it.*
→ ***As long as** organic food becomes cheaper, more people will want to buy it.*

Μπορούμε να χρησιμοποιήσουμε *unless* σε προτάσεις του first και του second conditional. Έχει τη σημασία του *if not*.
→ *We can't stop forest fires **unless** more people volunteer to help us.*
→ *I wouldn't buy genetically modified food **unless** I knew it was safe to eat.*

Μπορούμε να χρησιμοποιήσουμε *otherwise* αντί για *if*. Σημαίνει 'αλλιώς'.
→ ***If** we **don't** protect natural habitats, more wild animals will become endangered.*
→ *We must protect natural habitats. **Otherwise**, more wild animals will become endangered.*

Μπορούμε να χρησιμοποιήσουμε *supposing* σε όλες τις υποθετικές προτάσεις. Σημαίνει 'αν υποθέσουμε', ή 'τι θα γινόταν αν'.
→ ***Supposing** you can't stand the noise, will you move from the city centre?*
→ ***Supposing** you were caught in a hurricane, what would you do?*
→ ***Supposing** they had built a nuclear plant here, would the local people have protested?*

Grammar Exercises

A Match.

1. If you go out in the rain,
2. If the forest had been protected,
3. If we run out of fossil fuels,
4. We wouldn't be here
5. Who would have informed you
6. Terry will study meteorology
7. What would you study
8. Crops never survive

a if we couldn't grow crops.
b if she passes her exams.
c you get wet.
d if you were a student?
e if there is no rain.
f we will need alternative sources of energy.
g if I hadn't told you about it?
h it would have provided a home for the local wildlife.

8 Grammar

B Complete the sentences with one word in each gap.

1. If we cause more deforestation, soil erosion _____ get worse.
2. It would be a crime _____ the problem of pollution was not addressed.
3. Who would _____ known if Kim hadn't told everybody about it?
4. What _____ happen to humans if the ozone layer got too thin?
5. If all the oil runs out, we will _____ be able to use cars.
6. We can't go sailing next weekend _____ the weather improves.
7. Nobody would have heard of the scientist if he _____ not published an important paper.
8. If I _____ you, I would finish my homework.

C Complete the mixed conditional sentences with the correct form of the verbs in brackets.

1. If we hadn't run out of dry wood, the campfire _____ (not be) so small now.
2. If they hadn't built so many factories near here, we _____ (have) cleaner air.
3. The ecosystem would be healthier if they _____ (not pollute) the water.
4. If the Industrial Revolution _____ (not take) place, what would the world be like today?
5. If the dinosaurs had survived, _____ (people/exist) today?
6. If you _____ (not install) solar panels, we wouldn't have hot water now.
7. If we'd studied harder, we _____ (feel) more confident about today's test.
8. If we hadn't heard about the tornado on the radio, we _____ (trap) inside our house right now.

D Circle the correct words.

1. Provided / Condition that you clean up, you cab stay in my flat.
2. Supposing / Supposed you got caught in a downpour, what would you do?
3. He can use my bike on / in condition that he returns it without a scratch.
4. If / Unless we do something fast, the planet is in danger of becoming uninhabitable.
5. As long as / Otherwise we seek permission, there shouldn't be a problem.
6. We will be late providing / if you don't hurry.
7. Supposing / Providing that you agree, we can plant some vegetables in the garden.
8. We must reduce emissions of greenhouse gases, otherwise / if our existence will be threatened.

Use your English

Exam Task

For questions **1–8**, complete the second sentence so that it has a similar meaning to the first sentence, using the word given. **Do not change the word given.** You must use between **two** and **five** words, including the word given.

1. If carbon dioxide emissions are not reduced, the greenhouse effect will get worse.
   UNLESS
   The greenhouse effect will get worse _____ reduced.

2. If, and only if we have reliable data, we will be able to make better weather predictions.
   AS
   As _____ we have reliable data, we will be able to make better weather predictions.

3. We can study the ecosystem provided that we have reliable data.
   ON
   We can study the ecosystem _____ we have reliable data.

4. A hurricane is the cause of all this damage.
   ACCOUNTS
   A hurricane _____ all this damage.

5. We think all the dinosaurs were killed as a result of a meteor strike.
   OUT
   We think all the dinosaurs _____ as a result of a meteor strike.

6. The speaker tried make people feel enthusiastic about the issue but failed.
   UP
   The speaker failed to _____ enthusiasm for the issue.

7. The world would be a very different place without the Industrial Revolution.
   HAPPENED
   If the Industrial Revolution _____, the world would be a very different place.

8. The storm passed and only a few trees were uprooted.
   BLEW
   The storm _____ only a few trees were uprooted.

9 And What Do You Do?

page 109

9.1 **stilts** (n) /stɪlts/
two long pieces of wood with places for your feet, which allow you to stand and walk high above the ground • *There were street performers on stilts doing tricks.* ❖ ξυλοπόδαρα

9.2 **attach** (v) /əˈtætʃ/
join or fasten one thing to another • *A photo was attached to the letter.*
❖ προσκολλάω, συνδέω, επισυνάπτω

Reading — page 110

9.3 **qualification** (n) /kwɒlɪfɪˈkeɪʃnz/
If you have a qualification, you have passed an exam to show you have a skill or knowledge in a subject. • *University qualifications are necessary these days if you want to find a good job.*
➢ qualify (v) ❖ τυπικά προσόντα

9.4 **lifeguard** (n) /ˈlaɪfɡɑːd/
sb who works at a beach or swimming pool and helps swimmers who are in danger • *The lifeguard ran into the water to help the swimmer who was in difficulty.* ❖ ναυαγοσώστης

9.5 **salesperson** (n) /ˈseɪlzˌpɜːsən/
sb who sells things • *She asked the salesperson to show her the range of make-up available.*
❖ πωλητής

9.6 **creativity** (n) /kriːeɪˈtɪvəti/
ability to make sth new and imaginative • *He is a creative artist and paints beautiful portraits.* ➢ create (v), creation (n), creative (adj) ❖ δημιουργικότητα

9.7 **leadership skills** (pl n) /ˈliːdəʃɪp skɪlz/
qualities that make sb a good leader • *A good manager needs to have great leadership skills.*
❖ ηγετικές ικανότητες

9.8 **neat** (adj) /niːt/
carefully done or arranged and looking nice • *Harry was wearing a neat blue suit.*
❖ προσεγμένος, καλοφτιαγμένος

9.9 **physical fitness** (n) /ˈfɪzɪkl ˈfɪtnɪs/
the condition of being strong and healthy • *You can improve your physical fitness by taking regular exercise.* ❖ φυσική κατάσταση

9.10 **reliability** (n) /rɪlaɪəˈbɪləti/
the quality that makes sb trusted or depended on • *John's employer appreciates him for his honesty and reliability.* ➢ rely (v), reliable (adj)
❖ αξιοπιστία
✎ Opp: unreliability

Word Focus — page 110

9.11 **workforce** (n) /ˈwɜːkfɔːs/
all the people who work for a company, organisation, etc • *Most of our workforce are women.* ❖ εργατικό δυναμικό

9.12 **bounce ideas off sb** (expr) /baʊns aɪˈdɪəz ɒf ˈsʌmbədi/
tell sb your ideas in order to get their opinion • *Can I bounce a couple of ideas off you?*
❖ παίρνω τη γνώμη κάποιου για τις ιδέες μου

9.13 **interaction** (n) /ˌɪntəˈrækʃn/
when two or more people communicate, work together, spend time with each other, etc • *What I love about teaching is the interaction with my students.* ➢ interact (v)
❖ επικοινωνία, συναναστροφή

9.14 **bearer of bad news** (expr) /ˈbeərər əv bæd njuːz/
sb who brings you bad news • *I hate to be the bearer of bad news, but I'm afraid you've failed your exam.* ❖ αυτός που φέρνει άσχημα νέα

9.15 **what makes sb tick** (expr) /wɒt meɪks ˈsʌmbədi tɪk/
what makes sb behave in the way that they do • *I've never understood what makes him tick.*
❖ ο τρόπος που λειτουργεί/σκέφτεται κάποιος

Reading — pages 110–111

9.16 **recruiter** (n) /rɪˈkruːtə(r)/
sb whose job is to find new people to join a company, organisation, etc • *As a recruiter, she interviews a lot of young people.* ➢ recruit (v), recruitment (n)
❖ υπεύθυνος προσλήψεων, εργοδότης

9.17 **candidate** (n) /ˈkændɪdeɪt/
sb who is being considered for a job • *The first candidate performed well in the job interview.* ❖ υποψήφιος

9.18 **position** (n) /pəˈzɪʃn/
a job • *The position of head teacher at the local primary school has been filled.*
❖ θέση εργασίας

9.19 **full-time** (adj) /fʊl taɪm/
for all the working hours of the day or week • *Emma is looking for a full-time job.*
➢ full time (adv) ❖ πλήρους απασχόλησης, με πλήρες ωράριο

9.20 **staff** (n) /stɑːf/
people who work at the same place • *The company has a large staff, many of whom have been working there for years.* ❖ προσωπικό

9.21	**receptionist** (n) /rɪˈsepʃənɪst/ a person in a hotel, office, etc who helps people when they arrive, answers the telephone, etc • *I told the receptionist that I wanted to see the manager.* ➣ reception (n) ❖ υπάλληλος υποδοχής, ρεσεψιονίστ	9.33	**job seeker** (n) /dʒɒb ˈsiːkə/ sb who is looking for a job • *There are a few things that all job seekers should think about before a job interview.* ❖ κάποιος που ψάχνει για δουλειά
9.22	**accountant** (n) /əˈkaʊntənt/ sb who keeps or examines the records of money received, paid and owed by a company or person • *He employs an accountant to deal with his company's finances.* ➣ accounting (n) ❖ λογιστής	9.34	**lack** (v) /læk/ not have any or enough of sth that you need • *He lacks the necessary skills for the job.* ➣ lack (n), lacking (adj) ❖ στερούμαι, δεν έχω
9.23	**client** (n) /ˈklaɪənt/ a customer; sb who pays for a service • *The clients were pleased with the service they received from the company.* ❖ πελάτης	9.35	**pride myself on sth** (expr) /praɪd maɪˈself ɒn ˈsʌmθɪŋ/ be proud of sth • *She prides herself on being a good cook.* ❖ καμαρώνω, υπερηφανεύομαι
9.24	**freelance** (adj) /ˈfriːlɑːns/ not working for one particular company but getting paid for each separate job you do • *The freelance journalist published articles in many different magazines.* ➣ freelancer (n) ❖ αυτοαπασχολούμενος	9.36	**match** (v) /mætʃ/ go well together • *Those pink shoes match your bag, so wear them.* ❖ ταιριάζω
9.25	**steady** (adj) /ˈstedi/ not changing or stopping • *He has a steady job.* ❖ σταθερός	9.37	**fit** (n) /fɪt/ used to say whether sb is right or suitable for a job, situation, etc. • *I think she's a perfect fit for our company.* ❖ κατάλληλος, που ταιριάζει/αρμόζει σε κάτι
9.26	**income** (n) /ˈɪŋkʌm/ money you earn • *Our income has dropped because my wife lost her job and no longer has a salary.* ❖ εισόδημα	9.38	**effective** (adj) /ɪˈfektɪv/ producing the result that is wanted • *Swimming is an effective way of keeping fit.* ➣ effect (n) ❖ αποτελεσματικός ✎ Opp: ineffective
9.27	**co-worker** (n) /ˈkoʊˌwɜːrkə(r)/ a person sb works with • *She invited all her friends and co-workers to her party.* ❖ συνάδελφος, συνεργάτης ✎ Syn: colleague	9.39	**put myself in sb's shoes** (expr) /pʊt maɪˈself ɪn ˈsəmˌbɑːdi ʃuːz/ imagine that you are in another person's situation • *Put yourself in my shoes. What would you do?* ❖ έρχομαι/βάζω τον εαυτό μου στη θέση κάποιου
9.28	**sociable** (adj) /ˈsəʊʃəbl/ friendly and enjoying being with other people • *She's a sociable person who gets on with everyone.* ❖ κοινωνικός	9.40	**feedback** (n) /ˈfiːdbæk/ comments about how useful or successful sth is • *They'll give you some feedback on your work so that you know what to do next time.* ❖ (εποικοδομητική) κριτική, σχόλια
9.29	**on behalf of sb** (expr) /ɒn bɪˈhɑːf əv ˈsʌmbədi/ instead of sb; as sb's representative • *On behalf of everyone in the office, I would like to thank you for your help.* ❖ εκ μέρους	9.41	**critical** (adj) /ˈkrɪtɪkl/ extremely important • *Their support is critical to our success.* ❖ κρίσιμος (για), υψίστης σημασίας
9.30	**vacancy** (n) /ˈveɪkənsi/ available job • *There is a vacancy at the local supermarket that I think I will apply for.* ➣ vacant (adj) ❖ κενή θέση εργασίας	9.42	**applicant** (n) /ˈæplɪkənt/ sb who has asked for a job in writing • *Three applicants were interviewed for the job.* ➣ apply (v), application (n) ❖ αιτών
9.31	**register** (n) /ˈredʒɪstə(r)/ an official list of names, items, etc • *He keeps a register of all his customers.* ➣ register (v) ❖ κατάλογος, μητρώο	9.43	**employer** (n) /ɪmˈplɔɪə(r)/ a person or company that pays other people to work for them • *Her employer offered to pay for her English lessons.* ➣ employ (v), employment, employee (n) ❖ εργοδότης
9.32	**hire** (v) /ˈhaɪə/ employ • *That company is hiring a new accountant, so why don't you apply?* ❖ προσλαμβάνω	9.44	**suit** (v) /suːt/ Colours, clothes, etc that suit you make you look attractive. • *Short skirts suit you as you have nice legs.* ❖ μου πηγαίνει

Work words

applicant	get the sack
apprentice	hire
be made redundant	job hunter
client	job seeker
co-worker	position
employee	recruiter
employer	sick leave
finance department	staff
freelance	vacancy
full-time	workforce

Vocabulary   page 112

9.45 enquiry (n) /ɪnˈkwaɪəri/
a question you ask to get information about sth • *We're getting hundreds of enquiries about this job.* ❖ ερώτηση

9.46 place (v) /ˈpleɪs/
put sth somewhere • *He placed the bag on the table.* ❖ βάζω, τοποθετώ

9.47 sales (pl n) /seɪls/
to do with selling • *He works in sales and it's his job to visit clients and persuade them to buy the product.* ❖ πωλήσεις

9.48 request (v) /rɪˈkwest/
ask for sth politely • *She requested our help, and we agreed to assist her.* ➤ request (n) ❖ ζητώ

9.49 apply (v) /əˈplaɪ/
make a formal written request for a job, a place in a university, etc • *You can apply for many jobs online nowadays.* ➤ application, applicant (n) ❖ κάνω αίτηση

9.50 assistant (n) /əˈsɪstənt/
sb whose job it is to help sb else • *The manager asked his assistant to print out the report.* ➤ assist (v) ❖ βοηθός

9.51 compute (v) /ˈkəmpjuːt/
calculate • *They haven't computed the results yet.* ➤ computer (v) ❖ υπολογίζω, λογαριάζω

9.52 commute (v) /kəˈmjuːt/
travel to work on public transport • *It takes her an hour to commute to work on the bus.* ➤ commuter (n) ❖ μετακινούμαι με μέσα μαζικής μεταφοράς

9.53 employee (n) /ɪmplɔːˈjiː/
sb who works for sb else • *There are two hundred employees in this company.* ➤ employ (v), employer, employment (n) ❖ υπάλληλος, εργαζόμενος

9.54 insurance (n) /ɪnˈʃɔːrəns/
an agreement in which you pay a company money and they pay your costs if you have an accident, injury, etc • *Insurance against theft was expensive, but she was happy to have it when her house was burgled.* ➤ insure (v) ❖ ασφάλεια

9.55 leave (n) /liːv/
time allowed away from work for holidays or because of illness • *John is on leave. He's gone to Barbados for two weeks.* ❖ άδεια

9.56 opening (n) /ˈəʊpənɪŋ/
a job vacancy • *When Janet leaves her job, there will be an opening in the sales department.* ❖ κενή θέση

9.57 finance department (n) /ˈfaɪnæns dɪˈpɑːtmənt/
the part of a company that manages the company's money • *The finance department arranged for the employees' salaries to be paid.* ❖ λογιστήριο

9.58 cover (n) /ˈkʌvə/
insurance • *If you don't have any cover, your possessions are not protected against theft or damage.* ➤ cover (v) ❖ κάλυψη

9.59 fire (v) /faɪə/
remove sb from their job, usually because they have done sth wrong • *He was fired because he never did any work.* ❖ απολύω
Syn: dismiss

9.60 dismiss (v) /dɪsˈmɪs/
remove sb from their job, usually because they have done sth wrong • *The boss dismissed her because she was always late for work.* ➤ dismissal (n) ❖ απολύω
Syn: fire

9.61 quit (v) /kwɪt/
give up your job • *Bob quit his job because he wanted to go back to university.* ❖ παραιτούμαι
Syn: resign

9.62 licence (n) /ˈlaɪsns/
an official piece of paper that shows you are allowed to have or do sth • *Do you have a driving licence?* ❖ άδεια

9.63 flight attendant (n) /flaɪt əˈtendənt/
sb who serves food and drink to passengers on a plane and looks after their safety and comfort • *The flight attendants asked us to fasten our seatbelts before take-off.* ❖ αεροσυνοδός

9.64 apprentice (n) /əˈprentɪs/
sb who works for an employer in order to learn a skill or job • *The electrician taught his apprentice how to install an alarm.* ❖ μαθητευόμενος

9.65 independent (adj) /ɪndɪˈpendənt/
not influenced or controlled by other people • *Paul left home at the age of twenty because he had a good job and wanted to be independent.* ➤ independence (n) ❖ ανεξάρτητος

9.66 **contract** (n) /ˈkɒntrækt/
a written agreement • *He signed a contract when he started as a new employee.*
❖ συμβόλαιο

9.67 **be made redundant** (expr) /biː meɪd rɪˈdʌndənt/
lose your job because your employer no longer needs you • *They were made redundant when the company closed and now they are all looking for employment.*
❖ απολύομαι λόγω έλλειψης δουλειάς

9.68 **promotional** (adj) /prəˈməʊʃənʊl/
intended to advertise sth • *The pizza chain handed out promotional leaflets with special offers.* ➣ promote (n), promotion (n)
❖ προωθητικός

9.69 **profitable** (adj) /ˈprɒfɪtəbl/
which makes money • *This product is profitable so we hope the company makes more money this year.*
➣ profit (v, n) ❖ επικερδής
✎ Opp: unprofitable

Phrasal verbs
fill in
hand out
hold down
keep up
knock down
move on
take on

Grammar — page 113

9.70 **graduate** (v) /ˈɡrædʒueɪt/
get a degree from a university • *He graduated with a degree in history and is looking for a teaching job.*
➣ graduate, graduation (n) ❖ αποφοιτώ

9.71 **personnel manager** (n) /ˌpɜːsəˈnel ˈmænɪdʒə(r)/
a person in a company who is in charge of dealing with all matters related to employees • *The personnel manager decided not to give her the job.* ❖ υπεύθυνος προσωπικού

9.72 **knock down** (phr v) /nɒk daʊn/
completely destroy a building so that it falls down • *The old factory will be knocked down next year.*
❖ κατεδαφίζω

9.73 **founder** (n) /ˈfaʊndə/
sb who establishes an organisation, city, business, etc • *Steve Jobs was one of the founders of Apple.*
➣ found (v) ❖ ιδρυτής

9.74 **grocery store** (n) /ˈɡrəʊsəri stɔː/
a shop that sells food and other things for the home • *Will you get some milk from the grocery store?* ❖ παντοπωλείο

9.75 **chestnut** (n) /ˈtʃestnʌt/
a smooth red-brown nut that you can eat • *They stopped to buy chestnuts from a street seller.*
❖ κάστανο

9.76 **boot** (n) /buːt/
the space at the back of a car which is for carrying luggage, shopping etc • *They put the bags in the boot and drove home.* ❖ πορτ-μπαγκάζ

9.77 **janitor** (n) /ˈdʒænɪtə/
a caretaker • *The school janitor locked the gates after all the students had gone home.*
❖ επιστάτης

9.78 **changing room** (n) /ˈtʃeɪndʒɪŋ ruːm/
a room where you change clothes for sport • *We put on our football kit in the changing room.*
❖ αποδυτήριο

9.79 **inspire** (v) /ɪnˈspaɪə/
make sb want to do sth • *Her story inspired me to write this poem.* ➣ inspiration (n), inspiring (adj)
❖ εμπνέω

9.80 **revenge** (n) /rɪˈvendʒ/
punishing sb who has harmed you • *She took revenge on her boss by smashing his car windows.*
❖ εκδίκηση

9.81 **bully** (n) /ˈbʊli/
sb who frightens or hurts sb who is weaker than they are • *The school bully was expelled for stealing the younger kids' lunch money.* ➣ bully (v) ❖ νταής

9.82 **best-seller** (n) /best-ˈselə/
a popular book which many people buy • *Her new book will be a best-seller. It's very good.*
❖ μπεστ σέλερ

Listening — page 114

9.83 **an eye for sth** (expr) /ən aɪ fə ˈsʌmθɪŋ/
When you have an eye for sth, you are good at noticing a particular type of thing. • *He has an eye for detail.* ❖ ικανότητα να διακρίνω εύκολα κάτι, 'μάτι που κόβει' (για κάτι)

9.84 **initiative** (n) /ɪˈnɪʃətɪv/
the ability to take action without waiting for sb to tell you what to do • *He took the initiative and contacted some new clients.* ❖ πρωτοβουλία

9.85 **fair** (n) /feə/
a large show where people from a particular industry meet and promote their products • *A lot of young people came to the careers fair to find out about different jobs.* ❖ έκθεση

9.86 **appeal (to)** (v) /əˈpiːl (tuː)/
be attractive or interesting to sb • *Living in the country doesn't appeal to me.* ➣ appeal (n)
❖ ελκύω, τραβάω

9.87 **current** (adj) /ˈkʌrənt/
happening or existing now • *What is your current address?* ❖ τωρινός, σημερινός

9.88 **job hunter** (n) /dʒɒb ˈhʌntə(r)/
sb who is looking for a job • *Hundreds of job hunters applied for an interview.*
❖ κάποιος που ψάχνει για δουλειά

9.89 **hand out** (phr v) /hænd aʊt/
give sth to each person in a group • *Could you hand out these papers, please?* ❖ μοιράζω

9.90 **CV** (n, abbrv) /siː viː/
a document that lists your education and previous jobs that you send to employers when you are looking for a job • *He enclosed a CV with his job application.* ❖ βιογραφικό
✎ NB: CV = curriculum vitae

9.91 **workshop** (n) /ˈwɜːkʃɒp/
a meeting where people try to improve their skills by doing practical exercises • *All new employees attend workshops when they start at this company.* ❖ εργαστήριο (μαθημάτων), σεμινάριο

9.92 **gain entrance** (expr) /geɪn ˈentrəns/
be allowed or able to enter a building or place • *The thieves gained entrance to the house through an open window.* ❖ αποκτώ πρόσβαση (σε χώρο)

Speaking page 115

9.93 **ideal** (adj) /aɪˈdiːəl/
perfect • *Teaching is an ideal job for somebody who likes children and is patient.* ❖ ιδανικός

9.94 **cashier** (n) /kæˈʃɪə/
sb whose job is to receive money in a shop • *I gave the cashier a fifty euro note and she gave me two euros change.* ❖ ταμίας

9.95 **butcher** (n) /ˈbʊtʃə/
sb who sells meat in a shop • *She bought a steak from the butcher.* ❖ κρεοπώλης

9.96 **seasonal** (adj) /ˈsiːzənl/
needed or happening during a particular season • *They hire seasonal workers during the summer months.* ❖ εποχιακός

9.97 **pick** (v) /pɪk/
remove a fruit, flower, etc from a tree or plant • *Let's pick some flowers.* ❖ μαζεύω, κόβω (λουλούδια, καρπούς, κλπ)

9.98 **gig** (n) /gɪg/
a performance by musicians or a comedian in front of an audience • *I'm in a band and we're doing our first gig on Saturday!* ❖ παράσταση

Grammar page 116

9.99 **briefcase** (n) /ˈbriːfkeɪs/
a flat case used for carrying papers • *The man was wearing a suit and carrying a briefcase.* ❖ χαρτοφύλακας

9.100 **translate** (v) /trænzˈleɪt/
change writing or speech into another language • *Can you translate this letter into Spanish?*
➣ translation (n), translator (n) ❖ μεταφράζω

9.101 **branch** (n) /brɑːntʃ/
one of a group of shops or businesses • *He works at the Kallithea branch of this bank.* ❖ υποκατάστημα

9.102 **reference** (n) /ˈrefrəns/
a letter with information about you, written by sb who knows you, especially to a new employer • *My old boss said he would write me a reference.*
➣ refer (v) ❖ σύσταση, συστατική επιστολή

9.103 **conference** (n) /ˈkɒnfərəns/
a formal meeting where a lot of people discuss important matters for several days • *We attended a week-long conference on the environment in Brussels.* ❖ συνέδριο

9.104 **on the spot** (expr) /ɒn ðə spɒt/
immediately • *The boss asked for a meeting, and so we held one there and then on the spot.* ❖ επί τόπου

Use your English page 117

9.105 **keep up** (phr v) /kiːp ʌp/
continue • *The boss told his staff to keep up the good work.* ❖ συνεχίζω

9.106 **fill in** (phr v) /fɪl ɪn/
complete • *He filled in an application form for a job in sales.* ❖ συμπληρώνω

9.107 **hold down** (phr v) /həʊld daʊn/
manage to keep a job • *He can't hold down a job and keeps getting fired.* ❖ κρατώ (μια δουλειά)

9.108 **move on** (phr v) /muːv ɒn/
leave your present job and start doing another one • *She was bored with her job and decided to move on.* ❖ προχωρώ, προοδεύω

9.109 **take on** (phr v) /teɪk ɒn/
employ • *They are taking on people at the supermarket, so you might get a job there.* ❖ προσλαμβάνω

9.110 **out of work** (expr) /aʊt əv wɜːk/
unemployed • *He has been out of work for a year now and still can't find a job.* ❖ άνεργος

9.111 **personal details** (pl n) /ˈpɜːsənəl ˈdiːteɪls/
information about sb like their name, date of birth, marital status, etc • *You must write your personal details at the top of the form.* ❖ προσωπικά στοιχεία

9.112 **take (a day) off** (expr) /teɪk (ə deɪ) ɒf/
have a period of time as a break from work • *You look tired. Why don't you take the day off?* ❖ παίρνω (μία μέρα) άδεια

9.113 **get the sack** (expr) /get ðə sæk/
be fired • *Cheryl hasn't got a job. She got the sack yesterday.* ❖ απολύομαι

9.114 overall (adj) /ˌəʊvəˈrɔːl/
including or considering everything; general
• *There are a few problems, but the overall situation is good.* ➣ overall (adv) ❖ γενικός, συνολικός

9.115 motivation (n) /məʊtɪˈveɪʃn/
willingness to do sth without needing to be forced to do it • *They aren't a bad football team but they lack the motivation to win.* ➣ motivate (v) ❖ κίνητρο

9.116 sick leave (n) /sɪk liːv/
time you take off work because you are ill • *When Mary caught the flu, she had to take sick leave.* ❖ αναρρωτική άδεια

9.117 be just around the corner (expr) /bi dʒəst əˈraʊnd ðə ˈkɔːnə(r)/
likely to happen soon; coming soon • *Summer is just around the corner.* ❖ πλησιάζω (σε χρόνο), έρχομαι σύντομα

> **No work**
> be made redundant
> dismiss
> fire
> get the sack
> out of work
> quit
> sick leave
> unemployed

Writing: a formal letter (2) page 118

9.118 interpersonal skills (n) /ˌɪntəˈpɜːsnl skɪlz/
the ability to create good relationships with other people • *A personnel manager needs strong interpersonal skills.* ❖ διαπροσωπικές δεξιότητες, ικανότητες ανάπτυξης καλών διαπροσωπικών σχέσεων

9.119 attitude (n) /ˈætɪtjuːd/
how you think and feel • *You need a positive attitude in order to cope with problems.* ❖ στάση, νοοτροπία

9.120 cheerful (adj) /ˈtʃɪəfl/ happy
• *Olga looks more cheerful since she started her new job.* ❖ χαρούμενος

9.121 upbeat (adj) /ʌpˈbiːt/
positive and happy • *The staff at this magazine are upbeat and always have a positive outlook.* ❖ αισιόδοξος

9.122 word processing (n) /wɜːd ˈprəʊsesɪŋ/
creating written documents on a computer • *She learned how to do word processing in her IT class at school.* ❖ επεξεργασία κειμένου

9.123 co-ordinator (n) /kəʊˈɔːdɪneɪtə/
sb who organises an activity so that the people involved in it work well together • *The activity co-ordinator makes sure that everyone works well together.* ➣ co-ordinate (v), co-ordination (n) ❖ συντονιστής

9.124 counsellor (n) /ˈkaʊnsələ/
sb who gives advice • *If you are being bullied at school, ask the counsellor for advice.* ➣ counsel (v), counselling (n) ❖ σύμβουλος

9.125 outgoing (adj) /ˈaʊtɡəʊɪŋ/
friendly and liking to talk to new people • *Sam has an outgoing personality.* ❖ εξωστρεφής, ανοιχτός

9.126 at your earliest convenience (expr) /æt jɔː ˈɜːliɪst kənˈviːniəns/
as soon as you like or can • *Please complete the enclosed form and return it to us at your earliest convenience.* ➣ convenient (adj) ❖ το συντομότερο δυνατόν

Video: Dinosaur Builder page 120

9.127 palaeontology (n) /ˌpæliɒnˈtɒlədʒi/
the study of ancient bones, plants, etc in rocks as a way of getting information about the history of life on earth • *Mr Richards is a palaeontology professor.* ➣ palaeontologist (n) ❖ παλαιοντολογία

9.128 craftsman (n) /ˈkrɑːftsmən/
sb who makes things skilfully with their hands • *Our wooden furniture was made by a craftsman.* ➣ craftsmanship (n) ❖ τεχνίτης

9.129 cast (n) /kɑːst/
an object made by pouring liquid into a mould and leaving it to become solid • *This ancient bronze cast was made by pouring melted metal into a mould.* ➣ cast (v) ❖ εκμαγείο

9.130 fossil (n) /ˈfɒsl/
remains of an animal or plant found in a rock • *Fossils found in rocks can tell us about life on Earth millions of years ago.* ❖ απολίθωμα

9.131 workshop (n) /ˈwɜːkʃɒp/
a place with machines and tools where you make things • *The mechanic's workshop was full of old car parts.* ❖ εργαστήρι

9.132 machinery (n) /məˈʃiːnəri/
machines • *The machinery in this factory is used to make cars.* ❖ μηχανήματα

9.133 bone (n) /bəʊn/
one of the hard parts of your body which are your skeleton • *The archaeologists found some bones that came from the skeleton of a young man.* ➣ bony (adj) ❖ οστό

9.134 liquid (n) /ˈlɪkwɪd/
a substance that can be poured like water • *The hot liquid was poured into the mould.* ❖ υγρό

9.135 mould (n) /məʊld/
a container of a certain shape • *She poured the jelly into the mould and then put it in the fridge.* ➣ mould (v) ❖ καλούπι

9.136 harden (v) /ˈhɑːdən/
go solid • *The biscuits will harden when you cook them in the oven.* ➢ hard (adj)
❖ σκληραίνω
✎ Opp: soften

9.137 display (n) /dɪsˈpleɪ/
an exhibit • *The children's favourite display at the museum was the dinosaur.* ➢ display (v)
❖ έκθεμα

9.138 mount (v) /maʊnt/
to put sth together • *We learnt how to mount skeletons in the workshop.* ❖ τοποθετώ, στήνω

9.139 actual (adj) /ˈæktʃuəl/
real • *I can't believe I saw an actual dinosaur skeleton at the museum.* ➢ actually (adv)
❖ πραγματικός

9.140 construct (v) /kənˈstrʌkt/
build • *The bridge was constructed in 1995.*
➢ construction (v) ❖ χτίζω, κατασκευάζω

9.141 skeleton (n) /ˈskelɪtn/
the bones of a whole animal or person • *We took photos of the dinosaur skeletons at the museum.*
❖ σκελετός

9.142 hole (n) /həʊl/
an empty space in something solid • *There's a hole in the wall here so you can see through to the next room.* ❖ τρύπα

9.143 drill (v) /drɪl/
make a hole in sth with a special tool • *He drilled a hole in the wall so he could hang a picture.*
➢ drill (n) ❖ τρυπώ (με τρυπάνι)

9.144 assemble (v) /əˈsembl/
put all the separate parts of sth together • *The bookcase was easy to assemble.* ❖ συναρμολογώ, μοντάρω

9.145 shape (v) /ʃeɪp/
make sth into a particular shape • *They use this tool to shape wood.* ➢ shape (n)
❖ δίνω σχήμα, πλάθω

9.146 missing (adj) /ˈmɪsɪŋ/
lost or not in the usual place • *The missing child hasn't been found yet.* ❖ χαμένος, που λείπει

9.147 recreate (v) /ˌriːkriːˈeɪt/
make sth from the past exist or happen again
• *The students are trying to recreate ancient tools from paper, glue and paint.* ❖ αναπαράγω

Vocabulary Exercises

A Match.

1	sales	☐	a	fitness
2	physical	☐	b	back
3	work	☐	c	leave
4	sick	☐	d	department
5	job	☐	e	processing
6	feed	☐	f	attendant
7	personnel	☐	g	skills
8	word	☐	h	force
9	finance	☐	i	room
10	leadership	☐	j	manager
11	flight	☐	k	person
12	changing	☐	l	seeker

B Complete each sentence with one word.

1 He has been out _____ work for six months.
2 Poor Jim got _____ sack.
3 That's great. Keep _____ the good work!
4 We need to take _____ more staff.
5 I'd like to bounce some ideas _____ you.
6 Please fill _____ this form.
7 Why can't you hold _____ a job?
8 Nobody likes to be the _____ of bad news.
9 Have you any idea what makes her _____?
10 It's time you moved _____ and did something new.

C Read the definition and complete the words.

1. the money you earn: i _ _ _ _ _
2. exams you have passed: q _ _ _ _ _ _ _ _ _ _ _ _ _
3. without a job: u _ _ _ _ _ _ _ _ _
4. how you think and feel: a _ _ _ _ _ _ _
5. carefully arranged and looking nice: n _ _ _
6. a person who establishes a business: f _ _ _ _ _ _
7. all the people who work for a company: w _ _ _ _ _ _ _ _
8. a customer: c _ _ _ _ _
9. a job vacancy: o _ _ _ _ _ _ _
10. a person you work with: c _ _ _ _ _ _ _ _
11. travel to work on public transport: c _-_ _ _ _ _
12. extremely important: c _ _ _ _ _ _ _

D Complete the sentences with these words.

| accountant | apprentice | butcher | candidate | cashier | craftsman |
| counsellor | graduate | janitor | lifeguard | receptionist | salesperson |

1. If you have a problem and need advice, you can talk to a(n) _____.
2. The _____ is learning to become a plumber.
3. A good _____ will persuade his clients to buy the company's products.
4. The _____ at the hotel gave me my key and I went upstairs.
5. Please pay the _____ at the till at the front of the shop.
6. The personnel manager has just finished interviewing the last _____ for the job.
7. When you leave, can you ask the _____ to lock up the building?
8. The _____ sells wonderful meat and sausages.
9. This furniture was made by a brilliant _____.
10. The only person who understands what happens to the money in this business is the _____.
11. Luckily, there was a _____ at the beach or you might have drowned.
12. The university _____ believed she would find a good job.

9 Grammar

9.1 Relative Clauses
Οι **relative clauses** δίνουν περισσότερες πληροφορίες για το υποκείμενο ή το αντικείμενο μιας πρότασης. Εισάγονται με τις παρακάτω λέξεις (relative pronouns-αναφορικές αντωνυμίες):
who για πρόσωπα   *when* για χρόνο
which για πράγματα ή ζώα   *where* για τοποθεσίες
whose για να δείξουμε κτήση ή ιδιοκτησία   *why* για να εξηγήσουμε το σκοπό

9.2 Defining Relative Clauses
Αυτό το είδος της αναφορικής πρότασης μας δίνει πληροφορίες που είναι απαραίτητες ώστε να καταλάβουμε για ποιο πρόσωπο ή για ποιο πράγμα μιλάει ο ομιλητής. Δε χρησιμοποιούμε κόμμα για να τη χωρίσουμε από την υπόλοιπη πρόταση. Στις **defining relative clauses** μπορούμε να χρησιμοποιήσουμε *that* στη θέση του *who* ή *which*.
→ *That's the hotel **where** I worked last summer.*   → *She's the secretary **who/that** works here part-time.*

Όταν το *who*, *which* ή το *that* είναι αντικείμενο της αναφορικής πρότασης, μπορούμε να το παραλείψουμε.
→ *He's the writer **(who)** they invited to give a talk on creative writing.*
→ *The application form **(which)** he filled in was for a sales position.*
→ *The lawyer **(that)** I consulted yesterday said he would help me.*

9.3 Non-defining Relative Clauses
Αυτό το είδος της αναφορικής πρότασης μας δίνει παραπάνω πληροφορίες που όμως δεν είναι απαραίτητες για να καταλάβουμε το νόημα της κύριας πρότασης. Χρησιμοποιούμε κόμμα πριν και μετά τη **non-defining relative clause** για να τη χωρίσουμε από την υπόλοιπη πρόταση. Δε χρησιμοποιούμε that με τις non-defining relative clauses.
→ *Stephen King, **who** worked as a janitor when he was young, is a very successful writer.*
→ *La Strada, **which** is looking for waiters, is one of the best restaurants in town.*

9.4 Participle Clauses
Υπάρχουν δύο είδη participles (μετοχές): η **present participle** – ενεργητική μετοχή (verb + *-ing*), και η **past participle** – παθητική μετοχή (verb + *-ed* ή άλλος ανώμαλος τύπος ρήματος).

Χρησιμοποιούμε participles σε **participle clauses** (δευτερεύουσες προτάσεις με μετοχή σε θέση ρήματος), ώστε να κάνουμε μια πρόταση συντομότερη. Μπορούν να αντικαταστήσουν το υποκείμενο και το ρήμα σε μια πρόταση όταν το υποκείμενο της κύριας και της δευτερεύουσας πρότασης είναι το ίδιο. Χρησιμοποιούμε present participle όταν το ρήμα είναι ενεργητικό (active), και past participle όταν το ρήμα είναι παθητικό (passive).
→ *Ronnie **wanted** to supplement his income, so he applied for a second job.*
→ ***Wanting** to supplement his income, Ronnie applied for a second job.*
→ *Because she **was given** a pay rise, my sister was able to buy a new computer.*
→ ***Given** a pay rise, my sister was able to buy a new computer.*

Μπορούμε να χρησιμοποιήσουμε μετοχή για να αντικαταστήσουμε την αναφορική αντωνυμία και το ρήμα.
→ *The cashier **who was accused of** stealing was fired.*
→ *The cashier **accused of** stealing was fired.*
→ *University graduates **who applied for** work at Job Find were hired immediately.*
→ *University graduates **applying for** work at Job Find were hired immediately.*

Μπορούμε επίσης να χρησιμοποιήσουμε μετοχή αορίστου (perfect participle), δηλαδή *having* + past participle για να ενώσουμε δύο προτάσεις που έχουν το ίδιο υποκείμενο.
Αυτό το κάνουμε όταν μια πράξη:
έχει ολοκληρωθεί πριν από μια άλλη πράξη.
→ ***She improved** her computer skills and then she applied for a better position.*
→ ***Having improved** her computer skills, she applied for a better position.*

συνεχιζόταν για ένα χρονικό διάστημα πριν αρχίσει μια άλλη πράξη.
→ ***He had been working** for the company for six years when he was promoted to personnel manager.*
→ ***Having worked** for the company for six years, he was promoted to personnel manager.*

Χρησιμοποιούμε την perfect participle στην ενεργητική και στην παθητική φωνή.
Ενεργητική φωνή: having + past participle (**Having made** *a big profit last year, the company gave the staff a rise.*)
Παθητική φωνή: having been + past participle (**Having been offered** *a better position abroad, he decided to sell his house and go.*)

Grammar Exercises

A Join the sentences using relative clauses.

1 Terry is the new accountant. He works in the finance department.

2 Tina Jones is the candidate we liked best. She was an apprentice here.

3 This is the cover. It is the most affordable.

4 Let me introduce you to Betty. You will be replacing her assistant.

5 London is my favourite city. It's where I had my first job.

6 He works in the bank. I work there.

7 Mrs Evans was born in 1969. Neil Armstrong and Buzz Aldrin walked on the moon then.

8 She moved to London to get a job. That was the reason.

B Circle the correct words.

1 Given / Giving the chance, he would have left his job on the spot.
2 Having / Have promoted Sue, Diana needs a new assistant.
3 A lifeguard saved / saving a swimmer has to react fast.
4 Spoken / Speaking loudly, he got his staff to pay attention.
5 Your desk is by the window looked / looking over the park.
6 He was caught having stolen / stealing the money.
7 The candidate left the interview disappointed / disappointing with her performance.
8 Faced / Facing with a new challenge, he felt under a lot of pressure.

C Complete the sentences with your own ideas.

1 Mr Smith is the boss _____
2 This is the town _____
3 That's the reason _____
4 These are the qualifications _____
5 Being scared of making a mistake, _____
6 My school, _____
7 Saturday is the day _____
8 His counsellor, _____

9 Grammar

D Choose the correct answers.

1. That is the company at ___ I work.
   a where   b which
2. He's the craftsman ___ workshop I attended.
   a who   b whose
3. The city ___ my university is situated is in the north.
   a where   b that
4. The reason ___ he fired you is that you are never punctual.
   a why   b which
5. The personal details ___ have written here don't seem accurate.
   a that   b you
6. Your ___ is one of the nicest actually, is on the third floor.
   a office, which   b office which
7. That was the day ___ everyone came to work late because of the bad weather.
   a where   b when
8. Jake Black, ___ you met at the conference, is our line manager.
   a who   b that

Use your English

Exam Task

For questions **1–10**, read the text below and decide which answer (**A**, **B**, **C** or **D**) best fits each gap.

The Best Job in the World

Have you ever wondered what the best job in the world might be? Well, Queensland, Australia came up with the answer: the **(1)** ___ of caretaker of the Great Barrier Reef islands. Benefits included a generous **(2)** ___ and free luxury accommodation with a pool. Thousands of **(3)** ___ tried to land this job, but only a handful were called for an interview and then only one was **(4)** ___. The lucky man was Ben Southall from the UK. No formal **(5)** ___ were necessary for the job, but **(6)** ___ had to be able to swim, dive, snorkel and sail.

The caretaker's duties included feeding fish and collecting the mail for Hamilton Island. The Queensland authorities also asked their new **(7)** ___ to create a blog, do video updates and take photos to promote the area. So how did Ben **(8)** ___ for this job? There was no need to post an application form with his personal **(9)** ___. He simply submitted an online video application on the Tourism Queensland website. Clearly, there was something about Ben that **(10)** ___ to the authorities!

1	A position	B lifeguard	C janitor	D schedule
2	A boot	B opening	C income	D shift
3	A staff	B co-ordinators	C applicants	D co-workers
4	A taken on	B kept up	C moved on	D filled in
5	A contracts	B tools	C forms	D qualifications
6	A candidates	B fellows	C apprentices	D markers
7	A boss	B employee	C buyer	D client
8	A commit	B attend	C notify	D apply
9	A experience	B details	C cover	D leave
10	A requested	B preferred	C liked	D appealed

10 Learn to Learn!

Reading — page 122

10.1 substance (n) /'sʌbstəns/
any solid, liquid or gas • *They spray the wood with a special substance to protect it from the sun.*
❖ ουσία

10.2 guide (v) /gaɪd/
show sb where to go • *Tom guided his blind elderly mother to the kitchen.* ➢ guide (n)
❖ οδηγώ, καθοδηγώ

10.3 blind (adj) /blaɪnd/
unable to see • *He is blind and feels his way along the street with a white stick.* ➢ blindness (n)
❖ τυφλός

Word Focus — page 122

10.4 adaptable (adj) /əˈdæptəbl/
able to change to suit different conditions
• *Humans are an adaptable species and can live in many different climates.* ➢ adapt (v), adaptation (n)
❖ προσαρμοστικός

10.5 praise (n) /preɪz/
expression of approval or admiration for sb or sth • *Our teacher gives us lots of praise when we do well in tests.* ➢ praise (v)
❖ έπαινος

10.6 distraction (n) /dɪsˈtrækʃn/
sth that prevents sb from concentrating on sth else • *I need to study somewhere without distractions.* ➢ distract (v) ❖ περισπασμός

10.7 assessment (n) /əˈsesmənt/
estimating the ability or quality of sth • *You've worked hard, so your assessment should be good.*
➢ assess (v) ❖ αξιολόγηση

10.8 stage (n) /steɪdʒ/
a step in a process or development • *The first stage of a guide dog's training is to teach it simple commands.* ❖ στάδιο

Reading — pages 122–123

10.9 non-profit organisation (n) /nɒn-ˈprɒfɪt ɔːɡənaɪzˈeɪʃn/
charity • *Save the Children is a non-profit organisation in the UK which raises money for children in need.* ❖ μη κερδοσκοπικός οργανισμός

10.10 breed (v) /briːd/
keep animals for the purpose of producing young
• *He breeds Labradors and his dogs have won many awards.* ➢ breed (n) ❖ εκτρέφω

10.11 spinal cord (n) /ˈspaɪnəl kɔːd/
the long string of nerves in your backbone that sends messages to and from your brain • *If you damage your spinal cord, you might become paralysed.* ❖ σπονδυλική στήλη

10.12 native to (adj) /ˈneɪtɪv tuː/
growing or living in one particular place
• *Pandas are native to China.* ➢ native (n)
❖ προέρχομαι από

10.13 inch (n) /ɪntʃ/
a measurement of about 2.5 cm • *Those trousers are an inch too long* ❖ ίντσα

10.14 lifespan (n) /ˈlaɪfspæn/
the average length of time that people, animals or plants will live • *Dogs have an average lifespan of fourteen years.* ❖ διάρκεια ζωής

10.15 lend a hand (expr) /lend ə hænd/
help • *I can't carry all these boxes. Could you lend a hand?* ❖ δίνω ένα χεράκι

10.16 companionship (n) /kəmˈpænɪənʃɪp/
when you are with sb you enjoy being with
• *Grandma needs companionship so she often visits her friends.* ➢ companion (n) ❖ συντροφιά

10.17 guide dog (n) /gaɪd dɒg/
a specially trained dog for blind people • *My aunt is blind and has a guide dog to help her get around.*
❖ σκύλος-οδηγός (για τους τυφλούς)

10.18 physical (adj) /ˈfɪzɪkl/
to do with the body • *We should judge people by their actions rather than from their physical appearance.* ➢ physically (adv) ❖ σωματικός

10.19 disability (noun) /ˌdɪsəˈbɪləti/
a condition that means you can't use part of your body easily or that you can't learn easily
• *Granddad has a physical disability, so he can't walk up stairs quickly.* ➢ disabled (adj)
❖ αναπηρία

10.20 quadriplegic (adj) /kwɒdrɪˈpliːdʒɪk/
sb who cannot move any part of their body below their neck • *He is quadriplegic but he has learnt to paint with his mouth.* ❖ τετραπληγικός

10.21 paralysed (adj) /ˈpærəlaɪzd/
unable to move part or all of your body • *She cannot walk because her pegs are paralysed.*
➢ paralyse (v), paralysis (n) ❖ παράλυτος

10.22 disease (n) /dɪˈziːz/
an illness affecting humans, animals or plants
• *A healthy diet reduces the risk of heart disease.*
❖ ασθένεια

10.23 embark (v) /ɪmˈbɑːk/
start • *After leaving school, he embarked on his university course.* ➢ embarkation (n) ❖ ξεκινώ

10.24 **master** (v) /ˈmɑːstə/
learn and become good at sth • *It takes a lot of practice to master the piano.* ➢ master (n)
❖ τελειοποιώ

10.25 **scratch** (v) /skrætʃ/
rub your nails on your skin • *Don't scratch that rash as you will make it worse.* ➢ scratch (n) ❖ ξύνω

10.26 **itch** (n) /ɪtʃ/
an uncomfortable feeling on your skin that makes you want to scratch it • *I have an itch on my back that I can't scratch.* ➢ itch (v) ❖ φαγούρα

10.27 **affection** (n) /əˈfekʃn/
a feeling of liking for a person • *Dogs show their owners lots of love and affection.*
❖ στοργή, συμπάθεια, αγάπη

10.28 **treat** (n) /triːt/
sth special that you give sb or do for them because they will enjoy it • *The trainer taught the dog to follow commands by giving it treats when it obeyed correctly.* ➢ treat (v) ❖ κέρασμα

10.29 **wheelchair** (n) /ˈwiːltʃeə/
a chair with wheels used by people who cannot walk • *He needs a wheelchair because his legs are paralysed.* ❖ αναπηρικό καροτσάκι

10.30 **laser pointer** (n) /ˈleɪzə ˈpɔɪntə/
a small tool that looks like a pen and uses a laser for pointing to things • *The speaker used a laser pointer to show us some data on the whiteboard.*
❖ δείκτης λέιζερ

10.31 **means** (n) /miːnz/
a way of doing sth • *We had no means of contacting them.* ❖ μέσο, τρόπος

10.32 **progress** (v) /prəˈgres/
improve; develop • *Your son has progressed well this term and has learnt a lot.* ➢ progress (n)
❖ προοδεύω

10.33 **schooling** (n) /ˈskuːlɪŋ/
education • *She completed all her schooling in Patras before going on to university in Athens.*
➢ school (v) ❖ εκπαίδευση

10.34 **placement** (n) /ˈpleɪsmənt/
finding a place for sb to work • *Many companies have a placement programme for young university graduates.* ➢ place (v) ❖ θέση, τοποθέτηση

10.35 **disabled** (adj) /dɪsˈeɪbld/
having an illness, injury or condition that makes it difficult to do things other people do • *Disabled athletes take part in the Paralympics.*
➢ disability (n) ❖ με ειδικές ανάγκες

10.36 **thorough** (adj) /ˈθʌrə/
careful and complete, with attention to detail
• *The police did a thorough search of the area.*
❖ διεξοδικός, σχολαστικός

10.37 **arrange** (v) /əˈreɪndʒ/
organise • *The teacher has arranged a trip to the museum for her class.* ➢ arrangement (n)
❖ κανονίζω

10.38 **lifelong** (adj) /ˈlaɪflɒŋ/
all your life • *Fred and Paul were lifelong friends; they had known each other since they were children.*
❖ δια βίου, για όλη (μου) τη ζωή

10.39 **get under way** (expr) /get ˈʌndə weɪ/
start • *The course has already got under way, so you cannot join it now.* ❖ αρχίζω

10.40 **partnership** (n) /ˈpɑːtnəʃɪp/
a relationship between two people • *The helper monkeys have lifelong partnerships with the people they assist.* ❖ συνεργασία

10.41 **welfare** (n) /ˈwelfeə/
health and happiness • *Parents are responsible for the welfare of their children.* ❖ ευημερία

10.42 **around the clock** (expr) /əˈraʊnd ðə klɒk/
happening all day and all night • *People who are very ill need care around the clock.*
❖ όλο το εικοσιτετράωρο

10.43 **generosity** (n) /dʒenəˈrɒsɪti/
willingness to give money or time in order to help people • *He showed great generosity when he gave money to the charity.* ➢ generous (n)
❖ γενναιοδωρία

10.44 **donor** (n) /ˈdəʊnə/
sb who gives money to charity • *The charity relies on donors for financial support.* ➢ donate (v), donation (n) ❖ δωρητής

10.45 **independence** (n) /ɪndɪˈpendəns/
not relying on other people • *When Juliet moved away from home, it took her a while to get used to her independence.* ➢ independent (n)
❖ ανεξαρτησία
✎ Opp: dependence

10.46 **launch** (v) /lɔːntʃ/
make a new product or service available to the public • *The company will launch the program in February.* ➢ launch (n) ❖ λανσάρω, ξεκινώ

10.47 **raise awareness** (expr) /reɪz əˈweənəs/
improve people's knowledge about sth
• *They've launched a new campaign to raise awareness of the dangers of smoking.*
❖ ενημερώνω

10.48 **mental** (adj) /ˈmentl/
relating to the mind and thinking • *He has amazing mental abilities and will do very well in his studies.* ➢ mentality (n) ❖ διανοητικός, νοητικός

10.49 **eyesight** (n) /ˈaɪsaɪt/
the ability to see • *She lost her eyesight, so she now has a guide dog.* ❖ όραση

10.50 **authentic** (adj) /ɔːˈθentɪk/
real and true • *The painting is not authentic – it's just a copy.* ❖ αυθεντικός, πραγματικός

10.51 **donate** (v) /dəʊˈneɪt/
give sth to charity • *Please donate what you can afford to our children's charity.*
➢ donation, donor (n) ❖ δωρίζω

10.52 **in recognition of** (expr) /ɪn ˌrekəgˈnɪʃn ɒv/
in order to show respect, admiration or express thanks for sth • *He was given a medal in recognition of his work.* ❖ ως αναγνώριση για

10.53 **bright** (adj) /braɪt/
clever • *He's very bright and got 100% in all his exams.* ❖ ευφυής

10.54 **dyslexic** (adj) /dɪsˈleksɪk/
having difficulty with reading and writing caused by the brain's inability to see the difference between some letter shapes • *There is a special reading programme for dyslexic students at our school.* ➤ dyslexia (n) ❖ δυσλεξικός

Being disabled
blind
disability
disabled
guide dog
paralysed
quadriplegic
wheelchair

Vocabulary page 124

10.55 **enrol** (v) /ɪnˈrəʊl/
join a school, university or course • *We enrolled for an English course at the language institute.* ➤ enrolment (n) ❖ εγγράφομαι

10.56 **raise** (v) /reɪz/
lift or move sth up • *She raised her eyes from her book and said hello.* ❖ σηκώνω

10.57 **rise** (v) /raɪz/
come or go upwards • *Smoke was rising from the burning building.* ❖ ανεβαίνω

10.58 **coach** (n) /kəʊtʃ/
sb who trains a sports team or athlete • *The football coach decided which players would take part in the match.* ➤ coach (v) ❖ προπονητής

10.59 **instructor** (n) /ɪnˈstrʌktə/
sb who teaches you a skill • *His driving instructor was patient and a good teacher.* ➤ instruct (v), instruction (n) ❖ εκπαιδευτής

10.60 **tutor** (n) /ˈtjuːtə/
a teacher • *Her private maths tutor gives her two lessons per week.* ➤ tutor (v) ❖ δάσκαλος/καθηγητής (συνήθως για ιδιαίτερα μαθήματα)

10.61 **civil engineering** (n) /ˈsɪvəl endʒɪˈnɪərɪŋ/
designing and building roads, bridges and buildings • *Vicky is studying civil engineering at university and wants to design luxury apartments.* ❖ πολιτική μηχανική

10.62 **tone up** (phr v) /təʊn ʌp/
improve the strength of your muscles • *You have really toned up your muscles since you enrolled at the gym.* ❖ τονώνω

10.63 **faculty** (n) /ˈfækʊlti/
a university department • *There are four hundred students in the faculty of history.* ❖ (πανεπιστημιακή) σχολή

10.64 **deadline** (n) /ˈdedlaɪn/
a day or time before which you must do sth • *Our deadline for the essay is 15 March.* ➤ ❖ προθεσμία

10.65 **assignment** (n) /əˈsaɪnmənt/
a piece of work that sb is given to do, often as part of their studies • *We have to complete one more written assignment by the end of the year.* ❖ εργασία

10.66 **primary education** (n) /ˈpraɪməri ˌedʒuˈkeɪʃn/
the education of children between the ages of about five and eleven • *When do children begin primary education in your country?* ❖ πρωτοβάθμια εκπαίδευση

10.67 **secondary school** (n) /ˈsekəndri skuːl/
a school for children between the ages of eleven and eighteen • *He has finished primary school so he is starting secondary school in September.* ❖ γυμνάσιο (δευτεροβάθμια εκπαίδευση)

10.68 **apprenticeship** (n) /əˈprentɪʃɪp/
a period of time when a young person works for an employer in order to learn a skill or job • *He did a two-year apprenticeship as an electrician.* ➤ apprentice (n) ❖ πρακτική εκπαίδευση, επαγγελματική μαθητεία

10.69 **scholarship** (n) /ˈskɒləʃɪp/
money given to a good student to help them continue their studies • *Anna won a scholarship to the University of Pittsburgh.* ❖ υποτροφία

10.70 **plumbing** (n) /ˈplʌmɪŋ/
repairing things such as water pipes, toilets, etc • *I've never really liked plumbing, but the pay is good.* ➤ plumber (n) ❖ η δουλειά του υδραυλικού

10.71 **tuition** (n) /tjuˈɪʃn/
teaching sth, especially to one person or a small group • *She had to have extra tuition before her exams.* ❖ διδασκαλία

10.72 **struggle** (v) /ˈstrʌgl/
try very hard to do sth that is not easy • *They are struggling to pay their bills.* ➤ struggle (n) ❖

10.73 **permit** (n) /ˈpɜːmɪt/
a piece of paper that gives you the right to do sth • *You need a permit to fish in the river.* ➤ permit (v) ❖ άδεια

10.74 **valid** (adj) /ˈvælɪd/
acceptable; that can be used • *Your passport is valid until February.* ❖ έγκυρος

Phrasal verbs
breeze through   figure out   look up
brush up   go over   pick up
drop out   hand in   tone up

Grammar — page 125

10.75 observatory (n) /əbˈsɜːvətri/
a building from which you observe space with a telescope • *They went on a school trip to the observatory and saw a film about planets.* ➢ observe (v) ❖ αστεροσκοπείο, πλανητάριο

Listening — page 126

10.76 have a go (expr) /həv ə ɡəʊ/
try to do sth • *I'll have a go at fixing your computer.* ❖ κάνω μια προσπάθεια/απόπειρα

10.77 stall (n) /stɔːl/
a large table or small shop with an open front where people sell goods • *She's at the fruit stall buying some apples.* ❖ πάγκος, περίπτερο

Grammar — page 128

10.78 insist (v) /ɪnˈsɪst/
say firmly that sth is true • *It was embarrassing when Dad insisted on driving me to university.* ➢ insistence (n), insistent (adj) ❖ επιμένω

10.79 secretarial course (n) /sekrɪˈtɜːriəl kɔːs/
lessons which teach you typing and other office skills • *After leaving school, she did a secretarial course.* ❖ σειρά μαθημάτων γραμματέων

10.80 boarding school (n) /ˈbɔːdɪŋ skuːl/
a school where pupils live • *The students at the boarding school were looking forward to going home in the holidays.* ❖ σχολείο με εσωτερικούς μαθητές

10.81 drop out (phr v) /drɒp aʊt/
leave a school or university before you have graduated • *He dropped out of his course after only a month.* ➢ drop-out (n) ❖ εγκαταλείπω

10.82 principal (n) /ˈprɪnsɪpl/
a head teacher • *He was sent to see the principal because he was misbehaving.* ❖ διευθυντής σχολείου

10.83 refuse (v) /rɪˈfjuːz/
say no • *She told him to tidy his room, but he refused, saying he liked it messy.* ➢ refusal (n) ❖ αρνούμαι

10.84 gap year (n) /ɡæp jɪə(r)/
a year between leaving school and starting university which some people spend working or travelling • *She worked in her father's firm during her gap year.* ❖ έτος διακοπών που παρεμβάλλεται μεταξύ τελευταίας τάξης λυκείου και πρώτου έτους πανεπιστημίου

10.85 shake hands (expr) /ʃeɪk hændz/
take sb's hand and move it up and down as a way of saying hello • *In my country, people shake hands when they first meet.* ❖ χαιρετώ δια χειραψίας, δίνω τα χέρια

Use your English — page 129

10.86 breeze through (phr v) /briːz θruː/
achieve sth easily • *He breezed through his exams and got excellent marks.* ❖ πετυχαίνω (εύκολα)

10.87 brush up (phr v) /brʌʃ ʌp/
practise and improve your skills of sth that you learnt in the past • *You should brush up your Italian before you visit Rome.* ❖ φρεσκάρω

10.88 figure out (phr v) /ˈfɪɡə aʊt/
understand sth • *They figured out the answer to the maths problem together.* ❖ υπολογίζω

10.89 go over (phr v) /ɡəʊ ˈəʊvə/
look at sth; revise • *You should go over the second chapter before the test.* ❖ κάνω επανάληψη

10.90 hand in (v) /hænd ɪn/
give in homework • *I handed in my homework and the next day the teacher returned it marked.* ❖ παραδίδω

10.91 look up (phr v) /lʊk ʌp/
find sth in a list • *Always look up any new words in a dictionary.* ❖ ψάχνω

10.92 pick up (phr v) /pɪk ʌp/
learn sth quickly • *Matt went to live in Italy and picked up Italian quickly.* ❖ μαθαίνω

10.93 submit (v) /sʌbˈmɪt/
give homework, a plan, etc to sb for them to approve, mark, etc • *We have to submit a history project at the end of term.* ➢ submission (n) ❖ παραδίδω

10.94 compulsory (adj) /kəmˈpʌlsəri/
Sth that is compulsory must be done because it is the law or a rule. • *It is compulsory to do maths at school.* ❖ υποχρεωτικός
✎ Opp: optional

10.95 memory (n) /ˈmeməri/
the ability to remember • *He has a good memory, so he remembers names easily.* ➢ memorise (v) ❖ μνήμη

10.96 class register (n) /klaːs ˈredʒɪstə/
a pupil attendance list • *The best pupil in the class is usually in charge of the class register.* ❖ απουσιολόγιο

10.97 ceremony (n) /ˈserəməni/
a social or religious event that includes a series of traditional actions • *We're going to the opening ceremony of the World Cup!* ❖ τελετή

Writing: a formal email — pages 130–131

10.98 exchange programme (n) /ɪksˈtʃeɪndʒ ˈprəʊɡræm/
a programme in which students go to a foreign country to study • *As part of the exchange programme, Maria spent a term at a school in Sweden.* ❖ πρόγραμμα ανταλλαγής μαθητών

10.99 **chunk** (n) /tʃʌŋk/
a large amount or part of sth • *A chunk of her essay had been copied off the internet.* ❖ (μεγάλο) κομμάτι, μέρος

Video: Aquarium on Wheels
page 132

10.100 **aquarium** (n) /əˈkweərɪəm/
a large glass container where fish are kept
• *We saw a shark at the aquarium!* ❖ ενυδρείο

10.101 **conservation** (n) /kɒnsəˈveɪʃn/
protection of the natural environment
• *The conservation of wildlife is critical if we want to prevent more species becoming extinct.*
➢ conserve (v), conservationist (n)
❖ διατήρηση και προστασία του περιβάλλοντος

10.102 **marine biology** (n)) /məˈriːn baɪˈɒlədʒi/
the study of life in the sea • *She loves the sea and wants to study marine biology.*
➢ marine biologist (n) ❖ θαλάσσια βιολογία

10.103 **specialise** (v) /speʃəlˈaɪz/
focus on a particular subject and become an expert in it • *After completing her medical degree she specialised in paediatrics.* ➢ specialist (n)
❖ ειδικεύομαι

10.104 **major** (v) /ˈmeɪdʒə/
study sth as your main subject at university
• *Jack is majoring in history at university.*
➢ major (n, adj) ❖ σπουδάζω

10.105 **advantageous** (adj) /ædvənˈteɪdʒəs/
helpful and likely to make you successful
• *The ability to speak foreign languages is advantageous when it comes to finding a job.*
➢ advantage (n) ❖ επωφελής

10.106 **hands-on** (adj) /hænds-ɒn/
when you are involved in doing sth and not only studying it • *I'd like to get some hands-on experience of the job.* ❖ με πρακτική εξάσκηση

School

assignment	primary education
boarding school	principal
class register	scholarship
drop out	schooling
dyslexic	secondary school
enrol	tuition
exchange programme	tutor

Vocabulary Exercises

A Read the definition and complete the words.

1 unable to move: p _ _ _ _ _ _ _ _
2 illness or injury of the body: d _ _ _ _ _ _ _ _ _
3 permanently unable to move any part of your body below our neck: q _ _ _ _ _ _ _ _ _ _ _
4 an illness: d _ _ _ _ _ _
5 a solid, liquid or gas: s _ _ _ _ _ _ _ _
6 an agreement between two people: p _ _ _ _ _ _ _ _ _
7 focus on one particular subject and become an expert in it: s _ _ _ _ _ _ _ _ _
8 make a new product or service available to the public: l _ _ _ _ _

B Complete the dialogue with the correct form of these words.

breeze   brush   drop   figure   go   hand   look   pick

Rory: What are you (1) _____ up in the dictionary, Greg?
Greg: I'm doing a French translation for homework and I'm trying to
        (2) _____ out what this sentence means. I don't suppose
        you could help?
Rory: No way, mate. I (3) _____ out of French last year. I don't like learning
        foreign languages.
Greg: But don't you speak Italian? You (4) _____ through the
        Italian exam last summer and you didn't even study.
Rory: Well, that's because my grandma's Italian. We visit her every year. She can't
        speak English, so I have just (5) _____ it up. But I would
        have to (6) _____ up if I wanted to live in Italy permanently.
        I'm a bit rusty.
Greg: Well, maybe I can phone my tutor and ask him to (7) _____
        over this chapter with me again. I hope he can come today as I have to
        (8) _____ in this translation in tomorrow.

C Choose the correct answers.

1 Maths is a(n) ___ subject at school – you have to do it.
   a mental   b adaptable   c compulsory
2 'I can't concentrate in this place. There are too many ___!' she said.
   a placements   b distractions   c apprenticeships
3 His tennis ___ made him go to the gym every day in order to get fit.
   a guide   b tutor   c coach
4 The twins were sent to ___ school in a town far away from their home in the country.
   a mastering   b progressing   c boarding
5 He ___ on a successful career as soon as he finished his studies.
   a embarked   b donated   c enrolled
6 Can you scratch a terrible ___ I have on my back?
   a donor   b inch   c itch
7 She's ___ and performs well in all her subjects.
   a distinct   b bright   c critical
8 The school has ___ a parents evening for Tuesday.
   a arranged   b reminded   c majored

D Match. Then write the words.

1   spinal   span   _____
2   civil   cord   _____
3   life   home   _____
4   exchange   ship   _____
5   scholar   line   _____
6   guide   chair   _____
7   foster   dog   _____
8   eye   engineering _____
9   dead   sight   _____
10 wheel   register   _____
11 class   pointer   _____
12 laser   programme   _____

10 Grammar

10.1 Reported Speech: Statements

Όταν μεταφέρουμε τον άμεσο λόγο σε πλάγιο (reported speech), οι χρόνοι που χρησιμοποιεί ο ομιλητής συνήθως αλλάζουν ως εξής:

Direct Speech	Reported Speech
Present Simple	**Past Simple**
'He **sleeps** in the dormitory,' she said.	She said (that) he **slept** in the dormitory.
Present Continuous	**Past Continuous**
'He **is learning** Chinese,' she said.	She said (that) he **was learning** Chinese.
Present Perfect Simple	**Past Perfect Simple**
'My sons **have graduated**,' he said.	He said (that) his sons **had graduated**.
Present Perfect Continuous	**Past Perfect Continuous**
'He **has been studying** hard,' she said.	She said (that) he **had been studying** hard.
Past Simple	**Past Perfect Simple**
'Tom **passed** the exam,' he said.	He said (that) Tom **had passed** the exam.
Past Continuous	**Past Perfect Continuous**
'He **was revising**,' she said.	She said (that) he **had been revising**.

Άλλες αλλαγές στους τύπους των ρημάτων είναι οι παρακάτω:

can	**could**
'He **can** count to ten,' she said.	She said (that) he **could** count to ten.
may	**might**
'She **may** get the scholarship,' he said.	He said (that) she **might** get the scholarship.
must	**had to**
'You **must** improve,' the teacher said.	The teacher said (that) I **had to** improve.
will	**would**
'We **will** solve the problem,' he said.	He said (that) they **would** solve the problem.

Σημείωση:
1. Τα ρήματα *say* και *tell* χρησιμοποιούνται συχνά στο reported speech. Το ρήμα *tell* ακολουθείται από αντικείμενο (object).
   → Our coach **said** we should avoid risks.
   → Our coach **told us** we should avoid risks.

2. Μπορούμε να παραλείψουμε τη λέξη *that*.
   → **Emma said that** she wanted to be a fashion designer.
   → **Emma said** she wanted to be a fashion designer.

3. Θυμήσου να αλλάξεις τις αντωνυμίες και τα κτητικά επίθετα όπου χρειάζεται.
   → '**We** have figured out the answer,' he said.
   → He said (that) **they** had figured out the answer.
   → 'I handed in **my** science project,' she said.
   → She said (that) **she** had handed in **her** science project.

4. Οι παρακάτω χρόνοι και λέξεις δεν αλλάζουν στο reported speech: Past Perfect Simple, Past Perfect Continuous, *would, could, might, should, ought to, used to, had better*, καθώς και *must/mustn't* όταν αναφέρονται σε συμπέρασμα.
   → 'You **should** book the morning tour at the museum,' he said.
   → He said (that) I **should** book the morning tour at the museum.

10.2 Reported Speech: Changes in time and place

Όταν μεταφέρουμε τον άμεσο λόγο σε πλάγιο, υπάρχουν συχνά αλλαγές στις λέξεις που δηλώνουν χρόνο και τόπο.

10 Grammar

now	then
'I'm playing the piano **now**,' she said.	She said she was playing the piano **then**.
today	that day
'She's leaving college **today**,' he said.	He said she was leaving college **that day**.
tonight	that night
'I'm studying **tonight**,' she said.	She said she was studying **that night**.
yesterday	the previous day/the day before
'I visited the zoo **yesterday**,' she said.	She said she had visited the zoo **the previous day/the day before**.
last week/month	the previous week/month/the week/month before
'He started boarding school **last week**,' she said.	She said he had started boarding school **the previous week/the week before**.
tomorrow	the next day/the following day
'I'll visit the careers counsellor **tomorrow**,' she said.	She said she would visit the careers counsellor **the next day/the following day**.
next week/month	the following week/month
'Ned is going on an exchange programme **next week**,' she said.	She said Ned was going on an exchange programme **the following week**.
this/these	that/those
'**This** is my laptop,' she said.	She said **that** was her laptop.
ago	before
'He read the book three days **ago**,' she said.	She said he had read the book three days **before**.
at the moment	at that moment
'He's filling in the application form **at the moment**,' she said.	She said he was filling in the application form **at that moment**.
here	there
'The test results are **here** in the office,' she said.	She said the test results were **there** in the office.

10.3 Reported Speech: Questions

Όταν μεταφέρουμε ερωτήσεις από τον άμεσο στον πλάγιο λόγο (reported speech), οι αλλαγές στους χρόνους, στις αντωνυμίες, στα κτητικά επίθετα, στο χρόνο και τον τόπο είναι όπως και στις καταφατικές προτάσεις του πλάγιου λόγου. Όμως στις ερωτήσεις στον πλάγιο λόγο, το ρήμα είναι στον καταφατικό τύπο. Επίσης δε χρησιμοποιούμε ερωτηματικό.

Όταν η άμεση ερώτηση περιέχει ερωτηματική λέξη (πχ who, why, how, when, where), τη χρησιμοποιούμε και στην πλάγια ερώτηση (reported question).
→ **When** did Luke enroll on the course?' he asked. → He asked **when** Luke had enrolled on the course.

Όταν η άμεση ερώτηση δεν περιέχει ερωτηματική λέξη, χρησιμοποιούμε if ή whether στην πλάγια ερώτηση (reported question).
→ 'Is the language institute near the centre of the city?' she asked.
→ She asked **if/whether** the language institute was near the centre of the city.

10.4 Reported Speech: Commands & Requests

Όταν μεταφέρουμε κάποια εντολή στο reported speech, συνήθως χρησιμοποιούμε tell + αντικείμενο + απαρέμφατο με to.
→ 'Stop talking in class!' he shouted at us. → 'Don't be late for class again!' the professor told me.
→ He **told us to stop** talking in class. → The professor **told me not to be** late for class again.

Όταν μεταφέρουμε στο reported speech ένα αίτημα, συνήθως χρησιμοποιούμε ask + αντικείμενο + απαρέμφατο με to.
→ 'Can you help me choose a gift?' she asked. → She **asked me to help** her choose a gift.

(Επίσης: *She asked if I could help her choose a gift.*)
→ *'Please don't leave the door open,'* she said. → *She **asked me not to leave** the door open.*

10.5 Reported Speech: Reporting Verbs

Εκτός από τα ρήματα *say, tell* και *ask*, μπορούμε να χρησιμοποιήσουμε και άλλα ρήματα για να μεταφέρουμε με μεγαλύτερη ακρίβεια τα λόγια κάποιου. Παρατήρησε τους διαφορετικούς τρόπους σύνταξης.

verb + full infinitive	
agree	'Yes, I'll help decorate the gift shop,' she said. She **agreed to help** decorate the gift shop.
claim	'I'm the best at decorating,' she said. She **claimed to be** the best at decorating.
decide	'I think I'll help decorate the gift shop,' she said. She **decided to help** decorate the gift shop.
refuse	'No, I won't help decorate the gift shop,' she said. She **refused to help** decorate the gift shop.
offer	'Shall I help decorate the gift shop?' she said. She **offered to help** decorate the gift shop.
promise	'Don't worry, I'll help decorate the gift shop,' she said. She **promised to help** decorate the gift shop.
verb + object + full infinitive	
advise	'If I were you, I'd be careful during training,' he said. He **advised me to be** careful during training.
encourage	'Come on, you can train harder,' he said. He **encouraged me to train** harder.
order	'Start training immediately!' he told me. He **ordered me to start** training immediately.
persuade	'You should be careful during training,' he said. 'You're right,' I answered. He **persuaded me to be** careful during training.
remind	'Remember to train every day,' he said. He **reminded me to train** every day.
warn	'Be careful during training!' he said. He **warned me to be** careful during training.
verb + gerund	
admit	'I lost your history book,' she said. She **admitted losing** my history book.
deny	'No, I didn't lose your history book,' she said. She **denied losing** my history book.
recommend	'You should buy another history book,' she said. She **recommended buying** another history book.
suggest	'Let's look for your history book,' she said. She **suggested looking** for my history book.
verb + preposition + gerund	
apologise for	'I'm sorry I didn't help you study for the exam,' he said. He **apologised for not helping** me study for the exam.
complain about/ of	'I've failed the exam again!' he said. He **complained of failing** the exam again.
insist on	'I will definitely help you study,' he said. He **insisted on helping** me study.

10 Grammar

verb + object + preposition + gerund	
accuse sb of	'I'm sure you broke the microscope,' he said. He **accused me of breaking** the microscope.
congratulate sb on	'You fixed the microscope! Well done!' he said. He **congratulated me on fixing** the microscope.
verb + that	
admit agree	'I'm going to take a gap year before I start university,' she said. She **announced that** she was going to take a gap year before she started university.
boast claim complain decide	'My parents won't let me take a gap year before I start university,' she said. She **complained that** her parents wouldn't let her take a gap year before she started university.
deny persuade remind warn	'We want you to explain why you want to take a gap year before you start university,' my parents said. My parents **demanded that** I explain why I wanted to take a gap year before I started university.

Grammar Exercises

A Circle.

1. The headmaster told / said us to behave.
2. We said that we had already done a test the next day / day before.
3. He asked whether / that I wanted to major in physics.
4. She said / told that the course had been cancelled.
5. Tom asked her does / if she went to secondary school.
6. Geoff told him stopping / to stop revising so much.
7. Yesterday they said we were / are going to have a test but we never did.
8. The lecturer asked us if / did we had taken notes.

B Complete the second sentence so they have a similar meaning to the first sentences. Use the words in bold.

1. 'I will hand back the reports tomorrow,' said the teacher.   **WOULD**
   The teacher said he _____ day.

2. 'Do you like the new dormitory?' the principal asked me.   **IF**
   The principal _____ the new dormitory.

3. 'Please don't spill any chemicals,' said Mr Jones to his class. **NOT**
   Mr Jones _____ any chemicals.

4. 'I think you should enrol on a secretarial course,' said Fay.   **ADVISED**
   Fay _____ on a secretarial course.

5. 'I'm sorry I forgot to phone you,' said Toby.   **FOR**
   Toby _____ not phoning me.

6. 'Don't forget to wake up early for the train,' Mum said to me.   **REMINDED**
   Mum _____ early for the train.

7. 'Yes, I stole the dictionary from the library,' said Lance.   **STEALING**
   Lance _____ the dictionary from the library.

8. 'Could you hand in your work on time?' said the teacher to her class. **TO**
   The teacher _____ their work on time.

C Write one word in each gap.

1. He apologised _____ being late.
2. The pupils denied _____ in the test.
3. The school has announced _____ Monday is a holiday.
4. Susan reminded her son _____ enrol at the language institute.
5. Mum encouraged us _____ go to university.
6. He complained again _____ his son's bad grades.
7. Dad reminded me _____ I had to do the washing up.
8. They accused me _____ being lazy.

D Read the dialogue and then change the direct speech into reported speech.

Sandra: Can you take notes for me this morning in the lecture?
Kelly: No, sorry. I'm not going to the lecture as I have a doctor's appointment.
Librarian: Please be quiet!
Jack: Hi girls. Do you want to accompany me to the lecture?
Sandra: No, Jack, because we won't be at the lecture.
Kelly: Oh, Jack. Could you take notes for us?
Jack: But I took notes for you last week!
Sandra: Jack's right, Kelly.

1. Sandra asked Kelly _____.
2. Kelly told _____.
3. The librarian told _____.
4. Jack asked _____.
5. Sandra said to Jack _____.
6. Kelly asked Jack to _____.
7. Jack said _____.
8. Sandra said to _____.

Use your English

Exam Task

For questions **1–12**, read the text below and think of the word which best fits each gap. Use only **one** word in each gap.

School Uniform

The UK is one of the few places **(1)** _____ school uniform is still compulsory. The reasons **(2)** _____ range from economic ones to those of social equality, depending on whom you talk to. But has anyone ever asked the pupils **(3)** _____ have to wear uniforms for their view? We talked to a few and here are their verdicts. Most primary school pupils **(4)** _____ us that they liked school uniform. Many junior schools have the same uniforms for boys and girls. Primary school pupils agreed **(5)** _____ their uniforms were comfortable. But when secondary school pupils were asked **(6)** _____ they liked their uniforms, answers varied.

Uniforms for boys are the typical trousers, shirt, blazer and tie, whereas for girls, skirts are usually compulsory. Girls complained that **(7)** _____ got cold in winter. Boys disliked ties but were told by principals **(8)** _____ to remove them until they got home. Girls, however, boasted **(9)** _____ they wore to school; it seems ties are quite a fashion statement at present.

It seems unlikely, though, that uniforms will disappear from schools however much the pupils dislike them. It is the parents who insist **(10)** _____ their children wearing uniforms. When asked why, they denied **(11)** _____ mean to their kids, but explained that uniforms make weekly life easier as they are cheaper than everyday clothes. They also told **(12)** _____ that uniforms discourage teenagers from competing over brand name garments and thus reduce tensions at school.

11 Wish You Were Here!

Word Focus — page 136

11.1 souvenir (n) /ˌsuːvəˈnɪə(r)/
sth you keep to remember a place or event • *I bought this model of the Eiffel Tower as a souvenir of Paris.* ❖ σουβενίρ, αναμνηστικό

11.2 day pack (n) /deɪ pæk/
a small bag you carry on your back with things for a day trip • *Did you put your camera in your day pack?* ❖ μικρή τσάντα πλάτης

11.3 on board (expr) /ɒn bɔːd/
on a ship or plane • *There were 45 people on board the ship.* ❖ πάνω σε (πλοίο ή αεροπλάνο)

11.4 accent (n) /ˈæksent/
a way of saying words which shows what country, area, etc. a person is from • *She spoke with an American accent.* ❖ προφορά

11.5 distinctive (adj) /dɪˈstɪŋktɪv/
sth that is distinctive is easy to recognise because it is different from other things • *This coffee has a distinctive smell.* ❖ χαρακτηριστικός, ιδιαίτερος

11.6 taxi rank (n) /ˈtæksi ræŋk/
a place where taxis wait for customers • *There was a long queue at the taxi rank.* ❖ πιάτσα ταξί

Reading — pages 136–137

11.7 overseas (adj) /ˌəʊvəˈsiːz/
in another country • *He's leaving the UK to work overseas in Germany.* ❖ στο εξωτερικό

11.8 my fill of sth (expr) /maɪ fɪl əv ˈsʌmθɪŋ/
as much of sth as you can eat or drink • *After eating our fill of pizza, it was time for ice cream!* ❖ όσο μπορεί να φάει/πιει κανείς (ώσπου να χορτάσει)

11.9 stunning (adj) /ˈstʌnɪŋ/
extremely beautiful • *They took some stunning photos of the Acropolis.* ➣ stun (v) ❖ εντυπωσιακός, καταπληκτικός

11.10 take my breath away (expr) /teɪk maɪ breθ əˈweɪ/
be very beautiful or surprising • *The view took my breath away.* ❖ μου κόβει την ανάσα, με συγκλονίζει

11.11 chaos (n) /ˈkeɪɒs/
a situation in which everything is happening in a confused way and nothing is organised • *The living room was in chaos after the party.* ❖ χάος

11.12 armed (with) (adj) /ɑːmd wɪð/
carrying sth you need • *Armed with my camera, I went out to see the sights.* ❖ εφοδιασμένος (με), 'οπλισμένος' (με)

11.13 phrase book (n) /freɪz bʊk/
a book with useful expressions in another language for tourists • *When we arrived at the airport, I bought a French phrase book.* ❖ μικρό βιβλίο με βασικές και χρήσιμες εκφράσεις σε μια ξένη γλώσσα

11.14 board (v) /bɔːd/
get on a plane, train, bus, etc • *He boarded the plane and then sat down in seat 3B before take-off.* ❖ επιβιβάζομαι

11.15 overhead compartment (n) /ˌəʊvəˈhed kəmˈpɑːtmənt/
a place where you can store small items of luggage in the cabin of a plane • *The flight attendant helped me put my bag in the overhead compartment.* ❖ ντουλάπι σε αεροπλάνο

11.16 settle into your seat (expr) /ˈsetl ˈɪntə jɔː siːt/
make yourself comfortable in your seat • *She settled into her seat and began reading her book.* ❖ βολεύομαι στη θέση μου

11.17 fellow (adj) /ˈfeləʊ/
used to talk about sb who is similar to you in some way or in the same situation as you • *Why don't you discuss your ideas with your fellow workers?* ❖ συν- (πχ συνεργάτης, συνεπιβάτης)

11.18 passenger (n) /ˈpæsɪndʒə/
sb travelling in a vehicle but not driving it • *Passengers are asked not to distract the driver.* ❖ επιβάτης

11.19 distressed (adj) /dɪˈstrest/
worried, upset or anxious • *We were all distressed by the news of Hannah's death.* ➣ distress (v, n) ❖ ταραγμένος, ανήσυχος

11.20 animatedly (adv) /ˈænɪmeɪtɪdli/
with a lot of interest and energy • *They were talking animatedly.* ➣ animated (adj) ❖ ζωηρά, έντονα

11.21 nod off (phr v) /nɒd ɒf/
fall asleep for a short time, especially when you do not intend to • *Grandpa kept nodding off in front of the TV.* ❖ με παίρνει ο ύπνος, 'κουτουλάω' (από τη νύστα)

11.22 snore (v) /snɔː(r)/
make a noise in your throat and nose when you are asleep • *My brother snores so loudly that I can hear him from my room!* ➣ snore (n) ❖ ροχαλίζω

11.23 sight (n) /saɪt/
an interesting place to visit • *The tourists visited all the sights in the city, but their favourite was the Parthenon.* ❖ αξιοθέατο

11.24 almond eyes (expr) /ˈɑːmənd aɪz/
eyes shaped like an almond (an oval nut with a hard shell) • *She had long blond hair and beautiful almond eyes.* ❖ αμυγδαλωτά μάτια

11.25 instructive (adj) /ɪnˈstrʌktɪv/
giving interesting or useful information
• *I found his presentation instructive.* ➢ instruct (v), instruction (n) ❖ εποικοδομητικός, κατατοπιστικός

11.26 insight (n) /ˈɪnsaɪt/
an understanding of a situation or of what sth is like • *The meeting gave me some insight into the problems we are facing.* ❖ γνώση, εικόνα, ιδέα

11.27 stride off (phr v) /straɪd ɒf/
walk away quickly with long steps • *He said goodbye and strode off towards the exit.*
❖ απομακρύνομαι με μεγάλα, γρήγορα βήματα

11.28 shove (v) /ʃʌv/
put sth somewhere roughly and carelessly
• *She shoved her books in her bag.* ❖ χώνω, σπρώχνω

11.29 tissue (n) /ˈtɪʃuː/
a thin piece of soft paper used for cleaning your nose • *He handed me a tissue and said, 'Please don't cry.'* ❖ χαρτομάντιλο

11.30 grip (v) /grɪp/
have a strong effect on sb or sth ➢ *Fear gripped me when I heard the news.* ❖ κυριεύω

11.31 penniless (adj) /ˈpenɪləs/
having no money at all • *I was penniless, so I asked my friend to give me £5.* ❖ απένταρος, αδέκαρος

11.32 racking sobs (expr) /ˈrækɪŋ sɒbz/
loud noises sb makes when they are crying with sudden, sharp breaths • *We could hear her racking sobs from the other room.* ❖ δυνατοί λυγμοί/ αναφιλητά

11.33 be over (expr) /bi ˈəʊvə(r)/
If sth is over, it has finished. • *Are your exams over yet?* ❖ τελειώνω

11.34 drawer (n) /drɔː(r)/
a thing like a box, which is part of a piece of furniture and used for keeping things in • *I keep all my photos in that drawer.* ❖ συρτάρι

11.35 terminal (n) /ˈtɜːmɪnl/
a building where people wait to get on planes, buses, etc • *Our flight leaves from Terminal 4.*
❖ σταθμός επιβίβασης/αποβίβασης

11.36 sheer (adj) /ʃɪə(r)/
complete; with nothing else except the thing mentioned • *It was sheer luck that nobody was hurt.* ❖ καθαρός, απόλυτος

11.37 extract (n) /ekstrækt/
a particular part of a book, film, etc that gives you an idea of what the whole thing is like • *She read us an extract from her new book.* ❖ απόσπασμα

11.38 liar (n) /ˈlaɪə(r)/
sb who says or writes things that are not true
• *I don't believe you! You're a liar!* ➢ lie (v, n) ❖ ψεύτης

11.39 vast (adj) /vɑːst/
extremely large • *Tom's parents have spent vast amounts of money on his education.* ❖ τεράστιος
✎ Syn: huge

11.40 turn in (sth) /tɜːn ɪn (sʌmθɪŋ)/
give sth to a person in authority • *Luckily, my stolen bag was turned in a few days later.*
❖ παραδίδω (στις αρχές)

11.41 domestic flight (n) /dəˈmestɪk flaɪt/
a flight to and from places in a country
• *All domestic flights leave from Terminal 1.*
❖ πτήση εσωτερικού

11.42 break down (phr v) /breɪk daʊn/
stop working • *I was late because my car broke down.* ❖ χαλάω

Vocabulary   page 138

11.43 bay (n) /beɪ/
coast where a circle of sea is formed • *The fishing boat sailed into the bay where the fishing village was situated* ❖ κόλπος

11.44 hostel (n) /ˈhɒstəl/
a house like a hotel where you can stay cheaply
• *The students didn't have a lot of money, so they stayed in a hostel while on holiday.*
❖ ξενώνας

11.45 isolated (adj) /ˈaɪsəleɪtɪd/
far from other places • *The hotel was nice, but it was isolated; the nearest town was five kilometres away.* ➢ isolate (v), isolation (n)
❖ απομονωμένος

11.46 quay (n) /kiː/
a place in a town or village where boats can be tied up • *He tied his fishing boat to the quay.*
❖ αποβάθρα

11.47 runway (n) /ˈrʌnweɪ/
a road used by planes to take off and land at an airport • *The plane accelerated along the runway and took off smoothly.*
❖ διάδρομος (προσγείωσης)

11.48 shuttle (n) /ˈʃʌtl/
a bus, train or plane that makes regular short journeys between two places • *There is a shuttle between the hotel and the airport.* ❖ λεωφορείο

11.49 customs (pl n) /ˈkʌstəmz/
the place where goods are checked when you enter a country • *She had to open her suitcase at customs for a check.* ❖ τελωνείο

11.50 departure lounge (n) /dɪˈpɑːtʃə laʊndʒ/
the place where you wait for a flight • *We waited two hours in the departure lounge for our flight.*
❖ αίθουσα αναχωρήσεων

11.51 harbour (n) /ˈhɑːbə/
an area of water next to the land where ships can be safe • *The ferry entered the harbour and when it stopped the passengers got off.* ❖ λιμάνι

11.52 dock (n) /dɒk/
a place in a port where ships are loaded and unloaded or repaired • *The ferry stopped at the dock.* ➢ dock (v) ❖ αποβάθρα

11.53 **guest-house** (n) /gest-haʊs/
a small hotel • *Mrs Jones turned her home into a guest-house after her children left home.* ❖ ξενώνας

11.54 **bed and breakfast** (n) /bed ən ˈbrekfəst/
a private house or small hotel where you can sleep and have breakfast • *It is cheaper to stay in a bed and breakfast than a hotel.* ❖ πανσιόν με ύπνο και πρόγευμα
✎ Also: B&B

11.55 **inn** (n) /ɪn/
a small hotel or pub in the countryside • *They stayed in a room at the village inn.* ❖ πανδοχείο

11.56 **distant** (adj) /ˈdɪstənt/
faraway • *Can you hear the sound of distant music?* ➣ distance (n) ❖ μακρινός

11.57 **faraway** (adj) /ˌfɑːrəˈweɪ/
not near • *They visited a faraway castle in the middle of the wilderness.* ❖ μακρινός

11.58 **vessel** (n) /ˈvesəl/
a ship • *The cruise liner was a large vessel with two thousand passengers.* ❖ πλοίο

11.59 **liner** (n) /ˈlaɪnə(r)/
a large ship that carries passengers • *The Monterey, a luxury ocean liner, left the port on 15 April.* ❖ πλοίο της γραμμής

11.60 **yacht** (n) /jɒt/
a large boat with a sail used for pleasure or sport • *The yacht sailed across the blue sea.* ❖ γιοτ, σκάφος

11.61 **cove** (n) /kəʊv/
a small secluded bay • *The yacht could not be seen from the open sea as it was in a cove.* ❖ ορμίσκος

11.62 **lagoon** (n) /ləˈguːn/
a lake of sea water that is partly separated from the sea by rocks, sand or coral • *There are many species of fish in this lagoon.* ❖ λιμνοθάλασσα

11.63 **gulf** (n) /ɡʌlf/
a large area of sea partly enclosed by land • *Large ships can enter the gulf and sail to the city.* ❖ κόλπος

11.64 **in-flight** (adj) /ˈɪnˈflaɪt/
happening or available during a flight • *Does Gold Air offer in-flight entertainment?* ❖ εντός/κατά τη διάρκεια της πτήσης

11.65 **excess** (adj) /ekses/
more than allowed • *Her suitcase weighed more than 23 kilos, so she had to pay for excess baggage.* ➣ excess (n) ❖ υπέρβαρος (για αποσκευές)

11.66 **boarding pass** (n) /ˈbɔːdɪŋ pɑːs/
a document which allows you to get on a plane • *Please show your boarding pass before you board the plane.* ❖ κάρτα επιβίβασης

11.67 **baggage** (n) /ˈbæɡɪdʒ/
luggage • *Her baggage consisted of small suitcase and her handbag.* ❖ αποσκευές

11.68 **cabin crew** (n) /ˈkæbɪn kruː/
the people who work on a plane • *She asked one of the cabin crew to bring her a glass of water.* ❖ πλήρωμα (αεροσυνοδοί)

11.69 **store** (v) /stɔː/
keep sth somewhere in order to use it later • *We store all the information on a computer.* ❖ αποθηκεύω, φυλάω

11.70 **declare** (v) /dɪˈkleə/
tell a customs official that you are carrying goods on which you have to pay tax when you enter a country • *The tourists had nothing to declare.* ❖ δηλώνω

11.71 **delay** (v) /dɪˈleɪ/
cause to be slow or late • *The plane was delayed for two hours because of ice on the runway.* ➣ delay (n) ❖ καθυστερώ

11.72 **ground** (v) /ɡraʊnd/
not allow to fly • *The plane was grounded due to engine problems.* ❖ γειώνω, καθηλώνω στο έδαφος, απαγορεύω την πτήση

11.73 **fog** (n) /fɒɡ/
thick cloud near the ground • *We can't see a thing in this fog.* ➣ foggy (adj) ❖ ομίχλη

Flying
baggage	glide
board	ground
boarding pass	in-flight
cabin crew	on board
check in	overhead compartment
customs	paraglide
delay	passenger
departure lounge	runway
domestic flight	terminal

Grammar   page 139

11.74 **backpacking** (n) /ˈbækpækɪŋ/
travelling for pleasure and carrying a backpack • *They went backpacking through Europe and stayed at cheap hostels.* ➣ backpack (v), backpacker (n) ❖ ταξιδεύω με σακίδιο πλάτης

11.75 **roam** (v) /rəʊm/
walk, wander • *We roamed around the countryside all afternoon.* ❖ περιπλανώμαι

11.76 **ridge** (n) /rɪdʒ/
a long, narrow area of high land at the top of a mountain • *They walked along the mountain ridge.* ❖ κορυφογραμμή

11.77 **fossil** (n) /ˈfɒsl/
a part of a dead plant or animal that has been in the ground for a very long time and has turned into rock • *This dinosaur fossil is millions of years old.* ❖ απολίθωμα

11.78 territory (n) /ˈterətri/
land of a particular type • *The explorers travelled through dangerous territory.* ➣ territorial (adj)
❖ περιοχή

11.79 track (n) /træk/
footprints or markings • *Those tracks in the sand are a sea turtle's.* ➣ track (v) ❖ ίχνος, αχνάρι, πατημασιά

Listening page 140

11.80 house swapping (n) /haʊs ˈswɒpɪŋ/
exchanging houses for the holiday period • *House-swapping is a cheap way to have a holiday because you don't have to pay for hotels.*
❖ ανταλλαγή κατοικίας

11.81 house sitting (n) /haʊs ˈsɪtɪŋ/
living in and looking after sb's house while they are away • *You can do some house sitting for your aunt while she is away and earn some money.*
❖ προσέχω ένα σπίτι

11.82 next to nothing (expr) /nekst tə ˈnʌθɪŋ/
almost nothing • *My mum knows next to nothing about computers.* ❖ σχεδόν τίποτα/καθόλου

11.83 property (n) /ˈprɒpəti/
a building or building and/or land • *Property is very expensive, which is why many people rent flats instead of buying.* ❖ ιδιοκτησία

11.84 more often than not (expr) /mɔːr ˈɒfn̩ ðən nɒt/
usually • *More often than not, Amy is late for school.*
❖ συχνά

11.85 not … any time soon (expr) /nɒt … ˈeni ˈtaɪm suːn/
used in negative sentences to talk about the near future • *We aren't going to visit them any time soon.*
❖ δεν θα … στο άμεσο μέλλον/σύντομα

11.86 luxurious (adj) /lʌkˈʒʊəriəs/
very comfortable and expensive • *The luxurious hotel had gold taps and silk sheets.* ➣ luxury (n)
❖ πολυτελής

11.87 get in touch (with) (expr) /get ɪn tʌtʃ (wɪð)/
contact • *While you are in Rome, get in touch with my cousin who lives there.* ❖ έρχομαι σε επαφή με

11.88 northern lights (n) /ˈnɔːðən laɪts/
coloured light that you sometimes see in the night sky in the most northern countries of the world • *We're going on a cruise around Norway and hope to see the northern lights.* ❖ Βόρειο Σέλας

Speaking page 141

11.89 versus (prep) /ˈvɜːsəs/
used to compare the advantages of two different things, ideas, etc • *It was the job of my dreams versus a job with a better salary – I couldn't decide.*
❖ σε αντιπαράθεση, εναντίον

11.90 city break (n) /ˈsɪti breɪk/
a short holiday in a city • *We went on a city break to London.* ❖ σύντομες διακοπές σε πόλη

11.91 camper van (n) /ˈkæmpə(r) væn/
a large vehicle that you can stay and sleep in when travelling • *They drove around Europe in their camper van.* ❖ τροχόσπιτο

11.92 broaden your horizons (expr) /ˈbrɔːdən maɪ həˈraɪzənz/
learn or experience new things • *Travelling has broadened his horizons; he has learned more about other people and cultures.* ❖ διευρύνω τους ορίζοντες

11.93 ashore (adv) /əˈʃɔː(r)/
on or towards land from an area of water
• *We swam ashore.* ❖ στην/προς την ακτή

11.94 put up (phr v) /pʊt ʌp/
place sth like a tent somewhere • *It took them hours to put up their tent.* ❖ στήνω (σκηνή)

11.95 pitch (a tent) (v) /pɪtʃ (ə tent)/
set up (a tent) somewhere • *Why don't we pitch our tent over there?* ❖ στήνω (σκηνή)

Grammar page 142

11.96 immensely (adv) /ɪˈmensli/
very much; extremely • *He's an immensely talented young actor.* ➣ immense (adj) ❖ υπερβολικά, πάρα πολύ

11.97 utterly (adv) /ˈʌtəli/
completely • *That was an utterly stupid thing to do!*
➣ utter (adj) ❖ εντελώς, απόλυτα

11.98 furious (adj) /ˈfjʊəriəs/
very angry • *David was furious when his son came home three hours late.* ➣ fury (n) ❖ έξαλλος, πολύ θυμωμένος

11.99 pretty (adv) /ˈprɪti/
to some extent; more than a little • *His English is pretty good.* ❖ αρκετά

11.100 slightly (adv) /ˈslaɪtli/
a little • *He's slightly taller than his brother.*
➣ slight (adj) ❖ ελαφρώς, λίγο

11.101 reasonably (adv) /ˈriːznəbli/
in a satisfactory way • *I did reasonably well in my exam.* ➣ reasonable (adj) ❖ επαρκώς

11.102 virtually (adv) /ˈvɜːtʃuəli/
almost • *It's virtually impossible to find a taxi in the city centre during rush hour.* ❖ σχεδόν

11.103 shutter (n) /ˈʃʌtə/
one of a pair of covers on the outside of a window that can be opened and closed • *Please close the shutters before you go to bed.* ❖ παραθυρόφυλλο

11.104 rusty (adj) /ˈrʌsti/
covered in the brownish-red substance that forms when iron gets wet • *The metal gate was rusty with age.* ➣ rust (v, n) ❖ σκουριασμένος

11.105 ridiculous (adj) /rɪˈdɪkjʊləs/
very silly • *You look ridiculous in that flowery swimming cap.* ➣ ridicule (v) ❖ γελοίος

Use your English page 143

11.106 book into (phr v) /bʊk ˈɪntu/
arrive at a hotel and say who you are, etc • *I have booked into this hotel for one night.* ➣ booking (n)
❖ κλείνω, κάνω κράτηση

11.107 check in (phr v) /tʃek ɪn/
arrive at a hotel and say who you are etc • *You cannot check in at the hotel before two.* ➣ check-in (n) ❖ υπογράφω κατά την άφιξη σε ξενοδοχείο
✎ Opp: check out

11.108 check out (phr v) /tʃek aʊt/
leave a hotel • *We checked out of the hotel and left for the airport.* ❖ πληρώνω και αναχωρώ από ξενοδοχείο
✎ Opp: check in

11.109 make for (phr v) /meɪk fɔː/
go towards • *As soon as the kids got to the beach, they made for the sea.* ❖ κατευθύνομαι προς

11.110 see sb off (phr v) /siː sʌmbədi ɒf/
go to the place where sb is leaving to say goodbye • *We saw John off at the airport.*
❖ ξεπροβοδίζω, συνοδεύω κάποιον μέχρι το σταθμό κλπ.

11.111 register (v) /ˈredʒɪstə(r)/
put your name on an official list • *I've just registered for the computer course.* ❖ εγγράφομαι, καταχωρώ το όνομά μου

11.112 a wealth of (expr) /welθ/
a large amount of sth • *There was a wealth of information at the travel agent's on good places to visit.* ❖ πληθώρα

Writing: a story (2)

pages 144–145

11.113 roll (v) /rəʊl/
move like a ball • *Tears rolled down the child's cheeks.* ❖ κυλώ

11.114 directions (pl n) /daɪˈrekʃənz/
instructions about how to get to a place
• *The receptionist gave us directions to the bay.*
➣ direct (v) ❖ οδηγίες

11.115 foolish (adj) /ˈfuːlɪʃ/
silly • *She felt foolish when she arrived in Greece in winter without a coat.* ➣ fool (n) ❖ ανόητος

11.116 pocket (n) /ˈpɒkɪt/
the part of a piece of clothing you can put things in • *He always keeps his car keys in his pocket.*
❖ τσέπη

11.117 over the moon (expr) /ˈəʊvə ðə muːn/
very happy • *We were over the moon when we heard the good news.* ❖ πανευτυχής, πετάω από τη χαρά μου

11.118 on top of the world (expr) /ɒn tɒp əv ðə wɜːld/
extremely happy • *I feel on top of the world because it's my wedding day.* ❖ πανευτυχής, πετάω από τη χαρά μου

11.119 speechless (adj) /ˈspiːtʃləs/
unable to speak because you are extremely surprised, upset, etc • *The news left me speechless.*
❖ άφωνος

11.120 too good to be true (expr) /tuː ɡʊd tə bi truː/
If sth is too good to be true, it is so good that you cannot believe it is real. • *A new car, a new house and the perfect job? It was too good to be true.*
❖ πολύ καλό για να είναι αληθινό

11.121 scared stiff (expr) /skeəd ˈstɪf/
very frightened • *She is scared stiff of flying, so she never travels by plane.* ❖ τρομοκρατημένος

11.122 gripped with fear (expr) /ɡrɪpt wɪð fɪə/
terrified • *They were gripped with fear all through the horror film.* ❖ τρομοκρατημένος

11.123 panic-stricken (adj) /ˈpænɪk-ˈstrɪkən/
in a great panic • *They were panic-stricken when they got lost in the mountains at night.*
❖ σε κατάσταση πανικού, πανικόβλητος

11.124 beat (v) /biːt/
make a regular sound or movement • *The cat was alive – its heart was still beating.* ❖ χτυπώ

11.125 my heart sinks (expr) /maɪ hɑːt sɪŋks/
feel hopeless • *His heart sank when he heard the flight had been cancelled.* ❖ νιώθω απελπισμένος, απογοητεύομαι

11.126 white as a sheet (expr) /waɪt æz ə ʃiːt/
white from fear • *She went as white as a sheet when she thought she had seen a ghost.*
❖ άσπρος σαν το πανί

11.127 my hair stands on end (expr) /maɪ heə stændz ɒn end/
If sth makes your hair stand on end, it makes you feel extremely frightened. • *It's a great horror film that will make your hair stand on end.* ❖ μου σηκώνεται η τρίχα, ανατριχιάζω

Video: Gliding Across the Gobi page 146

11.128 glide (v) /ɡlaɪd/
fly without using an engine • *The birds often glide over the houses near the sea.* ➣ glider (v)
❖ γλιστρώ

11.129 sand dune (n) /sænd djuːn/
a hill of sand in a desert or by the sea
• *The camels had no problem walking on the sand dunes.* ❖ αμμόλοφος

11.130 paraglide (v) /ˈpærəglaɪd/
jump from a mountain side and float in the air with a special type of parachute • *He paraglided over the countryside and admired the view.* ➢ paraglider (v) ❖ ελεύθερη πτήση με αλεξίπτωτο πλαγιάς

11.131 arid (adj) /ˈærɪd/
very dry because it has very little rain • *It never rained in the hot arid desert.*
❖ ξηρός, άνυδρος

11.132 attempt (n) /əˈtempt/
effort to do sth • *Her attempt to finish the marathon succeeded and she did it in four hours.*
➢ attempt (v) ❖ προσπάθεια

11.133 shade (n) /ʃeɪd/
shelter from the direct light of the sun made by sth blocking it • *They stood in the shade under a tree.* ➢ shade (v) ❖ σκιά

Natural features
bay	lagoon
cove	ridge
gulf	sand dune
harbour	

Vocabulary Exercises

A Choose the correct answers.

1 They booked ___ a hotel they had found online.
  a to
  b into

2 Will you ___ us off at the airport when we leave?
  a see
  b set

3 He nodded ___ in front of the TV.
  a off
  b down

4 They got out of their car and ___ for the beach.
  a rolled
  b made

5 What time do we have to check ___ of our rooms?
  a in
  b out

6 She said goodbye and ___ off in the opposite direction.
  a strode
  b boarded

7 Someone found my wallet and turned it ___ to the police.
  a in
  b up

8 Please give me a lift to work. My car has broken ___.
  a down
  b up

B Complete the sentences with these words.

| baggage | board | customs | drawer | flight | hostel | insights | lounge | rank | shade | shutters | souvenirs |

1 You will have to pay for excess _____, sir.
2 The students said the dormitory at the cheap _____ they stayed in was dirty.
3 The sun is too strong, so I'm moving to the _____ under this tree.
4 Her luggage was checked at _____ when she arrived in Frankfurt.
5 We bought some nice _____ to remind us of our holiday.
6 There were about 250 people on _____ the plane that went missing.
7 I waited for a few minutes at the taxi _____ before one turned up.
8 They closed the window _____ to keep the room cool on the hot summer day.
9 We waited patiently in the departure _____ for our flight to be announced.
10 My holiday in Japan gave me some valuable _____ into a new culture and way of life.
11 She keeps her passport in the third _____ from the top.
12 I don't need a passport. I'm on a domestic _____ from Athens to Thessaloniki.

C Match.

1. She set out to explore the city, armed
2. The view was so beautiful it took
3. We stayed at a very nice bed
4. She settled into
5. Our holidays will be
6. They were over
7. He turned as white
8. It was sheer

a and breakfast on the way to London.
b the moon when they won a weekend in Paris.
c with nothing but a guide book.
d bad luck that we had the accident.
e as a sheet when he heard a noise from the roof.
f over in a few days.
g her seat and read a magazine.
h my breath away.

D Circle.

1. The ferry stopped at the quay / vessel to let the passengers disembark.
2. There is a retreat / shuttle bus every half hour from the airport to the hotel.
3. They tracked / roamed around town for the entire afternoon.
4. The tourists swam all day in the little cove / vessel.
5. All the planes were grounded / pitched because of the fog.
6. The plane landed safely on the harbour / runway.
7. The children were scared / gripped stiff when the lights went out and they were alone in the old house.
8. You did pretty / utterly well in the test but you could have done better.

11 Grammar

11.1 Comparison of Adjectives & Adverbs

Χρησιμοποιούμε comparative για να συγκρίνουμε δύο πρόσωπα ή πράγματα, ή το τρόπο που έγιναν δυο πράξεις. Συνήθως σχηματίζουμε το comparative προσθέτοντας την κατάληξη -er στο επίθετο ή το επίρρημα. Αν το επίθετο ή το επίρρημα έχει περισσότερες από δύο συλλαβές, τότε χρησιμοποιούμε τη λέξη more. Συχνά χρησιμοποιούμε τη λέξη than μετά από το comparative.
→ The Greek islands are **more crowded** in summer **than** in winter.
→ You can sleep **more comfortably** in a hotel **than** in a tent.

Χρησιμοποιούμε superlative για να συγκρίνουμε ένα πρόσωπο ή πράγμα με άλλα ομοειδή πρόσωπα ή πράγματα. Συνήθως σχηματίζουμε το superlative προσθέτοντας την κατάληξη -est στο επίθετο ή το επίρρημα. Αν το επίθετο ή το επίρρημα έχουν περισσότερες από δύο συλλαβές, τότε χρησιμοποιούμε τη λέξη most. Πριν από το superlative χρησιμοποιούμε τη λέξη the.
→ What's **the longest** river in the world?
→ Pete finished his breakfast **the most slowly** of all the other hotel guests.

Ορθογραφία:
bi**g** → bi**gg**er/bi**gg**est   larg**e** → larg**er**/larg**est**   eas**y** → eas**ier**/eas**iest**

Υπάρχουν επίθετα και επιρρήματα που είναι ανώμαλα και σχηματίζουν το comparative και superlative με διαφορετικούς τρόπους.

Adjective/Adverb	Comparative	Superlative
good/well	better	the best
bad/badly	worse	the worst
many/more	more	the most
much	more	the most
little	less	the least
far	farther/further	the farthest/furthest

→ Travelling to India was **less expensive than** we had expected.

Σημείωση:
1 Κάποιες λέξεις όπως *hard, late, straight* και *fast* είναι και επίθετα και επιρρήματα.
   → She's a **fast** driver.
   → She drives **fast**.
2 Υπάρχουν λέξεις που τελειώνουν σε –ly, όπως *friendly, lovely, silly* και *ugly*, αλλά δεν είναι επιρρήματα, είναι επίθετα.
   → The wild flowers were **lovely**.
3 Οι λέξεις *hardly* (= barely, μόλις, σχεδόν δεν) και *lately* (= recently, πρόσφατα) δεν είναι τα επιρρήματα των λέξεων *hard* και *late*.
   → Hassan **hardly** had any time to get to the airport in time to catch his flight.
   → I haven't been fishing **lately**.

11.2 Other comparative structures

Χρησιμοποιούμε *as* + επίθετο/επίρρημα + *as* για να δείξουμε ότι δύο πρόσωπα ή πράγματα είναι με κάποιο τρόπο παρόμοια.
→ Is snorkeling **as tiring as** horseback riding?

Χρησιμοποιούμε *not as/so ... as* για να δείξουμε ότι ένα πρόσωπο ή πράγμα έχει μια ιδιότητα σε μικρότερο βαθμό από ένα άλλο.
→ Madrid is**n't so cold as** Oslo in winter.

Χρησιμοποιούμε *the* + comparative (συγκριτικός), *the* + comparative (συγκριτικός), για να δείξουμε ότι όσο κάτι αυξάνεται ή μειώνεται, τόσο επηρεάζει κάτι άλλο.
→ **The heavier** the suitcase, **the more** money you will pay for excess baggage.

11 Grammar

11.3 *Too, Enough, So & Such*

Χρησιμοποιούμε *too* + επίθετο/επίρρημα για να δείξουμε ότι κάτι είναι περισσότερο από αυτό που θέλουμε ή χρειαζόμαστε.

→ *The weather was **too cold** to go swimming in the lagoon.*
→ *The taxi was going **too fast** for me to see the name of the hotel.*

Χρησιμοποιούμε επίθετο/επίρρημα + *enough* ή *enough* + ουσιαστικό για να δείξουμε ότι κάτι είναι ή δεν είναι τόσο όσο θέλουμε ή χρειαζόμαστε.
→ *Going fishing isn't **challenging enough** for my brother.*
→ *We have **enough photos** to show our friends when we get back.*

Χρησιμοποιούμε *so* και *such* για να τονίσουμε κάτι. Είναι πιο εμφατικά από το *very*.
Χρησιμοποιούμε *so* + επίθετο/επίρρημα.
→ *The view from the top of the skyscraper was **so incredible**!*
Χρησιμοποιούμε *such* + (επίθετο +) ουσιαστικό.
→ *He is **such an experienced pilot**!*

Μπορούμε επίσης να χρησιμοποιήσουμε *so* και *such* για να δώσουμε έμφαση στα χαρακτηριστικά που οδηγούν σε ένα συγκεκριμένο αποτέλεσμα ή πράξη.
→ *The overhead compartment on the plane was **so small that** I couldn't put my bag in it.*
→ *Visiting Victoria Falls was **such an amazing experience that** we talked about it for days.*

11.4 Gradable Adjectives

Τα διαβαθμίσιμα επίθετα μπορούν να:
ποικίλουν σε ένταση ή βαθμό.
→ *The fog is dense today, but it was **very dense** yesterday.*
χρησιμοποιηθούν με επιρρήματα διαβάθμισης όπως *a little, extremely, fairly, hugely, immensely, intensely, rather, reasonably, slightly, unusually, very*, κλπ.
→ *Horse riding is **extremely enjoyable**, but bareback riding is **rather uncomfortable**.*
σχηματίσουν το συγκριτικό και τον υπερθετικό βαθμό.
→ *The dinosaur museum was **more interesting than** the snake museum, and the exhibits from the Jurassic period were **the most interesting** of all.*

11.5 Non-gradable Adjectives

Τα μη-διαβαθμίσιμα επίθετα:
δεν μπορούν να ποικίλουν σε ένταση ή βαθμό γιατί ήδη εκφράζουν κάτι που είναι στο ανώτατο όριο.
→ *Dad was **furious** because the hotel had lost our passports.*
→ *We found some **incredible** bargains at the duty-free shop.*
συχνά χρησιμοποιούνται μόνα τους.
→ *The village was **dead**. There was nobody to ask for directions.*
→ *The hike lasted five hours and the kids were **exhausted**.*
μπορούν να χρησιμοποιηθούν μόνο με μη-διαβαθμιστικά επιρρήματα όπως είναι τα *absolutely, utterly, completely, totally*, κλπ.
→ *The moonlit nights on the cruise were **absolutely perfect**.*
→ *We didn't expect the beach to be **completely empty**.*

Σημείωση: Τα επιρρήματα *really, fairly, pretty* και *quite* συχνά χρησιμοποιούνται με διαβαθμίσιμα και μη-διαβαθμίσιμα επίθετα.
→ *The travel agent was **really helpful**.*
→ *Kevin must be **pretty starving** after walking around the city all day.*

11.6 Adjective Order

Όταν χρησιμοποιούμε δύο ή περισσότερα επίθετα για να περιγράψουμε κάποιον ή κάτι, συνήθως τα βάζουμε σύμφωνα με την παρακάτω σειρά.

opinion	size	shape	age	colour	origin	material	NOUN
charming	small	round	antique	white	Italian	porcelain	vase
nice	big	square	new	brown	German	wooden	table
lovely	large	long	old	beige	French	linen	tablecloth

→ We stayed at a **romantic old stone** inn while we were in Austria.
→ I found some **unusual Mexican silver** jewellery in the souvenir shop.

Grammar Exercises

A Write one word in each gap.

1 The more I travel, the _____ I broaden my horizons.
2 This guest-house is much more comfortable _____ the other one.
3 I enjoyed the visit to the museum as much _____ the trip to the beach.
4 Rome is the _____ beautiful city in the world.
5 The tortoise is the slowest _____ all the animals in the park.
6 The curator described the exhibits _____ vividly than the guide book did.
7 It was _____ a long delay that we missed the shuttle to the city hotel.
8 The plane was _____ old that all the passengers were panic-stricken.

B Complete the sentences with your own ideas.

1 The hostel was so _____.
2 This retreat is more _____.
3 The sea lions were the _____.
4 The boat was such _____.
5 Swimming is as _____.
6 Athens is the most _____.
7 The tourist spoke more _____.
8 This cove is much _____.

C Put the words in the correct order.

1 first / at / we / felt / starving / hungry / after / a / few / but / hours / we / were / rather
_____

2 the / was / day / but / the / sea / cold / absolutely / was / freezing
_____

3 beautiful / they / brown / stayed / in / a / lodge / wooden
_____

4 a / old / bought / silk / red / she / scarf / wonderful
_____

5 my / it / sight / the / so / away / was / breath / stunning / that / took
_____

6 I / expensive / can't / find / swimsuit / my / blue
_____

11 Grammar

Use your English

Exam Task

For questions **1–8**, read the text below. Use the word given in capitals at the end of some of the lines to form a word that fits in the gap **in the same line**.

The Terminal

A rather irritating film is the movie *The Terminal* starring Tom Hanks. He plays an unfortunate traveller who arrives in the US after a coup has taken place in his own country. The airport authorities won't let him enter the US, so he finds himself stuck in the airport. Despite having nothing to (1) _____ , his bags are searched at customs. He cannot speak English well, so it is (2) _____ impossible for him to understand what is going on. In disbelief, he realises that he cannot leave the (3) _____ lounge and he feels absolutely (4) _____ .
The whole situation is so unlikely in real life that despite a good performance by the leading man, the film seems a little (5) _____ to say the least.

This unfortunate traveller, who is understandably (6) _____ , stays in this airport for so long that he learns English and even gets a job. Viewers must feel (7) _____ relieved when the film starts to move a little faster, but the scenario is so unlikely that even the (8) _____ Catherine Zeta-Jones does not save the day.

DECLARATION

VIRTUAL
DEPART
FURY

FOOL

DISTRESS

IMMENSE
STUN

12 Fit for Life

Reading — page 148

12.1 **sea urchin** (n) /siː ˈɜːtʃɪn/
a sea animal shaped like a ball with spikes
• *She stepped on a sea urchin and it was really painful.* ❖ αχινός

12.2 **oyster** (n) /ˈɔɪstə/
a type of shellfish • *He ate the oyster raw with a little lemon.* ❖ στρείδι

12.3 **bean** (n) /biːn/
a small, thin green vegetable with seeds in it that you can eat • *Do you like traditional Greek bean soup?* ❖ φασόλι

12.4 **seaweed** (n) /ˈsiːwiːd/
plants which grows in the sea • *There was a lot of seaweed on the shore after the storm.*
❖ φύκια

12.5 **scorpion** (n) /ˈskɔːpɪən/
an animal like an insect with sting in its tail
• *He lifted a stone and there was a scorpion under it.*
❖ σκορπιός

12.6 **snail** (n) /ˈsneɪl/
a small soft animal that moves slowly and has a hard shell on its back • *After the rain there were lots of snails in the garden.* ❖ σαλιγκάρι

Word Focus — page 148

12.7 **delicacy** (n) /ˈdelɪkəsi/
delicious food that is expensive or rare
• *Smoked salmon is one of her favourite delicacies.*
➣ delicate (adj) ❖ λιχουδιά

12.8 **termite** (n) /ˈtɜːmaɪt/
a small insect like an ant • *Termites have destroyed the wooden doors in his house.*
❖ τερμίτης

12.9 **termite mound** (n) /ˈtɜːmaɪt maʊnd/
a nest built by termites (= small insects that eat wood and live in organised groups)
• *There were huge termite mounds all over the area.* ❖ φωλιά τερμιτών

12.10 **squirm** (v) /skwɜːm/
move with a wriggling motion • *The child squirmed in his chair because he wanted to go to the toilet.* ❖ στριφογυρίζω

12.11 **wriggle** (v) /ˈrɪɡl/
twist and turn • *Sit still and stop wriggling!*
❖ στριφογυρίζω

12.12 **motion** (n) /ˈməʊʃn/
the act or process of moving • *He jumped off the train while it was still in motion.* ❖ κίνηση

12.13 **abundant** (adj) /əˈbʌndənt/
existing in large numbers or amounts
• *Water is abundant in this region.*
➣ abundance (n) ❖ άφθονος
✎ Opp: scarce

12.14 **pulp** (n) /pʌlp/
soft material containing a lot of water • *Mash the strawberries to a pulp and eat them with honey and yoghurt.* ❖ πολτός

12.15 **tingle** (v) /ˈtɪŋɡl/
create a slightly painful sensation • *My leg fell asleep and now it's tingling.* ➣ tingling (n)
❖ τσούζω

Reading — pages 148–149

12.16 **for the sake of** (expr) /fə ðə seɪk ɒv/
If you do sth for the sake of sb or sth, you do it in order to help, please or improve them. • *He left his job for the sake of his health.* ❖ για χάρη/για το καλό του ...

12.17 **stick to** (phr v) /stɪk tə/
continue doing sth even though it may be difficult • *Let's stick to our original plan.*
❖ παραμένω σε, δεν αποκλίνω από

12.18 **balanced diet** (expr) /ˈbælənst ˈdaɪət/
a diet that is healthy because it contains the right foods in the right amounts • *Athletes need to eat a balanced diet.* ❖ ισορροπημένη διατροφή

12.19 **opt (for)** (v) /ɒpt (fɔː)/
choose • *She opted for a chicken burger as she isn't keen on red meat.* ➣ option (n)
❖ επιλέγω

12.20 **low-fat** (adj) /ləʊ-fæt/
containing only a little fat • *This low-fat yoghurt is tasteless!* ❖ χαμηλός σε λιπαρά

12.21 **intake** (n) /ˈɪnteɪk/
the amount of food or drink you consume
• *The doctor said his intake of salt was too high.*
❖ κατανάλωση

12.22 **conservative** (adj) /kənˈsɜːvətɪv/
not very open to anything new • *Grandpa is a bit conservative, so he never wants to try foreign food.*
❖ συντηρητικός

12.23 **bug** (n) /bʌɡ/
an insect • *The birds were eating little bugs in the grass.* ❖ έντομο

12.24 **pop** (v) /pɒp/
put sth somewhere quickly • *Pop this pill in your mouth and swallow it.* ❖ βάζω

12.25 **crawl** (v) /krɔːl/
move slowly • *The ant crawled up the leaf.*
❖ περπατώ (για έντομα), έρπω

12.26 **swallow** (v) /ˈswɒləʊ/
when sth goes from your mouth to your stomach
• *The little boy swallowed a toy and his parents had to take him to the doctor.* ❖ καταπίνω

12.27 **crunchy** (adj) /ˈkrʌntʃi/
Crunchy food is firm and makes a noise when you bite it. • *These nuts are nice and crunchy.*
❖ τραγανός

12.28 **grasshopper** (n) /ˈgrɑːshɒpə/
an insect with long back legs for jumping
• *The bird ate the grasshopper.* ❖ ακρίδα

12.29 **deep-fried** (adj) /diːp-fraɪd/
cooked in lots of hot oil • *Deep-fried fish and chips is a traditional British takeaway.*
➢ deep-fry (v) ❖ τηγανητός

12.30 **cockroach** (n) /ˈkɒkrəʊtʃ/
an insect that many people find disgusting
• *Mum screamed because there was a cockroach in the kitchen.* ❖ κατσαρίδα

12.31 **creepy-crawly** (n) /ˈkriːpi-ˈkrɔːli/
an insect • *Little George puts creepy-crawlies in his sister's hair, which makes her scream.* ❖ ζουζούνι

12.32 **tasty** (adj) /ˈteɪsti/
delicious • *This meal is very tasty. Can I have some more?* ➢ taste (v, n) ❖ νόστιμος
✎ Opp: tasteless

12.33 **magnesium** (n) /mɒgˈniːzɪəm/
a white, silvery coloured metal • *He takes vitamins and magnesium every day while training for the marathon.* ❖ μαγνήσιο

12.34 **iron** (n) /aɪən/
a common hard metal • *If you are anaemic, take some iron.* ❖ σίδηρος

12.35 **skip** (v) /skɪp/
not do sth that you usually do or should do • *She was hungry because she had skipped breakfast.*
❖ παραλείπω

12.36 **processed food** (n) /ˈprəʊsest fuːd/
food with substances added to it in order to preserve it or improve its colour • *Processed food has many preservatives so it isn't good for you.*
❖ επεξεργασμένα τρόφιμα

12.37 **unknowingly** (adv) /ʌnˈnəʊwɪŋli/
not realising what you are doing • *The king unknowingly drank poison and died.* ❖ εν αγνοία

12.38 **make your mouth water** (expr)
/meɪk jɔː maʊθ ˈwɔːtə/
If food makes your mouth water, it smells or looks so good you want to eat it. • *Just looking at the food made my mouth water.* ❖ μου τρέχουν τα σάλια

12.39 **whiff** (n) /wɪf/
a slight smell (often bad) • *He got a whiff of fried onions from next door.* ❖ μυρωδιά

12.40 **put off** (phr v) /pʊt ɒf/
make sb dislike or not want to do sth • *I didn't try the food – the smell put me off.* ❖ απωθώ, αποτρέπω

12.41 **spike** (n) /ˈspaɪk/
sth long and thin with a sharp point • *There are spikes all over this fruit, so I can't touch it.*
➢ spiky (n) ❖ ακίδα, αγκάθι

12.42 **sharp** (adj) /ʃɑːp/
able to cut easily • *He cut himself on the sharp knife.* ➢ sharpen (v) ❖ κοφτερός
✎ Opp: blunt

12.43 **garlic** (n) /ˈgɑːlɪk/
a plant like a small onion with a strong smell
• *I don't eat tzatziki because I don't like garlic.*
❖ σκόρδο

12.44 **fibre** (n) /ˈfaɪbə/
the part of food that your body cannot digest
• *There is a lot of fibre in fruit and vegetables.*
❖ φυτικές ίνες

12.45 **packed** (adj) /pækt/
containing a lot of one thing • *Fresh fruit salad is packed with vitamins.* ❖ γεμάτος, πλήρης

12.46 **carbohydrate** (n) /kɑːbəˈhaɪdreɪt/
a substance that is found in foods like sugar, bread and potatoes and which provides your body with energy • *Bread and sugar are high in carbohydrates.* ❖ υδατάνθρακας

12.47 **boost** (n) /buːst/
sth that helps sb or sth improve or increase
• *Passing that test was such a boost to her confidence.* ➢ boost (v) ❖ τόνωση, ενίσχυση

12.48 **bitter** (adj) /ˈbɪtə/
having a sharp strong taste • *This food is too bitter to eat.* ➢ bitterness (n) ❖ πικρός

12.49 **root** (n) /ruːt/
the part of a plant which is under the ground
• *Carrots and potatoes are my favourite root vegetables.* ❖ ρίζα

12.50 **fall to** (phr v) /fɔːl tuː/
If a job falls to sb, they are responsible for doing it. • *After every meal, it always falls to Mary to wash the dishes.* ❖ πέφτω σε

12.51 **grate** (v) /greɪt/
cut into very small pieces using a tool with a rough surface • *Please grate some cheese over my pasta.* ➢ grater (n) ❖ τρίβω (τυρί, ντομάτα, κλπ)

12.52 **squeeze** (v) /skwiːz/
press sth firmly in order to get liquid out of it
• *Squeeze the lemons and pour the juice into a glass.*
❖ στίβω

12.53 **strainer** (n) /streɪnə/
a kitchen tool with lots of small holes in it that is used for separating solids from liquids • *We need the strainer because the pasta is ready.* ➢ strain (v)
❖ σουρωτήρι

12.54 **paste** (n) /peɪst/
a soft smooth food made by crushing sth
• *Mix the flour and water into a paste and then add salt.* ❖ πάστα, αλοιφή

12.55 chubby (adj) /ˈtʃʌbi/
slightly fat in a pleasant way • *She was a beautiful baby with brown hair and chubby cheeks.*
❖ στρουμπουλός

12.56 porcupine (n) /ˈpɔːkjupaɪn/
an animal with spikes on its back • *The porcupine is well protected from predators with its long sharp spikes.* ❖ σκαντζόχοιρος

12.57 pinch (n) /pɪntʃ/
a very small amount • *Add a pinch of salt and the soup is ready.* ❖ πρέζα

12.58 toxin (n) /ˈtɒksɪn/
a poison • *There are many toxins in the polluted river, so don't go fishing there.* ➢ toxic (adj)
❖ τοξίνη

12.59 fatal (adj) /ˈfeɪtl/
deadly • *He never looked after his health and at the age of 60 he died of a fatal heart attack.*
➢ fatality ❖ μοιραίος

12.60 thrill (n) /θrɪl/
an exciting experience • *People do bungee-jumping for the thrill of the experience.* ➢ thrill (v), thrilling (adj) ❖ συγκίνηση, συγκλονιστική εμπειρία

12.61 plentiful (adj) /ˈplentɪfl/
abundant • *Fruit is plentiful in the summer.*
❖ άφθονος

12.62 thorn (n) /θɔːn/
a small sharp pointed part of a plant • *Careful! Those roses have thorns.* ❖ αγκάθι

12.63 husk (n) /hʌsk/
the dry outer part of some seeds and nuts
• *Remove the husk and put the corn on a plate.*
❖ φλοιός

12.64 odour (n) /ˈəʊdə(r)/
a smell, especially an unpleasant one • *How can I remove the odour of cooking from my curtains?*
❖ (δυσάρεστη) οσμή, μυρωδιά

12.65 overpowering (adj) /ˌəʊvəˈpaʊərɪŋ/
very strong or powerful • *There's an overpowering smell of fish in the kitchen.* ➢ overpower (v)
❖ ακατάσχετος

Describing food
bitter   low-fat
crunchy   tasty
deep-fried

Insects
bug   grasshopper
cockroach   termite
creepy-crawly

Vocabulary
page 150

12.66 mineral (n) /ˈmɪnərəl/
a natural substance found in food which your body needs to stay healthy • *Calcium is a mineral found naturally in milk.* ❖ μέταλλα
(πχ μαγνήσιο, ασβέστιο κλπ)

12.67 digest (v) /daɪˈdʒest/
change food in your stomach into substances that your body can use • *Some people can't digest dairy products easily.* ➢ digestion (n), digestive (adj)
❖ χωνεύω

12.68 calcium (n) /ˈkælsɪəm/
a mineral that is necessary for strong bones
• *Children need calcium for their bones to grow well.*
❖ ασβέστιο

12.69 cure (n) /kjʊə/
sth that makes you well • *Grandma always said a cup of tea is a cure for any problem.*
➢ cure (v) ❖ θεραπεία

12.70 workout (n) /ˈwɜːkaʊt/
an exercise routine • *He does a workout every evening at the gym.* ❖ προπόνηση

12.71 obese (adj) /əʊˈbiːs/
very fat • *He weighed 120 kilos and was warned by his doctor that he was obese.*
➢ obesity (n) ❖ παχύσαρκος

12.72 session (n) /ˈseʃn/
a period of time spent doing a particular activity
• *The athlete broke his leg in a training session.*
❖ συνεδρία, συνεδρίαση

12.73 immune (adj) /ɪˈmjuːn/
If you are immune to a disease, you cannot catch it. • *I had chickenpox when I was a child, so I am immune to it.* ➢ immunity (n) ❖ έχω ανοσία

12.74 operate (v) /ˈɒpəreɪt/
cut into sb's body to repair or remove a part that is damaged • *The surgeon must operate on you to remove your appendix.* ➢ operation (n)
❖ εγχειρίζω

12.75 sick of (adj) /sɪk ɒv/
fed up with • *I'm sick of this wet weather. I wish it were sunny.* ❖ βαρέθηκα

12.76 diabetes (pl n) /daɪəˈbiːtiːz/
a condition when sb has too much sugar in their blood • *He has diabetes, so he cannot eat sweets.*
➢ diabetic (n) ❖ ζάχαρο

12.77 break out (in sth) (phr v) /breɪk aʊt (ɪn ˈsʌmθɪŋ)/
If you break out in a rash, spots, etc, they suddenly appear on your skin. • *I break out in spots if I eat chocolate.* ❖ γεμίζω με, βγάζω (π.χ. εξάνθημα)

12.78 surgeon (n) /ˈsɜːdʒn/
a doctor who performs operations • *The surgeon operated on my knee.* ➢ surgery (n), surgical (adj)
❖ χειρούργος

12.79 chickenpox (n) /ˈtʃɪkɪn pɒks/
an infectious illness which causes spots on your skin and a fever • *The child caught chickenpox at nursery school.* ❖ ανεμοβλογιά

12.80 braces (pl n) /ˈbreɪsɪz/
metal wires that people wear on their teeth to make them grow straight • *Charlie got braces because his front teeth stick out.* ❖ σιδεράκια

12.81 contact lenses (pl n) /ˈkɒntækt ˈlensɪz/
a small round piece of plastic that you put on your eye to help you see clearly • *The actor had to wear blue contact lenses for the role.* ❖ φακοί επαφής

12.82 first-aid kit (n) /fɜːst-eɪd kɪt/
a box with things you need in case sb is hurt • *There is a first-aid kit in the bathroom with some painkillers in it.* ❖ φαρμακείο με πρώτες βοήθειες

12.83 hot water bottle (n) /hɒt ˈwɔːtə ˈbɒtl/
a rubber container full of hot water, used to make a bed warm • *It was a very cold night so I put a hot water bottle in my bed to keep me warm.* ❖ θερμοφόρα

12.84 stethoscope (n) /ˈsteθəskəʊp/
an instrument used for listening to sb's chest • *The doctor listened to my heart with a stethoscope.* ❖ στηθοσκόπιο

Grammar page 151

12.85 sneeze (v) /sniːz/
If you sneeze, air suddenly comes from your nose, making a noise. • *Pepper can make you sneeze.* ➢ sneeze (n) ❖ φτερνίζομαι

Listening page 152

12.86 apply (v) /əˈplaɪ/
put sth such as paint or cream on a surface • *Apply the cream to your face.* ❖ απλώνω, βάζω

12.87 commentator (n) /ˈkɒmənteɪtə(r)/
sb who describes an event while it is happening on television or radio
• *Why do sports commentators always shout?*
❖ παρουσιαστής, σχολιαστής

12.88 pork (n) /pɔːk/
meat from a pig • *Do you eat pork?*
❖ χοιρινό κρέας

Speaking page 153

12.89 be obsessed (with) (expr) /bi əbˈsest wɪð/
think or worry about sth all the time so that you cannot think about anything else • *He's so obsessed with money!* ➢ obsession (n) ❖ έχω μανία (με), με απασχολεί κάτι υπερβολικά

Grammar page 154

12.90 shift (n) /ʃɪft/
a period of time during the day or night when sb works • *Are you on the night shift this week?*
❖ βάρδια

12.91 under no circumstances (expr) /ˈʌndə nəʊ ˈsɜːkəmstənsɪz/
not for any reason • *Under no circumstances should you open that door.* ❖ σε καμία περίπτωση

12.92 miracle (n) /ˈmɪrəkl/
sth that happens or works in a way that you did not expect was possible • *There is no miracle cure for cancer.* ❖ θαυματουργός, θαύμα

12.93 anti-wrinkle cream (n) /ænti rɪŋkl kriːm/
a cream that promises to stop or reduce the signs of ageing on sb's skin • *Do anti-wrinkle creams really work?* ❖ αντιρυτιδική κρέμα

12.94 wound (n) /wuːnd/
an injury made by a knife or bullet • *The soldier's wound prevented me from walking.* ➢ wound (v), wounded (adj) ❖ πληγή, τραύμα

12.95 gauze (n) /gɔːz/
thin cotton with very small holes in it that is used for tying around a wound • *The nurse placed gauze over the cut to keep it clean.* ❖ γάζα

12.96 infected (adj) /ɪnˈfektɪd/
full of bacteria (= small living things that can cause disease) • *The cut on her finger had become infected.* ➢ infect (v), infection (n)
❖ μολυσμένος

12.97 low-calorie (adj) /ləʊ-ˈkæləri/
Low-calorie food has few calories (units for measuring the amount of energy that food will produce) • *Eat low-calorie food to lose weight.*
❖ χαμηλό σε θερμίδες

12.98 elegant (adj) /ˈelɪɡənt/
attractive and designed well • *She was wearing an elegant blue dress.* ➢ elegance (n)
❖ καλαίσθητος, σικάτος

12.99 crisp (adj) /krɪsp/
pleasantly hard when you bite it • *He bit into the crisp biscuit.* ❖ τραγανός

12.100 powdered (adj) /ˈpaʊdəd/
• *I don't like powdered milk in my coffee.* ➢ powder (n, v) ❖ σε σκόνη

12.101 ingredient (n) /ɪŋˈɡriːdiənt/
one of the foods that you use to make a particular food • *The main ingredient in bread is flour.*
❖ συστατικό

12.102 oven (n) /ˈʌvn/
a piece of equipment shaped like a box with a door on the front in which food is cooked
• *She took the cake out of the oven.* ❖ φούρνος

Use your English page 155

12.103 come round (phr v) /kʌm raʊnd/
become conscious again • *She fainted and it took a few minutes for her to come round.*
❖ συνέρχομαι

12.104 come down with (phr v) /kʌm daʊn wɪð/
get an illness • *He's not going to work as he's come down with a cold.* ❖ αρρωσταίνω

12.105 fight off (phr v) /faɪt ɒf/
try hard to get rid of sth like an illness • *Regular exercise improves your immune system, which helps you fight off infections.* ❖ καταπολεμώ

12.106 get over (phr v) /ɡet ˈəʊvə/
get better from an illness • *It took me ten days to get over that terrible flu.* ❖ ξεπερνώ, αναρρώνω

12.107 pass out (phr v) /pɑːs aʊt/
faint; lose consciousness • *It was so hot and airless in the room that I passed out.* ❖ λιποθυμώ

12.108 resist (v) /rɪˈzɪst/
not be harmed by sth • *If you drink this hot soup, it will help you resist a bad cold.* ➢ resistance (n)
❖ καταπολεμώ

12.109 faint (v) /feɪnt/
lose consciousness • *Mum fainted when she heard the bad news.* ❖ λιποθυμώ

12.110 recover (v) /rɪˈkʌvə/
get better after an illness • *He recovered from his cold and went back to work.* ➢ recovery (n)
❖ συνέρχομαι, αναρρώνω

12.111 flu (n) /fluː/
a common illness like a very bad cold, which you can get from other people • *Mike is still in bed with the flu.* ❖ γρίπη

12.112 sufficient (adj) /səˈfɪʃənt/
enough • *Is there a sufficient amount of milk in the fridge for the weekend?* ➢ sufficiently (adv)
❖ αρκετός

12.113 supply (n) /səˈplaɪ/
an amount of sth that is available for use • *Always take a large supply of food with you when you go camping.* ➢ supply (v) ❖ απόθεμα, προμήθειες

12.114 nutrient (n) /ˈnjuːtrɪənt/
a chemical or food that plants and animals need to live and grow • *There are nutrients in the ground which help plants grow.* ❖ θρεπτική ουσία

12.115 intake (n) /ˈɪnteɪk/
the amount of sth that you eat or drink
• *You need to reduce your daily sugar intake.*
❖ κατανάλωση

12.116 recovery (n) /rɪˈkʌvəri/
when you are well again after an illness
• *The doctor says she will make a full recovery.*
➢ recover (v) ❖ ανάρρωση

12.117 appetite (n) /ˈæpɪtaɪt/
a desire for food • *He has an enormous appetite and eats enough for three people.*
➢ appetising (adj) ❖ όρεξη

12.118 temperature (n) /ˈtemprətʃə/
how hot or cold sb is • *Mum took my temperature with a thermometer.* ❖ θερμοκρασία

12.119 prescription (n) /prɪˈskrɪpʃn/
a piece of paper where a doctor writes what medicine a sick person should get from a pharmacist • *The doctor gave her a prescription for painkillers.* ➢ prescribe (v) ❖ συνταγή (γιατρού)

12.120 in bad shape (expr) /ɪn bæd ʃeɪp/
unfit • *Dave is in bad shape. He should start working out.* ❖ σε κακή φόρμα

12.121 under the weather (expr) /ˈʌndə ðə ˈweðə/
ill; not feeling very well • *I'm feeling under the weather, so I think I'll stay in bed.* ❖ αδιάθετος

12.122 up and about (expr) /ʌp ənd əˈbaʊt/
recovered • *He was ill in bed last week, but now he's up and about again.*
❖ υγιής και όρθιος

Writing: a review

pages 156–157

12.123 all in all (expr) /ɔːl ɪn ɔːl/
considering everything • *All in all, it was a good year.* ❖ γενικά, λαμβάνοντας τα πάντα υπόψη

12.124 chill out (phr v) /tʃɪl aʊt/
relax • *They chill out in front of the TV in the evening.* ❖ χαλαρώνω

12.125 reasonable (adj) /ˈriːzənəbl/
fair and sensible • *The prices at this shop are reasonable, so I'm sure you can afford to buy that shirt.* ❖ λογικός

12.126 convenient (adj) /kənˈviːniənt/
easy to get to; near a place • *Our new flat is very convenient for our school.*
➢ convenience (n) ❖ βολικός
✎ Opp: inconvenient

12.127 brand new (adj) /ˌbrænd ˈnjuː/
completely new • *This is my brand new car!*
❖ ολοκαίνουριος

12.128 spotless (adj) /ˈspɒtləs/
very clean • *The house was spotless after she had finished the housework.* ❖ πεντακάθαρος

12.129 state of the art (adj) /steɪt əv ðiː ɑːt/
very modern • *The equipment at this gym is state of the art.* ❖ τελευταίας τεχνολογίας

12.130 membership (n) /ˈmembəʃɪp/
the state of being a member of a group or a club, etc • *At our gym, you get a free T-shirt and a bag when you pay for your membership.*
❖ ιδιότητα μέλους

12.131 bland (adj) /blænd/
not having a strong or interesting taste • *The restaurant was nice, but the food was bland.*
❖ άνοστος, άγευστος

12.132 overpriced (adj) /ˌəʊvəˈpraɪst/
more expensive than sth is worth • *The clothes in this shop are overpriced.* ❖ υπερτιμημένος, πανάκριβος

12.133 fully-booked (adj) /ˈfʊli-bʊkt/
A fully-booked flight, performance, etc has no more seats available. • *We couldn't reserve a table at the restaurant as it was fully-booked.* ❖ γεμάτος, κλεισμένος

Video: Living in the Slow Lane page 158

12.134 slow lane (n) /sləʊ leɪn/
a calm and relaxed lifestyle • *He lives life in the slow lane and never rushes about.* ❖ ήρεμη ζωή

12.135 movement (n) /ˈmuːvmənt/
a group of people with the same ideas or beliefs • *The LAA movement are trying to stop animal testing.* ❖ κίνημα

12.136 brand (n) /brænd/
a product made by a particular company that has a particular name or design • *My favourite brand of chocolate is Ion.* ❖ μάρκα

12.137 die out (phr v) /daɪ aʊt/
when a species or a tradition disappears • *It's sad, but many traditions are dying out.* ❖ εξαφανίζομαι (για είδη ή παραδόσεις)

12.138 preserve (v) /prɪˈzɜːv/
protect • *The old way of life in this village is being preserved by the locals.* ➢ preservation (n) ❖ προστατεύω

12.139 step in (phr v) /step ɪn/
become involved in sth • *They were going to knock down the building, but the mayor stepped in and saved it.* ❖ επεμβαίνω για να βοηθήσω

12.140 promote (v) /prəˈməʊt/
help sell sth by advertising it • *They are promoting organic food products at the market.* ➢ promotion (n) ❖ προωθώ

Phrasal verbs

break out in sth	get over
chill out	pass out
come down with	put off
come round	step in
die out	stick to
fight off	

Vocabulary Exercises

A Complete the table.

Nouns	Adjectives
taste	1
crunch	2
bitterness	3
reason	4
fatality	5
plenty	6
abundance	7
balance	8

B Match. Then write the words.

1 grass — pox _____
2 first-aid — roach _____
3 chicken — bottle _____
4 hot water — lenses _____
5 cock — weed _____
6 sea — hopper _____
7 contact — mound _____
8 termite — kit _____

C Choose the correct answers.

1. This cheese is a rare ___ and you can't buy it most supermarkets.
   a delicacy   b pulp   c paste

2. A ___ diet is essential for good health.
   a filling   b processed   c balanced

3. I'm not very hungry, so I'll opt ___ a light salad for lunch.
   a into   b up   c for

4. It's not wise to ___ breakfast as it gives you an energy boost you need.
   a skip   b grate   c digest

5. The secret ___ in this recipe is honey.
   a calcium   b ingredient   c mineral

6. You should start eating well and exercising for the ___ of your health.
   a motion   b sake   c whiff

7. Green peppers are good for you. They're ___ with vitamin C.
   a packed   b filled   c boosted

8. She is ___ in her tastes, so I doubt if she will eat Malaysian food.
   a catching   b spotless   c conservative

D Choose the correct answers.

1. If you are allergic to milk, it ___
   a will make you strong.   b will make you feel sick.

2. When something makes your mouth water, ___
   a you feel hungry.   b you feel full.

3. If a job falls to you, ___
   a you manage to avoid it.   b you become responsible for it.

4. A low-calorie diet ___
   a is fattening.   b helps you lose weight.

5. Somebody who is scared of creepy crawlies ___
   a doesn't like birds.   b doesn't like insects.

6. If you are obsessed with something, ___
   a you are tired of it.   b you think about it all the time.

7. When you are under the weather, you ___
   a feel ill.   b feel cold.

8. Somebody who is sick of their job ___
   a hates it.   b got fired.

12 Grammar

12.1 Wish & If only

Χρησιμοποιούμε *wish* για να μιλήσουμε για μια κατάσταση ή πράξη για την οποία δεν είμαστε ικανοποιημένοι ή ευχαριστημένοι, ή για να πούμε ότι θα θέλαμε κάτι να είναι διαφορετικό.

Χρησιμοποιούμε *wish* + past tense για να μιλήσουμε για το παρόν ή το μέλλον.
→ *I **wish** I **weren't** allergic to dairy products.*

Χρησιμοποιούμε *wish* + past perfect για να μιλήσουμε για το παρελθόν.
→ *I **wish** I **had remembered** to bring my glasses.*

Χρησιμοποιούμε *wish* + *would* + bare infinitive όταν μιλάμε για τις ενοχλητικές συνήθειες των άλλων, ή όταν θα θέλαμε κάτι να είναι διαφορετικό στο μέλλον. Το χρησιμοποιούμε για πράξεις και όχι για καταστάσεις. Το χρησιμοποιούμε μόνο όταν τα υποκείμενα είναι διαφορετικά.
→ *I **wish** you **would reduce** your intake of sugar.*
→ *I **wish** more health-food restaurants **would open** up in the area.*

Μπορούμε να χρησιμοποιήσουμε *If only* στη θέση του *wish* σε καταφατικές και αρνητικές προτάσεις.
→ ***If only** the local gym had an indoor swimming pool.*
→ ***If only** I hadn't dropped my contact lenses on the street.*

12.2 Had better

Συνήθως χρησιμοποιούμε *had better* για να δώσουμε μια συμβουλή για μια συγκεκριμένη περίπτωση στο παρόν ή στο μέλλον. Ακολουθείται από απαρέμφατο χωρίς *to*.
→ *You**'d better stay** home if you have a runny nose.*

Σημείωση: Κάποιες φορές χρησιμοποιούμε *had better* για να εκφράσουμε μια απειλή.
→ *You**'d better not bring** those snails in the house or you'll be in big trouble!*

12.3 It's (about/high) time

Μπορούμε να χρησιμοποιήσουμε *it's time*, *it's about time* και *it's high time* + past simple για να μιλήσουμε για κάτι που έπρεπε να έχει ήδη γίνει στο παρόν.
→ ***It's time** you **learned** about the food pyramid.*
→ ***It's about time** she **saw** a doctor about her cough.*
→ ***It's high time** Jack **got rid of** that old bike.*

12.4 Would rather

Χρησιμοποιούμε *would rather* για να δείξουμε κάποια προτίμηση στο παρόν ή στο μέλλον. Χρησιμοποιούμε *would rather* + απαρέμφατο χωρίς *to* όταν μιλάμε για τον εαυτό μας.
→ *I **would rather make** a salad than order a pizza.*

Χρησιμοποιούμε *would rather* + αντωνυμία + past tense, όταν μιλάμε για κάποιο άλλο πρόσωπο στο παρόν ή στο μέλλον.
→ *I**'d rather you didn't borrow** the hot water bottle without asking first.*

12.5 Would prefer & Prefer

Χρησιμοποιούμε *would prefer* για να δείξουμε προτίμηση σε μια συγκεκριμένη περίπτωση (και όχι γενικά).
Μπορούμε να χρησιμοποιήσουμε:
would prefer + ουσιαστικό
→ *'Would you like mayonnaise or butter in your sandwich?' 'I**'d prefer mayonnaise**.'*
would prefer + full infinitive
→ *I **would prefer to go** to the gym tonight.*
would prefer + full infinitive + *rather than* + bare infinitive.
→ *I **would prefer to bake** some cookies tonight **rather than watch** TV.*

Χρησιμοποιούμε *prefer* για να δείξουμε γενική προτίμηση.
Μπορούμε να χρησιμοποιήσουμε:
prefer + ουσιαστικό
→ My grandfather **prefers tea** (to coffee).
prefer + full infinitive + *than* + bare infinitive
→ My grandfather **prefers to drink** tea **than drink** coffee.
prefer + -ing + to + -ing
→ My grandfather **prefers drinking** tea **to drinking** coffee.

Σημείωση: Μπορούμε επίσης να χρησιμοποιήσουμε *prefer* με *rather than*.
→ My grandfather **prefers** to drink tea **rather than** (drink) coffee.

12.6 Be used to & Get used to

Χρησιμοποιούμε *be used to* + γερούνδιο/ουσιαστικό για να μιλήσουμε για πράξεις ή καταστάσεις που μας είναι συνηθισμένες ή οικείες.
→ Boris **is used to meeting** people from different cultures because he is an anthropologist.

Χρησιμοποιούμε *get used to* + γερούνδιο/ουσιαστικό για να πούμε ότι μια πράξη ή κατάσταση αρχίζει να γίνεται συνηθισμένη ή οικεία.
→ She **is getting used to wearing** glasses.

Σημείωση: Τα ρήματα *be* και *get* αλλάζουν ανάλογα με το χρόνο του ρήματος που χρειάζεται η πρόταση.
→ Brenda **was used to making** her own yoghurt as she'd lived on a farm.
→ I**'ve been getting used to doing** a daily workout.

12.7 Inversion

Μπορούμε να χρησιμοποιήσουμε φράσεις όπως *never, not only ... but also ..., under no circumstances, little, rarely/seldom, not once, only then, no sooner ... than..., hardly ... when ...* στην αρχή μιας πρότασης για να δώσουμε έμφαση. Όταν το κάνουμε αυτό, η σειρά των λέξεων αλλάζει. Αυτό ονομάζεται inversion (αντιστροφή).
→ **Felix has never eaten** junk food.
→ **Never has Felix eaten** junk food.
→ **Dairy products are not only** tasty, **but** they are **also** good for you.
→ **Not only are dairy products** tasty, **but** they are **also** good for you.
→ **You shouldn't go** near a poisonous snake **under any circumstances**.
→ **Under no circumstances should you go** near a poisonous snake.
→ **He had no idea** his younger sister was suffering from anorexia.
→ **Little did he know** his younger sister was suffering from anorexia.
→ **We rarely/seldom use** butter as we prefer margarine.
→ **Rarely/Seldom do we use** butter as we prefer margarine.
→ **My best friend didn't tell me once** that he was suffering from high blood pressure.
→ **Not once did my best friend tell me** that he was suffering from high blood pressure.
→ **I didn't realise how unhealthy my diet was until** I visited the doctor.
→ I visited the doctor. **Only then did I realise how unhealthy my diet was.**
→ Clara passed out **as soon as she saw** the cockroach.
→ **No sooner had Clara seen** the cockroach **than** she passed out.
→ **When the kids came** home from school, their mum gave them chocolate chip cookies and milk.
→ **Hardly had the kids come** home from school **when** their mum gave them chocolate chip cookies and milk.

Σημείωση: Μπορούμε να χρησιμοποιήσουμε την αντιστροφή και σε κάποια είδη του υποθετικού λόγου (conditional). Η αντεστραμμένη μορφή αντικαθιστά την πρόταση με το *if*.
→ **Had I known** she didn't eat meat, I would have made a vegetarian meal.
→ **If I had known** she didn't eat meat, I would have made a vegetarian meal.
→ **Should you decide** to take part in the marathon, we can train together.
→ **If you decide** to take part in the marathon, we can train together.

12 Grammar

Grammar Exercises

A Match.

1. I'm getting fat and I wish
2. He would rather
3. He would prefer
4. It's high
5. Jack likes sport but prefers
6. You look tired, so you had
7. I would rather you
8. Janet is sick again. If

a. to chill out at home tonight.
b. time you paid your gym fees.
c. I could stick to a diet.
d. better get some rest.
e. only she had been more careful.
f. didn't skip meals.
g. go to a restaurant than cook.
h. playing football to playing basketball.

B Circle.

1. I wish you would take / had taken up a sport or do some exercise.
2. If only we wouldn't walk / hadn't walked in the hot sun yesterday.
3. You had better include / including more fibre in your diet.
4. I prefer work / working out in the gym.
5. It's about time you stop / stopped smoking.
6. I wish I didn't eat / hadn't eaten those snails.
7. She would rather become / became a surgeon than a pediatrician.
8. We would prefer skipping / to skip dessert.

C Complete the sentences with these words.

| are | get | had | little | once | only | seldom | sooner | then | under |

1. No _____ had she got over one cold than she caught another.
2. I still can't _____ used to eating foreign food.
3. _____ no circumstances should you eat a pufferfish.
4. _____ did he know that his obesity would cause a heart attack.
5. We _____ used to our fitness regime after doing it for a couple of months.
6. _____ does he go the park now that it gets dark early.
7. Not _____ have we got oysters on the menu, but also fresh sea urchins.
8. Not _____ has he told me if he likes my cooking.
9. _____ we known the restaurant was fully-booked, we would have gone elsewhere.
10. Only _____ did they realise that this was an emergency.

Use your English

Exam Task

For questions **1–8**, complete the second sentence so that it has a similar meaning to the first sentence, using the word given. **Do not change the word given.** You must use between **two** and **five** words, including the word given.

1 George works out and has a balanced diet.
 ONLY
 George not _____ has a balanced diet.

2 Her father told her she must never take up paragliding.
 CIRCUMSTANCES
 Her father told her that _____ take up paragliding.

3 Although he felt under the weather, he didn't know he was seriously ill.
 LITTLE
 Although he felt under the weather, _____ he was seriously ill.

4 I think you should see a doctor immediately.
 BETTER
 I think you _____ immediately.

5 You should have phoned for the takeaway ages ago.
 HIGH
 It is _____ for the takeaway.

6 It was freezing, so we made hot chocolate as soon as we got home.
 SOONER
 It was freezing, so _____ home than we made hot chocolate.

7 The doctor has never given me a prescription.
 ONCE
 Not _____ me a prescription.

8 I am really sorry you aren't here with me.
 ONLY
 If _____ you were here with me.

Alphabetical Word List

An alphabetical list of all the words that appear in the Companion follows. The number next to the entry shows where the word appears.

(the) press 3.54

A

a bite to eat 6.68
a fair bit 6.26
a wealth of 11.112
abandoned 4.94
abolishment 7.149
abroad 2.153
absence 1.111
abundant 12.13
accent 11.4
access 3.46
accommodation 4.88
accomplish 6.134
accomplished 3.69
accomplishment 3.55
account 3.82
account for 8.23
accountant 9.22
accuse 7.84
achieve 1.154
achievement 6.38
acid rain 8.105
acrophobia 1.134
activate 1.45
actual 9.139
adapt 5.101
adaptable 10.4
addict 5.72
admire 4.137
admit 8.84
adolescent 7.120
adopt 1.54
adoptive parent 7.154
advancement 2.105
advantageous 10.105
adventure seeker 6.79
affair 8.1
affect 1.83
affection 10.27
against the law 7.138
agent 3.127
aggressive 5.70
agriculture 2.103
air force 2.117
airborne 8.10
all in all 12.123
alley 4.16
alley 6.44
almond eyes 11.24
alone 1.85
alongside 3.51
alternative 7.25
alternative energy 4.134
amateur 3.97
amazement 1.70
amputate 5.121

amputee 5.122
amusement park 6.4
an eye for sth 9.83
ancestor 3.34
anger management 7.56
animal shelter 6.11
animatedly 11.20
announce 1.68
annoy 1.95
annually 6.93
answering machine 5.55
antiquities 3.45
anti-wrinkle cream 12.93
anxiety 1.6
anxiety 4.110
anxious 1.117
appeal (to) 9.86
appetite 12.117
appliance 5.95
applicant 9.42
apply 9.49
apply 12.86
appreciate 4.138
apprentice 9.64
apprenticeship 10.68
approach 4.47
approval 7.59
aqua park 6.98
aquarium 10.100
archaeologist 2.106
arid 11.131
armed (with) 11.12
armed robber 1.40
around-the-clock 10.42
arrange 10.37
arrest 7.97
arrogant 3.147
arson 7.5
artificial 5.119
artificial intelligence 5.100
ashore 11.93
aspect 2.50
aspect 5.109
assemble 9.144
assessment 10.7
assignment 10.65
assistant 9.50
Assyrian 2.111
asteroid 3.16
astounding 5.135
astrophysicist 5.21
at a loss for words 1.66
at a price 3.126
at last 3.149
at your earliest convenience 9.126
atmosphere 5.17
attach 9.2
attempt 5.123
attend 1.149

attendance 7.55
attitude 9.119
attraction 6.13
audition 3.114
auditory 5.68
authentic 10.50
authority 7.58
automatic 1.14
availability 2.1
avenue 4.43
aviator 3.95
award 1.90
award 6.58
aware (of) 1.30
awe 6.16

B

background 1.162
backpacking 11.74
baggage 11.67
balanced diet 12.18
bank 7.110
barely 2.18
barricade 3.3
bat 5.29
bay 11.43
be in agony 1.63
be just around the corner 9.117
be made redundant 9.67
be obsessed (with) 12.89
be over 11.33
be worth the effort 2.146
beam 5.8
bean 12.3
bearer of bad news 9.14
beat 11.124
bed and breakfast 11.54
behind the scenes 3.132
belief 2.48
beloved 1.79
benefit 1.163
best-seller 9.82
beyond 1.174
billionaire 8.80
bitter 12.48
bitterly 3.148
blade 8.21
bland 12.131
blanket 8.49
blind 10.3
block out 8.107
blow over 8.108
board 6.45
board 11.14
board up 4.96
boarding pass 11.66
boarding school 10.80
body language 1.3

boiling 6.89
bold 4.145
bone 9.133
book into 11.106
boost 12.47
boot 9.76
bottle up 1.127
bounce 5.31
bounce ideas off sb 9.12
bound 6.8
boundary 2.7
braces 12.80
branch 9.101
brand 12.136
brand new 12.127
break down 11.42
break in 3.111
break out 1.53
break out (in sth) 12.77
breathe 1.140
breathe out 8.128
breed 10.10
breeze through 10.86
breezy 8.12
briefcase 9.99
bright 10.53
brighten up 4.99
bring to justice 7.117
broaden your horizons 11.92
browse 6.69
brush up 10.87
bucket 4.144
bug 12.23
bully 9.81
bump into 6.42
bumper car 6.17
burglar alarm 7.127
burglary 7.6
burial place 3.9
burst into 1.128
burst into flames 8.109
bury 3.30
butcher 9.95
buzz 4.19
by all accounts 3.131

C

cabin crew 11.68
calcium 12.68
call back 2.120
call for 2.125
call in 2.126
call off 2.121
call on 2.124
call out 2.123
call round 2.119
call up 2.122
calm down 1.129

146

camper van   11.91
canal   2.59
cancel   2.131
candidate   9.17
canvas   4.98
canyon   6.117
capable   6.55
capture   5.37
caravan   2.81
carbohydrate   12.46
carbon dioxide   8.45
carry out   1.35
carton   4.90
carve   8.7
case   7.39
cash machine   5.56
cashier   9.94
cast   9.129
catalogue   6.94
catch fire   8.114
catch on   2.29
cease   4.132
celebrity   3.8
cement   4.122
ceremony   10.97
chain   2.28
chain   6.9
challenge   4.124
changing room   9.78
chaos   11.11
charity   6.21
charm   3.22
charm   4.100
chatter   3.58
chatty   1.148
cheat   1.82
check in   11.107
check out   11.108
check-out   5.83
cheer up   1.108
cheerful   9.120
chemical reaction   8.129
chestnut   9.75
chicken out   1.130
chickenpox   12.79
chill out   12.124
choir   2.163
chubby   12.55
chunk   10.99
circuit   6.46
circulate   3.118
citizen   4.63
city break   11.90
civil engineering   10.61
civilisation   2.67
claim   4.74
class register   10.96
claustrophobia   1.135
clean record   7.65
clerk   7.74
client   9.23
cliff   1.104
climate change   2.26
coach   10.58
coal   8.53
coast   4.70
coastal   8.35

cockroach   12.30
coin   3.18
collapse   4.61
colleague   6.43
column   5.107
come across   4.117
come down with   12.104
come in for   3.116
come round   12.103
come to a halt   4.131
come to life   4.97
come up with   2.98
comment   3.83
commentator   12.87
commercial   4.36
commit   7.77
commit suicide   3.29
commitment   6.113
common sense   4.17
communicate   1.4
community   1.168
community member   2.156
community service   7.49
commute   9.52
companionship   10.16
company   2.22
compass   6.72
complain   8.85
complicated   5.43
compulsory   10.94
compute   9.51
computer hacking   7.7
concentrate (on)   1.31
concept   2.49
concern   2.35
concerned   6.22
conclude   2.152
conditions   2.44
conduct   2.80
conference   9.103
confess   7.82
confidence   1.71
Confucianism   3.158
confused   7.118
connect   2.23
connected (to)   1.43
conquer   2.89
conscious   1.28
consequence   7.64
consequently   5.114
conservation   10.101
conservative   12.22
conserve   8.56
consider   7.143
consist of   6.130
constant   4.64
construct   9.140
construction   4.123
consult   6.123
consume   8.57
contact lens   12.81
container   6.80
contestant   3.90
contract   9.66
contribute   2.91
convenient   12.126
conventional   7.62

convey   1.87
convinced   3.49
convinced   4.87
co-operation   2.38
coordinates   6.81
co-ordinator   9.123
cope (with)   1.145
cosmonaut   3.99
cosmopolitan   1.164
cost   5.66
costly   5.3
couch   3.140
counsellor   9.124
count   5.59
count (for)   7.61
course   6.47
court   6.48
court   7.20
courtroom   7.29
cove   11.61
cover   9.58
co-worker   9.27
craftsman   9.128
cramped   4.7
crawl   12.25
creativity   9.6
creepy-crawly   12.31
criminal act   7.32
crisp   12.99
critical   9.41
criticise   8.98
criticism   3.121
crop   8.17
crude oil   8.58
crumbling   4.95
crunchy   12.27
cuisine   2.65
culprit   7.119
cultural ambassador   1.157
cultural awareness   2.149
culture   1.175
cure   12.69
curfew   7.146
current   8.62
current   9.87
current affairs   5.111
custom   1.155
customs   11.49
CV   9.90

D

dairy product   2.30
date back (to)   2.114
day pack   11.2
deadline   10.64
deadly   7.92
deal   4.148
deal   6.65
deal with   1.21
decade   3.25
declare   11.70
decline v   3.171
decrease   8.133
deep-fried   12.29
defeat   3.27
defence   7.36

defendant   7.30
deforestation   8.60
defy   6.2
degrade   5.25
degree   6.32
delay   11.71
delicacy   12.7
delta   8.63
demolish   7.95
demonstrator   7.96
density   4.111
deny   7.69
departure lounge   11.50
depend (on)   5.110
depend on   4.15
depiction   2.110
deport   7.130
depression   1.132
depth   5.40
descent   6.118
deserve   5.105
desire   1.142
desperately   3.143
destination   8.121
destroy   2.12
detect   5.44
deter   7.122
determination   5.11
determine   5.30
device   5.85
devote   7.38
diabetes   12.76
die out   12.137
dietary   2.39
dig   2.107
digest   12.67
digital camera   5.79
dimension   4.136
directions   11.114
disability   10.19
disabled   10.35
disadvantaged person   4.12
disappointed   1.110
disapproval   7.60
disastrous   1.137
discount   6.92
discourage   8.95
discrimination   4.2
disease   10.22
disgrace   3.73
disgust   1.5
dismiss   7.85
dismiss   9.60
disorientated   5.127
display   9.137
distant   11.56
distinct   1.153
distinctive   4.92
distinctive   11.5
distort   5.9
distraction   10.6
distressed   11.19
district   2.159
divorce   5.98
do away with   7.131
do business   2.144
dock   11.52

147

dog sledding 2.66
domestic flight 11.41
domesticate 2.82
donate 10.51
donor 10.44
down 1.125
downpour 8.64
downtown 1.124
draught 8.39
drawback 5.113
drawer 11.34
drill 9.143
drive-through 2.62
drop out 10.81
drought 8.40
dump 8.122
dutiful 3.173
dweller 4.62
dynasty 3.163
dyslexic 10.54

E

eager 1.96
earthquake 3.36
echo 5.32
ecosystem 8.36
ecstatic 7.113
edge 2.8
effect 1.84
effective 9.38
effectively 2.147
efficient 2.75
effort 3.56
effortless 6.126
elect 2.88
electrician 2.127
electricity 4.127
electricity supply 5.93
elegant 12.98
eligible 7.42
embark 10.23
emission 8.42
emit 5.12
emotion 1.1
empire 2.133
employee 9.53
employer 9.43
employment 2.13
enable 1.57
endangered 8.102
enemy 3.53
engage (in) 6.35
enquire 8.86
enquiry 9.45
enrich 2.151
enrol 10.55
entertainment 3.105
enthusiasm 1.93
entirely 4.85
entitled 5.108
entrance fee 6.116
envelope 3.136
environmentally-friendly 8.99
equation 5.81
Equator 8.15
erosion 8.61
essential 4.135

establish 2.94
estate agent 4.59
estimate 4.93
ethnicity 1.165
evaluate 1.52
evaporation 8.37
event 2.43
eventually 3.157
evident 5.73
evolutionary 1.49
excavation 3.40
excess 11.65
excessive 1.136
exchange 2.55
exchange programme 10.98
excursion 5.47
exhaust fumes 8.124
exhausted 7.114
exhibit 6.60
expand 2.53
expansion 4.120
experience 1.89
experience 1.78
explode 1.123
exploration 4.141
explorer 3.96
explosion 8.77
export 2.68
expose 5.128
express 1.61
express doubt 8.97
extend 2.54
extensive 2.76
external modem 5.77
extinct 8.103
extract 11.37
extraordinary 5.28
extreme 1.115
extremely 1.48
eyesight 10.49

F

facial expression 1.2
faculty 10.63
fail (to) 3.41
faint 12.109
fair 9.85
fairness 2.167
fall to 12.50
fan 3.81
fancy 8.76
faraway 11.57
farming 2.99
fatal 12.59
faulty 5.80
favela 4.5
fearful 1.22
feedback 9.40
feel up to sth 6.83
fellow 11.17
fibre 12.44
field 1.170
field 6.49
fight off 12.105
figure 3.63
figure out 10.88
fill in 9.106

film projector 5.76
filthy 5.54
finance department 9.57
financial 7.3
find out 1.8
findings 6.39
fine 7.37
finish line 6.59
fire 9.59
fire department 7.50
first-aid kit 12.82
fit 9.37
fit 7.121
fit (with) 5.38
fixed 3.104
flame 6.84
flatmate 4.28
flight attendant 9.63
flock 1.46
floe 8.135
flood 2.102
flow 8.69
flu 12.111
focus (on) 1.56
fog 11.73
fool 3.160
foolish 11.115
for the sake of 12.16
forbidden 5.82
forces 3.26
foreign 2.21
forensic scientist 7.126
form 2.92
fortunate 4.13
fossil 9.130
fossil 11.77
fossil fuel 4.129
foster home 7.150
found 2.84
foundation 3.164
founder 9.73
fraction 1.51
freak out 1.105
freelance 9.24
freeze over 8.110
fright 1.88
frostbite 5.130
full-time 9.19
fully-booked 12.133
fumes 8.48
function 4.126
fundamentally 4.140
furious 11.98
fury 1.72

G

gadget 5.84
gain 7.66
gain entrance 9.92
gang 7.46
gap year 10.84
garlic 12.43
gathering place 7.145
gauze 12.95
gear 6.73
gene 1.100
generate 5.52

generation 4.142
generator 8.22
generosity 10.43
genetically modified food 8.91
geocaching 6.77
geological feature 5.42
get away 1.143
get away with 7.132
get in touch (with) 11.87
get over 12.106
get the sack 9.113
get together 6.101
get tough 7.142
get under (my) skin 1.69
get under way 10.39
ghost town 4.104
gifted 3.67
gig 9.98
give up 2.17
give yourself up 7.133
glide 11.128
global warming 8.125
globalisation 2.4
go around 3.91
go missing 1.80
go over 10.89
goods 2.2
gossip 3.59
grab 6.67
gradual 8.41
graduate 9.70
grasp 2.141
grasshopper 12.28
grassy 8.67
grate 12.51
grateful 1.151
grave 3.32
gravity 6.3
greenhouse effect 8.126
greenhouse gas 8.47
grip 11.30
gripped with fear 11.122
gritty 4.4
grocery store 9.74
ground 11.72
guarantee 3.70
guard 3.88
guardian 7.23
guess 1.7
guest-house 11.53
guide 10.2
guide dog 10.17
gulf 11.63
gust 8.6

H

habitat 8.65
hack into 5.88
hand in 10.90
hand out 9.89
handle 2.100
hands-on 10.106
hang out 4.101
harbour 11.51
harden 9.136
hardened criminal 7.89
harness 8.16

harsh   7.78
have a go   10.76
have in common   3.109
have stars in my eyes   3.75
head out   6.108
health-care worker   4.83
hearing   7.28
heir   3.1
hide-and-seek   6.78
highly   3.87
highway   2.61
hijack   7.105
hiking   6.70
hilarious   1.147
hire   9.32
hit   3.62
hoist   8.13
hold down   9.107
hold up   7.90
hole   9.142
holy   3.7
homeland   2.69
homeless   7.157
hometown   4.72
honesty   2.129
hook up to   5.89
host   6.54
host city   6.88
hostage   7.80
hostel   11.44
hot water bottle   12.83
house   2.113
house sitting   11.81
house swapping   11.80
household name   3.10
household waste   8.104
humid   8.78
hunch (over)   6.24
hurricane   8.26
husk   12.63
hybrid   6.119

I

I couldn't agree more.   4.84
ideal   9.93
identity   2.24
idiot   5.94
illegal parking   7.8
illuminate   2.116
image   1.34
immensely   11.96
immigrant   1.158
immigrate   2.155
immune   12.73
impact   2.36
implement   5.136
import   2.77
impression   2.134
in advance   3.48
in bad shape   12.120
in earnest   5.10
in orbit   5.19
in private   3.124
in public   3.123
in recognition of   10.52
in the public eye   3.85
inability   1.112

inadequate   7.16
inappropriate   1.146
inch   10.13
incident   7.148
income   9.26
incredible   2.104
independence   10.45
independent   9.65
indicate   6.28
indifferent   7.115
individual   4.119
industrial   4.37
Industrial Revolution   8.132
industry   3.106
ineffective   7.17
infected   12.96
in-flight   11.64
influence   2.70
influential   3.64
inform   8.87
ingredient   12.101
inhabitant   4.27
initial   5.22
initiative   9.84
inland   4.71
inn   11.55
inner-city   4.38
innocent bystander   7.104
innovative   4.143
insecure   4.14
insight   11.26
insist   10.78
inspect   6.133
inspiration   3.13
inspire   9.79
instinctively   1.15
instructive   11.25
instructor   10.59
insurance   9.54
intake   12.21
intake   12.115
interact   5.102
interaction   9.13
interactive   5.49
international   2.40
interpersonal skills   9.118
introduce   1.166
introverted   5.96
inventive   4.147
invest (in)   4.133
investigate   7.108
involve   1.138
iron   12.34
irrational   1.116
irrelevant   5.4
irrigation   8.70
isolated   11.45
issue   7.57
itch   10.26

J

janitor   9.77
jaw-dropping   6.15
job hunter   9.88
job seeker   9.33
joy   1.73
judge   7.33

judge   7.73
judicial system   7.63
junction   4.48
jury   7.18
jury duty   7.53
justice   3.169
juvenile   7.15

K

keen   8.117
keep sb going   6.14
keep up   9.105
key   2.150
kick-off   6.100
kidnapping   7.9
knock down   9.72
knowledge   2.46
laboratory   4.89

L

lack (of)   1.119
lack   9.34
ladder   4.58
lagoon   11.62
lamp post   3.115
land   2.79
land   3.94
landlady   4.30
landlord   4.29
landscape   1.160
large-scale   8.119
laser pointer   10.30
launch   3.101
launch   10.46
lawyer   7.72
lead to   1.25
leadership skills   9.7
leap   3.139
leave   9.55
lecture   5.48
lecturer   3.44
left-handed   1.97
lend a hand   10.15
lethal   7.139
level   4.65
liar   11.38
licence   9.62
lie   3.50
life in the fast lane   4.115
lifeguard   9.4
lifelong   10.38
lifespan   10.14
lifestyle   2.32
lightning   8.31
limb   5.120
limitation   5.71
liner   11.59
liquid   9.134
litter   8.101
live up to   3.107
lively   2.166
load   6.82
loaded   7.91
loaf   4.91
local   2.27
local council   4.26

location   3.31
lodger   4.31
loneliness   1.131
lonely   1.86
long-lasting   7.41
look down on   3.117
look forward to   3.144
look up   10.91
looks   3.23
lose   5.63
loudspeaker   5.34
lounge   6.36
low   4.76
low-calorie   12.97
lower   6.131
low-fat   12.20
luxurious   11.86
lyrics   2.11

M

machinery   9.132
magnesium   12.33
mainly   4.73
maintain   6.85
major   2.115
major (in)   10.104
majority   4.42
make a getaway   7.112
make a living   1.169
make for   11.109
make your mouth water   12.38
man-made   3.39
manufacture   2.14
marine biology   10.102
marked   3.65
martial art   7.152
mass   8.27
massive   3.61
master   10.24
match   9.36
match-fixing   3.72
mature   6.34
mausoleum   3.28
mayor   2.42
means   10.31
meanwhile   3.154
measure   5.60
mechanism   1.20
medical condition   2.137
meet expectations   3.120
melt   8.130
membership   12.130
memory   10.95
mental   10.48
mental health   4.82
mention   3.47
mentor   7.151
meteorological   8.120
methane   8.46
middle-class   4.9
mind   1.29
mineral   12.66
minority   6.25
miracle   12.92
mirror   6.87
misdemeanour   7.52
misery   1.74

miss   5.64
miss out (on sth)   6.91
missing   9.146
mission   3.102
moist   8.28
moisture   8.34
monitor   3.14
mood swings   4.81
moral   3.165
more often than not   11.84
motion   12.12
motivation   9.115
motor   1.17
mould   9.135
mount   9.138
move into   4.102
move on   9.108
move out   4.57
movement   12.135
mugged   4.3
multicultural   1.159
mummy   2.64
municipal   7.22
mural   2.160
murder   3.24
muscle   1.18
my fill of sth   11.8
my hair stands on end   11.127
my heart sinks   11.125

N

name sb/sth after sb/th   5.23
nasty   8.82
nation   2.165
native to   10.12
natural disaster   2.164
natural gas   8.52
natural resource   8.38
neat   9.8
neighbourhood   2.154
nerve   1.19
nervous   3.153
nervous system   1.11
network   2.71
neuroscientist   1.10
neutral   1.16
nevertheless   5.116
next to nothing   11.82
night on the town   4.106
nod off   11.21
non-profit organisation   10.9
northern lights   11.88
not … any time soon   11.85
not long afterwards   3.150
notorious   3.66
nutrient   12.114

O

obese   12.71
object   7.100
objective   6.129
observatory   10.75
observer   1.37
obvious   1.76
occupant   4.32

occupy   7.1
occur   1.102
occurrence   2.51
odour   12.64
offence   7.13
offender   7.27
officer   7.102
oil   8.51
old people's home   7.51
Olympic Torch Relay   6.86
omission   8.43
on a regular basis   4.68
on a voluntary basis   7.31
on behalf of sb   9.29
on board   11.3
on display   6.115
on my behalf   3.128
on the edge of (my) seat   1.65
on the rise   4.78
on the run   4.24
on the spot   9.104
on top of the world   11.118
opening   9.56
operate   4.80
operate   12.74
operating system   5.99
oppose   7.158
opt (for)   12.19
optimism   1.92
orbit   3.15
organic   8.92
organisation   2.158
originate   5.51
out of curiosity   1.64
out of the blue   3.151
out of work   9.110
outgoing   9.125
outing   6.74
outskirts   4.39
oven   12.102
over the moon   11.117
overall   9.114
overcome   1.81
overhead compartment   11.15
overhear   1.120
overpowering   12.65
overpriced   12.132
over-rated   1.118
overseas   11.7
oversleep   2.118
overwhelm   5.67
own up   7.134
oyster   12.2

P

packed   12.45
paint the town red   4.107
palaeontology   9.127
pale   1.122
panic-stricken   11.123
parachute   3.98
paraglide   11.130
paralysed   10.21
parking meter   4.46
participant   1.39
particular   1.13

partnership   10.40
part-time   6.110
pass (a) sentence (on sb)   7.70
pass on   1.99
pass out   12.107
passenger   11.18
paste   12.54
pastry shop   4.22
patch   8.115
path   6.71
pattern   8.14
pavement   4.45
pay off   6.125
peace and quiet   4.113
peak   6.132
pedestrian   4.21
pedestrian area   4.52
peer   7.26
penniless   11.31
perceive   1.59
permit   10.73
personal details   9.111
personnel manager   9.71
persuasiveness   3.19
pessimistic   8.116
petrol   4.128
PhD   5.133
phenomenon   2.52
photovoltaic panel   8.94
phrase book   11.13
physical   10.18
physical fitness   9.9
pick   9.97
pick up   10.92
pickpocketing   7.10
piece   6.61
pinch   12.57
ping   5.35
pitch   6.50
pitch (a tent)   11.95
place   9.46
placement   10.34
plain   5.41
plain clothes   7.88
plead guilty   7.44
pleasant   3.20
pleasure   2.145
plentiful   12.61
plot   8.100
plug in   5.90
plumbing   10.70
plus   1.152
plus side   4.18
pocket   11.116
point out   5.16
policy   3.172
poor   1.113
pop   12.24
porcupine   12.56
pork   12.88
port   2.72
portable   6.75
portrait   1.156
position   2.96
position   9.18
posture   1.23
potential   2.34

pottery   2.86
pour   1.41
poverty   1.77
powdered   12.100
power   8.2
power plant   8.127
PR   3.77
practise   1.167
praise   10.5
precise   5.18
predict   8.88
prescription   12.119
preserve   12.138
press conference   3.129
pretty (adv)   11.99
prevention   7.123
prey   1.50
price   5.65
pride myself on sth   9.35
primary education   10.66
principal   10.82
privacy   3.84
private   4.118
procedure   7.48
proceed   6.90
proceedings   7.43
process   1.24
processed food   12.36
professional   2.139
profit   2.6
profitable   9.69
progress   10.32
prohibit   8.96
promote   12.140
promotional   9.68
proof   5.45
proper   2.74
property   11.83
proposal   7.144
prosecution   7.35
prosper   3.174
prosperity   3.170
prosthesis   5.118
protest   7.2
proud   1.91
prove   1.36
provide   2.56
publicity   3.76
publish   4.125
pulp   12.14
pulse   5.13
punctual   6.6
punish   7.4
punishment   7.71
pushing and shoving   4.109
put away   7.135
put forward   3.43
put myself in sb's shoes   9.39
put off   12.40
put up   11.94

Q

quadriplegic   10.20
qualification   9.3
qualified   3.68
quality   4.79

quay   11.46
quest   3.5
question   7.103
quit   9.61
quote   3.159

R

racking sobs   11.32
radical   6.10
rafting   6.19
raging   7.107
rainfall   8.33
raise   2.161
raise   7.153
raise   10.56
raise awareness   10.47
range   6.29
range of movement   5.2
ransom   7.106
rapid   1.139
rash   8.83
rationalise   1.55
raw   8.59
react   1.32
reactor   8.71
reasonable   12.125
reasonably   11.101
recent   2.148
receptionist   9.21
recharge   5.78
recipient   7.147
recommend   1.150
record   2.93
record   5.39
recover   12.110
recovery   12.116
recreate   9.147
recruiter   9.16
recycled   8.73
recycling bin   8.90
reduce   8.75
refer   7.21
reference   9.102
reflect   2.162
reflect   5.36
refuse   10.83
regard   1.173
region   1.42
register   9.31
register   11.111
regret   3.112
regular   2.101
regulate   4.67
reindeer   2.58
relative   2.157
release   3.79
release   5.61
release   7.141
relevant   6.112
reliability   9.10
reliant (on)   5.86
relief   2.138
rely (on)   5.106
remain   3.33
remains   8.50
remote   5.87

removal   7.125
remove   3.113
renewable   8.54
rent   4.35
reoffend   7.68
reputation   2.132
request   9.48
require   2.128
resemble   3.108
reserve   6.40
resident   4.8
residential   4.40
resist   12.108
resources   4.11
respect   2.25
respect your elders   3.162
respond (to)   1.60
response   1.26
responsibility   2.130
responsible (for)   1.44
restless   6.31
restore   3.168
restricted   8.79
retired   3.166
reveal   3.86
revenge   9.80
review   3.89
revolutionary   5.5
revolutionise   5.14
ride   6.12
ridge   11.76
ridiculous   11.105
ring   6.51
rink   6.52
rip open   3.135
rise   7.24
rise   10.57
rising seas   3.38
roadway   2.73
roam   11.75
robbery   7.11
robotic   1.58
rock face   5.134
rocket scientist   5.20
roll   11.113
rollercoaster   6.18
roof   4.56
root   12.49
rotation   8.5
royal   3.12
royalty   3.103
rude   3.146
ruin   2.108
rule   3.167
rumour   3.60
run   1.161
run into   6.102
run out   4.130
run out (of sth)   5.53
runway   11.47
rural   4.66
rusty   11.104

S

sacred   3.6
salary   4.75

sales   9.47
salesperson   9.5
sample   6.33
sand dune   11.129
scandal   3.74
scared stiff   11.121
scholarship   10.69
schooling   10.33
scorpion   12.5
scratch   10.25
screen   6.109
screening   6.111
screenplay   5.104
sea urchin   12.1
seashore   6.64
seasonal   9.96
seat   6.57
seaweed   12.4
secondary school   10.67
secretarial course   10.79
security camera   7.101
see off   11.110
see through   7.136
seek permission   8.89
self-defence   7.140
self-esteem   7.67
sensation   5.131
sentence   7.34
service   5.24
services   2.3
session   12.72
set off   5.91
set out (to do sth)   5.126
setting   4.139
settle down   4.103
settle down   6.41
settle into your seat   11.16
settlement   4.6
severe   1.114
sewing machine   5.57
shackled   6.7
shade   11.133
shake hands   10.85
shake like a leaf   3.137
shame   1.75
shape   9.145
sharp   6.5
sharp   12.42
sheer   11.36
shellfish   8.81
shift   12.90
ship   2.15
shock of my life   3.134
shove   11.28
show up   6.103
shrink   8.131
shuffle   6.66
shut down   5.92
shutter   11.103
shuttle   11.48
sick leave   9.116
sick of   12.75
sight   11.23
silhouette   3.17
similar   2.33
sit around   6.104
sit back   6.105

site   3.35
skeleton   9.141
skip   12.35
slam   1.94
slavery   7.155
sleep in   6.106
slight   8.134
slightly   11.100
slow lane   12.134
slum   4.1
smile from ear to ear   3.138
smooth   8.113
snail   12.6
sneeze   12.85
snore   11.22
soaking wet   8.66
sociable   9.28
social networking   3.78
socialise   5.115
society   2.47
solid   4.121
sonar mapping   5.27
sophisticated   5.1
sore   1.121
soul   7.156
source   2.5
souvenir   11.1
space   2.135
spacecraft   3.100
specialise   10.103
species   8.72
specific   1.133
spectacular   5.6
spectator   6.56
speech   1.62
speechless   11.119
speed bump   4.51
speed camera   4.54
speed limit   4.55
speeding   7.76
spice   2.60
spike   12.41
spill   2.90
spin   8.4
spinal cord   10.11
split up   3.122
sponsor   3.71
spotless   12.128
spray   7.98
spread   1.9
spring up   2.95
squander   6.23
square kilometre   4.112
squatter   4.33
squeeze   12.52
squirm   12.10
stable   5.97
stadium   3.92
staff   9.20
stage   3.11
stage   10.8
stall   10.77
standard of living   4.77
start out as   3.93
starving   1.126
state of the art   12.129
statement   7.81

151

steady   9.25
steel   8.18
steep   6.120
step in   12.139
stethoscope   12.84
stick to   12.17
still   1.33
still   1.38
stilts   9.1
stimulant   5.69
store   11.69
storey   8.19
strainer   12.53
street sign   4.50
stressed   1.103
stretch   2.136
stride off   11.27
strike   8.30
stringed instrument   3.21
stroll   6.62
structure   5.33
struggle   10.72
study   1.12
stuff   8.93
stunned   3.141
stunning   11.9
stunt   6.1
submit   10.93
subsequent   7.54
substance   10.1
suburb   4.41
successor   5.26
suffer   5.124
sufficient   12.112
suit   9.44
sum up   2.140
supervisor   6.114
supply   12.113
support   2.20
supporter   3.80
surgeon   12.78
surgery   5.132
surrender   7.137
survive   2.19
suspect   7.86
suspect   7.93
swallow   12.26
swap   2.57
sweep   8.68
sympathetic   7.116

T

take (a day) off   9.112
take advantage (of)   4.116
take my breath away   11.10
take off   1.47
take on   5.103
take on   9.109
talk of the town   4.105
tasty   12.32
taxi rank   11.6
tear   8.9
temperature   12.118
temple   2.109
tenant   4.34

tend to   1.101
terminal   11.35
termite   12.8
termite mound   12.9
terrain   6.124
terrified   1.109
territory   11.78
textile   2.85
thanks to   5.15
the accused   7.83
the authorities   7.129
the elements   5.129
theft   7.45
theme park   6.97
thorn   12.62
thorough   10.36
thrill   12.60
thrive   4.114
thus   5.117
tidal wave   3.37
tingle   12.15
tissue   11.29
title   3.2
to make matters worse   3.152
to my astonishment   3.130
to my mind   2.143
tolerance   2.9
tomb   3.42
tone up   10.62
too good to be true   11.120
tool   5.62
top (with)   8.20
tornado   8.3
torrential   8.32
torrential   8.106
tournament   6.99
town hall   4.60
town hall   4.108
town planner   4.69
toxin   12.58
track   6.53
track   11.79
trade   2.41
trade route   2.78
traffic light   4.49
train   1.171
trait   1.98
transfer   2.83
translate   9.100
trap   8.44
treat   1.144
treat   10.28
tree-lined   4.44
trekker   6.76
trend   3.119
trial   7.19
tribe   2.87
troupe   6.96
trust   6.121
try   7.14
tube   8.24
tuition   10.71
turn down   6.107
turn in (sth)   11.40
turn into   8.74
turn out   3.145

turn up   1.107
tutor   10.60
typical   4.23

U

ultimate   6.128
uncontrollable   1.141
uncover   7.109
under no circumstances   12.91
under pressure   3.125
under the weather   12.121
undercover   7.87
unemployed   2.16
unevenly   8.11
unexpectedly   3.156
uninhibited   4.146
uniqueness   2.31
universal   2.45
universe   4.20
unknowingly   12.37
unpleasant   8.123
up and about   12.122
up to a point   4.86
upbeat   9.121
update   5.74
upright   8.25
uproot   8.29
urban   4.10
usable   8.55
utterly   11.97

V

vacancy   9.30
vacate   7.128
valid   5.46
valid   10.74
vandalism   7.12
vanish without a trace   3.110
vast   11.39
vending machine   5.58
venom   3.4
venue   6.95
verdict   7.79
verdict   7.124
versus   11.89
vertical   6.127
vessel   11.58
victim   4.25
victim   7.40
victimless   7.111
victorious   3.52
victory   3.57
view   2.142
virtually   11.102
virus protection   5.75
visual   1.27
volunteer work   6.27

W

wander   5.125
wander   6.63
warlord   3.161

warmly   3.142
warrior   2.112
wasteful   5.7
water cannon   7.99
waterfall   6.122
waterway   2.97
weaken   8.118
wealthy   2.37
weapon   7.47
wear away   8.111
weird   1.106
welfare   10.41
what makes sb tick   9.15
what's more   5.112
wheel   7.94
wheelchair   10.29
whiff   12.39
whip up   8.8
white as a sheet   11.126
willingness   2.10
wind turbine   5.50
windmill   2.63
wipe out   8.112
with regret   1.67
without a doubt   3.133
without warning   3.155
witness   7.75
word processing skills   9.122
workforce   9.11
workout   12.70
workshop   9.91
workshop   9.131
worthwhile   6.37
worthy   6.20
wound   12.94
wriggle   12.11

Y

yacht   11.60
youth   6.30

Z

zebra crossing   4.53